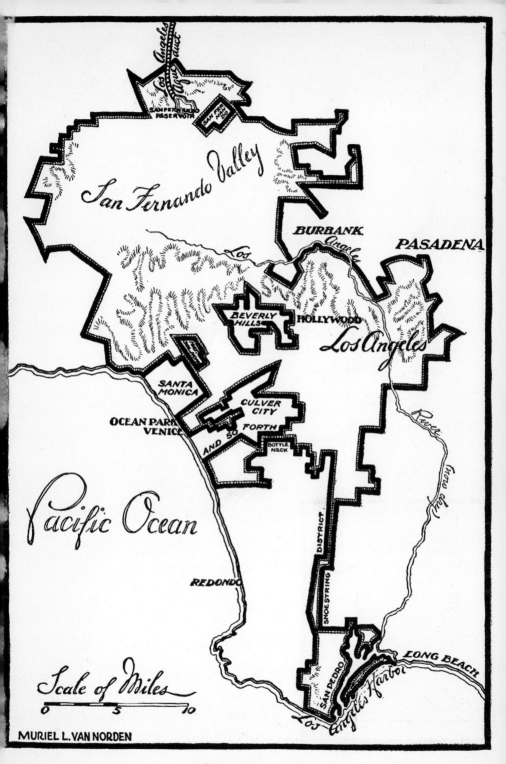

LOS ANGELES

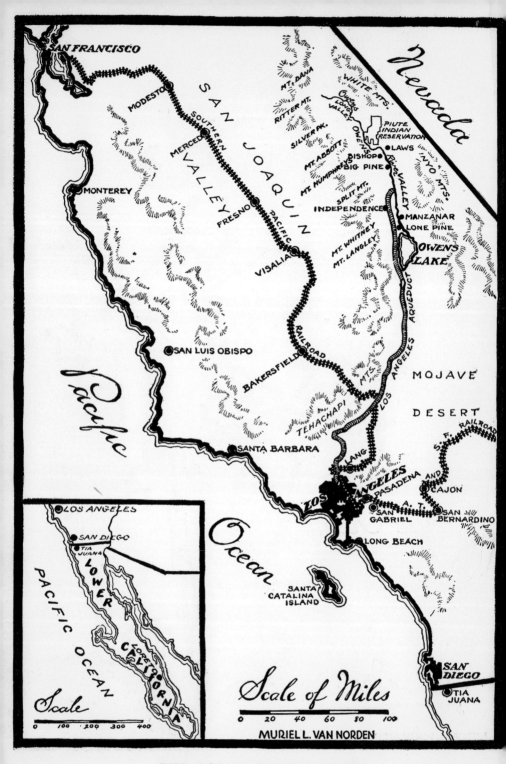

THE SCENE OF THE BOOK

THE WESTERN SCENE

OUTPOST OF EMPIRE
THE STORY OF THE FOUNDING OF SAN FRANCISCO
by Herbert Eugene Bolton, Ph.D., LL.D.
SATHER PROFESSOR OF HISTORY AND DIRECTOR OF THE BANCROFT
LIBRARY, UNIVERSITY OF CALIFORNIA
With 11 maps and 66 illustrations

A HISTORY OF THE PACIFIC NORTHWEST
by George W. Fuller
LIBRARIAN, SPOKANE PUBLIC LIBRARY
With 8 maps and 30 illustrations

THE MACADAM TRAIL
TEN THOUSAND MILES BY MOTOR COACH
by Mary Day Winn
Illustrated by E. H. Suydam

DANCING GODS
INDIAN CEREMONIALS OF NEW MEXICO AND ARIZONA
by Erna Fergusson
With 16 illustrations

ZUÑI FOLK TALES
Collected and Translated by Frank Hamilton Cushing
With an Introduction by Mary Austin and a Foreword by J. W. Powell

Coming: A new book about San Francisco by Herbert Asbury,
author of *The Gangs of New York.*

THESE ARE BORZOI BOOKS PUBLISHED BY ALFRED A. KNOPF

LOS ANGELES

LOS ANGELES

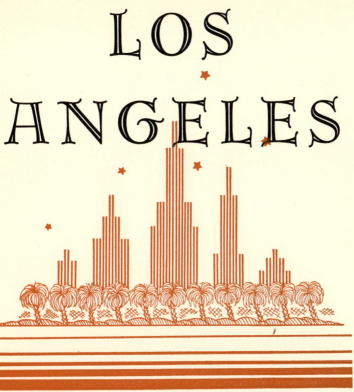

MORROW MAYO

ILLUSTRATED

New York Mcmxxxiii

ALFRED · A · KNOPF

" That is all very well," replied Candide, *" but let us cultivate our garden."*

— VOLTAIRE

Table of Contents

PART ONE

THE BIRTH OF LOS ANGELES   3
ENTER THE GRINGO   16
HELL-HOLE OF THE WEST   31

PART TWO

ON THE WINGS OF IRON HORSES   57
BOOM! BOOM!   74
TAPPING THE MIDDLE WEST   89
HUNTINGTON — THE HARBOR FIGHT   107
OIL, ORANGES, IOWA   128

PART THREE

HATRED IN THE SUNSHINE   139
DYNAMITE OR GAS?   155
A BLACK "BARGAIN-DAY" FOR LABOR   173
THE FRUITS OF "VICTORY"   189

PART FOUR

ABBOT KINNEY'S DREAM   203

PASADENA — MILLIONAIRES' RETREAT   211

THE RAPE OF OWENS VALLEY   220

HOLLYWOOD   247

PART FIVE

AIMEE SEMPLE McPHERSON   269

STRANGE INTERLUDE — THE HICKMAN
    HORROR   293

SCIENCE VS. RELIGION PLUS MILLIKAN   304

LOS ANGELES — TODAY AND TOMORROW   319

BIBLIOGRAPHICAL NOTE   331

INDEX   follows page 337

List of Illustrations

MAP OF LOS ANGELES

THE SCENE OF THE BOOK

{ *Front*
endleaf

THE PLAZA, THE CHURCH OF OUR LADY
THE QUEEN OF THE ANGELS, AND
"SONORA TOWN," IN 1869   24

THE CALLE DE LOS NEGROS   52

AN IMPROMPTU HANGING   52

LOS ANGELES WHEN THE SANTA FE RAIL-
ROAD ARRIVED   64

SOME OF THE FIRST ARRIVALS OF THE
GREAT BOOM   76

LOS ANGELES HARBOR IN 1873   108

SANTA MONICA   124

ORANGE GROVES   134

THE LOS ANGELES *TIMES* BUILDING   156

Some of the Bizarre Restaurants
and Refreshment Stands   178

Street Scene in Venice   206

The Arroyo Seco Bridge   214

A View of the Los Angeles Aqueduct   238

A "Premeer"   260

Mrs. Aimee Semple McPherson   272

Aimee Leaves for the Holy Land   290

An Airplane View of the Angel
City Today   324

PART ONE

The Birth of Los Angeles

*M*an's first conquest of California was simply a foot-race, with England and Russia moving down the Pacific coast, and Spain moving up. Spain was faster on her feet.

In the winter of 1769 two great men met at Loreto, six hundred miles south of Tia Juana, and got Spain going. One was José de Gálvez, the *Visitador-General;* the other was Junípero Serra, Franciscan father of all the California missions. In quick succession they started four expeditions into the unknown North, two by sea and two by land. One land party and both ships came to grief: incompetence and scurvy hit them. But the fourth expedition was in more capable hands.

On March 9, 1769 General Gaspar de Portolá rode north out of Loreto, leading Father Serra, six lesser Franciscan padres, seventy-five Spanish soldiers, and a gang of Mexican muleteers. He proposed to reach the Bay of Monterey by land or die in the attempt. Four months later the party straggled into the uninhabited sand-spit of San Diego, having traveled perhaps nine hundred miles through a terrible country and worse weather. They were saddle-sore and footsore, full of sand-fleas and cockle-burrs, sun-baked and weary. But they were in San Diego.

Father Serra stopped, for his ulcerated leg was giving him trouble, and, moreover, he had work to do. Accordingly, on the 16th of July, with a few stupid Indians looking on, he erected a rustic cross, the Spanish soldiers threw a bell over the limb of a sycamore tree and rang it, and Father Serra said mass. Thus he planted the germ of the Mission San Diego de Alcalá, the first bead on that golden rosary which was soon to sparkle in the sunshine for a thousand miles up the Pacific seaboard. Later Father Serra, game leg and all, walked every mile of that wonderful necklace (which he called *El Camino Real*—The King's Highway), not once, but several times. He was the greatest Marathon walker ever heard of.

But Portolá didn't linger in San Diego. Two days before the spiritual ceremonies, he took half the party, mounted his horse, and moved on. Due north he plugged for sixty miles, through a glaring desert of cactus, sagebrush, and chaparral shimmering under a fierce July heat; then he swung northwest, heading back to the receding sea. Obviously, the Bay of Monterey must be near the water. Now the Spaniards struggled over a sandy sun-shot plain; now they rested in the occasional shade of clumps of tall sycamore trees; now they fought through almost impassable low jungles of brambles, nettles, scrub palms, and serpentine grapevines. Portolá and his two holy men were making geography as well as history; they were mapping the changing landscape and naming the salient features of it after the saints. They were sniffing exotic perfumes, eying strange brilliant birds, meeting grizzly bears, coyotes, and rattlesnakes innumerable. It was not the southern California of to-day. No civilized man had ever been through that country before.

In the heat of morning the party came to a slim green river, caressed by weeping willows. It was a pleasure. They pitched camp gratefully, threw themselves into the cool water, broke out the winebags, took it easy, and fished. But not for too long. The earth beneath them suddenly quivered like a muscle dancer. That afternoon, according to the diary of Father Juan Crespi (historian of the party), the place was jiggled by four earthquakes, and that night by three more, and the seventh, at dawn, was a whopper. The slim river leaped from its channel, the weeping willows swayed drunkenly, horses and men were knocked flat. General Portolá picked himself up, named this stream *El Río del Dulcísimo Nombre de Jesús de los Temblores* (The River of the Sweetest Name of Jesus of the Earthquakes), crossed himself, and backed off.

Next morning at sunrise they came to a bigger river. The day was a very important day, August 2, the Fran-ciscan feast-day of Our Lady of the Angels. But the Spaniards, now shy of rivers, paused only long enough to name this one Portiuncula (after the little church in Assisi where St. Francis used to pray) and to cele-brate the day with a quick mass. Then they forded the stream, hurrying on. In a moment, however, some-thing stopped them. Beating through the heavy growth of alders, willows, and cottonwoods, they emerged un-expectedly into a clearing occupied by three hundred thatched-pole huts; the home of a tribe of circus freaks.

These queer folk, it seems, were left stranded on our western shore, along with the Rocky Mountain goat and the saber-toothed tiger, when Asia split and the Pacific rolled in between. Their bird's-nest village of Yang-na (or Yank-na, as the patriotic John Steven Mc-Groarty calls it) decorated a small piece of mesa land in a sharp bend of the river. How long they had been there before 1769 the ethnographers do not tell us; in any event, it was too long. Aborigines somewhat like them probably saw Cabrillo when he touched at San Pedro in 1542, and it is of record that Indians ran from Viscaino when he landed at San Diego in 1603. But so far as we know, the Yangs themselves had never laid eyes on a civilized man until these Spaniards crashed through the underbrush and hove into their astonished view.

Surprised, and pleasantly so, the Yangs came galloping forward, " howling like wolves," says Father Crespi, "but showing no hostility." These Oriental barbarians were "small, squat in stature, of a dingy brown color." They had little slant eyes, big flat noses, high cheekbones, wispy chin whiskers, and enormous mouths. The males were absolutely nude, the squaws sported a few alluring rabbit skins; the faces of all were smeared with paint. . . . Spanish blunderbusses roared into action. Firing from sheer amazement, the Spanish soldiers bumped off a score of these Little Nemos before Portolá could stop them. But, generally speaking, the strange encounter was marked by complete amiability.

So there they were: General Portolá, two Franciscan priests, thirty-four Spanish soldiers, twenty Mexican muleteers, and a mob of burlesque Indians. The southern California sun was shining brightly, and nothing disturbed the tranquillity of the scene except the melancholy cry of some weird river-bird. Behind the assemblage rose the brown sunburnt hills, and in the distance the Sierra Madre mountains.

Portolá was delighted. He dismounted from his heavily caparisoned steed, rammed the point of his sword into the ground, and waved aloft his plumed hat. The General was hot, dirty, tired; no doubt he called for the wine-bearer. His staff and the two Franciscan friars joined him, the Spanish soldiers rallied round, the Mexican muleteers stood back with their beasts at a respectful distance, the small Indians looked on, wide-eyed with admiration and wonder. Father Crespi declared, according to his diary: " This spot has all the resources for a large town "; and Portolá agreed. Why not? Here were six hundred gregarious, comic-strip savages, docile, friendly; all waiting to be converted and put to useful labor.

Señor Portolá, that devout man, gazed out over the river. He searched for a name for this place, this site of a future town, and, happily, the name was there. For had not the Spaniards just celebrated a special and particular feast-day, dedicated, not to a mere saint, but to the Blessed Virgin herself? The General raised the gurgling goat's-bladder of red wine. Some say he made a formal speech, beginning: "In the name of God, the Pope, and the Sovereign King of Spain . . ." but that is guess-work. But whatever the unknown details, whatever his exact words, Portolá did then and there solemnly decree that on this favored heathen spot should stand *El Pueblo de Nuestra Señora la Reina de Los*

Ángeles. Or, in unworthy English, "The Town of Our Lady the Queen of the Angels."

Having thus conceived and named the forthcoming municipality, Portolá moved on. Incidentally, he reached the Bay of Monterey.

II

The Spanish conquest of California worked, not haphazardly, but according to Hoyle. Hence the California missions were built first, to mother the embryonic towns; and one of the richest was created to nurture Portolá's dream-city. On September 8, 1771, at a lovely spot nine miles from the unborn Los Angeles, Father Serra founded the Mission San Gabriel Arcángel, where it stands to this day. A miracle attended the event.

The priests were scouting for a location, according to Saunders and Chase, when a mob of disapproving gentile Indians came dashing out of the woods. These savages, unlike the Yangs, were hostile and armed for battle. Yelling fiercely and brandishing their weapons, they bore down on the padres. Unfortunately, no Spanish soldiers were near at the moment. So the fathers quickly ransacked their baggage, got out a canvas on which was painted an image of the Virgin, and held it up. The savages, subdued by the vision — but perhaps I had better quote from Father Francisco Palou's original record, which reposes today in the Cathedral of St. Vibiana at Los Angeles:

"No sooner was this held up to the view of the excited throng than they all, subdued by the Vision, threw down their bows and arrows and came running hastily forward. The chief cast at the feet of the Sovereign

Queen the beads and trinkets which he wore about his neck, as a sign of greatest respect. . . . They invited all the people from the surrounding villages who in great numbers, men, women, and children, kept coming to see the Most Holy Virgin, bringing with them loads of various grains, which they left at the feet of Our Lady Most Holy, supposing She needed food the same as the rest."

The following day a Spanish corporal made love to the chief's squaw, and the chief attacked the soldier. Now, the Digger Indians of California, as Gertrude Atherton has pointed out, "were so lethargic that they rarely fought." But sometimes, on great provocation, they did, and this was one of the times. It was, so far as I can ascertain, the *only* time that one of them ever engaged in mortal combat with a Spanish soldier; hence I describe the battle. Fortified with a quart of *pishibata*, an early variety of white mule, the chief got back about fifty yards, steadied himself with a few preliminary whoops and jumps, and charged the home-wrecker with a wooden spear. When he got close enough, the Corporal cut him down with a musket ball and then hacked off the chief's noble head and draped it on a pole for other Diggers to contemplate. It was an old Spanish custom.

Aided by such temporal coaxing, the Mission fathers went to work on the Indians with great enthusiasm. There were seven thousand non-Catholic Diggers within a radius of twenty-five miles, comprising thirty tribes, each jabbering a different lingo. Having no name for these aborigines, the padres lumped together all those in the immediate vicinity, christening them Gabrielinos, in honor of the Angel Gabriel, thus making a permanent

contribution to ethnology. The good priests gathered
these morons into the fold, baptized them, prayed over
them, and then put them to work constructing huge
adobe buildings, growing wheat, and herding cattle.
Missionary zeal in California was not so subtle then as it
is today. Proselyting was often done with a club; an un-
saved Indian was apt to be one who could outrun a friar.
Still, the Franciscans did not actually force these savages
into the Holy Roman Church, for the woods remained
full of non-Catholic Diggers. Mainly, they lured them in
with beads and lumps of sugar!

Once in the fold, of course, that was different. Once
a Digger was baptized, there was no backsliding. His
soul thenceforth belonged to God, and the work of his
hands to the King of Spain. In less than no time, therefore, the Angel Gabriel Mission became a veritable bee-
hive of industry, embracing half a dozen large buildings
and the huts of a thousand Indian slaves, male and
female. These dingy neophytes worked nine hours a
day and prayed three.

Located in one of the potentially richest valleys in the
world, the Angel Gabriel Mission became the " Mother
of Agriculture" in California. In those days, as today,
the cheap-looking, porous, sandy soil of southern California — given water — would grow anything. The
padres started irrigating it. At once they raised onions,
corn, beans, peas, wheat, flax, and hemp. At once they
planted orchards of lemons, figs, pomegranates, dates,
olives, limes, peaches, apples, and pears. These priests
grew at San Gabriel the first wine grapes and the first
oranges ever seen in the Golden State. They assaulted
the soil with religious fervor; they kept the road to
Mexico hot, bringing up seeds, horses, cattle, farm im-

plements, masons, blacksmiths, engineers—everything available with which to turn a desert into an agricultural paradise.

The Indians were taught how to slaughter cattle, convert fat into tallow, tan hides, and worship the Christian God. Some of the Diggers sulked, and many retained their anti-Catholic prejudices. For a long time they strangled to death every child born of an Indian squaw and a Spanish soldier. The involved Catholic religion was as incomprehensible to them as the revised Einstein hypothesis. Nevertheless, the countryside was built up. And when it was built up sufficiently, or ten years after the founding of the Angel Gabriel Mission, Los Angeles appeared, as if by magic, to beautify and adorn it.

III

The City of the Angels was created in 1781 "to serve as a guarantee of the stability of California." San José, founded in 1777 with soldiers and subdued Indians, was a failure, and no other pueblo was under way. The Spaniards, to be sure, now had eleven missions and forts going, and most of them were thriving; but as yet there were no *bona fide* towns. And without independent civil communities, separate and distinct from spiritual plantations and military garrisons, the whole Spanish program was held up. Worse, there was no human material at hand with which to build a town. All the various tribes of California Indians were carefully examined and found to be hopeless. "It was impossible," Edwin Markham once wrote, "to train them into reasonable beings." The Spaniards, therefore, were somewhat upset, but by no means nonplussed. They knew the answer: *pobladores.*

Accordingly, Felipe de Neve, the first Military Governor of California, told Captain Fernando de Rivera to take a company of soldiers and go down to the Mexican states of Sonora and Sinaloa and get him some villagers—twenty-four men with families. "These colonists, Captain," said de Neve in writing, "must be healthy and industrious, and men of character, so that they will set the natives a good example." Two months later we find Rivera in Sonora rounding up homesteaders. "He probably painted a glowing picture," says one Los Angeles historian, " for he had been in the country seven years, and there is no record of anyone living in Southern California that long without becoming enamored of the climate."

In the meantime the Governor went down the Portiuncula River a quarter of a mile from Yang-na. Using Indian labor from the Angel Gabriel Mission, he had the sagebrush and wild mustard cleared from a piece of land 275 yards long by 180 yards wide, and then from a number of smaller plots, 55 feet wide and 110 feet long, each facing the larger rectangle. Near by, a part of the countryside was staked off into a series of fourteen-acre parcels. The net result of these labors was something that resembled a sort of glorified, unoccupied tennis-court in the desert, surrounded by empty polo-fields.

But it was not. It was Los Angeles. "This large rectangle," said the Governor, "is the Plaza, the smaller ones facing it are the residential town sites, and the fields near by constitute the acreage property." There remained, therefore, only one more thing to be done. The Governor sent his horsemen galloping out into the wilderness to mark off the "city limits." When they had done so, "Los Angeles," without anybody in it, covered thirty-six square miles! Señor de Neve was the first California subdivider.

It was not long, however, before the soldiers arrived with the population. They arrived, to be exact, at the Angel Gabriel Mission on August 18, 1781, after a forced march of one hundred days through alkaline dust and desert heat. There were only twelve settlers with their families (instead of twenty-four), twelve men, eleven women, and twenty-one children. The newcomers were heartily welcomed by the good padres. Then they were placed in quarantine, for smallpox had broken out among them.

It must be recorded that the first Angelenos, observed in the Ellis Island of the Mission, were nothing to boast about. Rivera seems to have taken what he could get, instead of what he desired. The names and ages of these involuntary colonists (which are matters of record) need not concern us here. The oldest paterfamilias was sixty-seven, the youngest nineteen. None of them could read or write. They were red, white, brown, black, and maybe yellow. Was one of the fathers, Antonio Miranda, a Chinaman? Historians have debated that question for years, and the controversy continues in Los Angeles to this day. Warner says Miranda *was* a Chinese; Bancroft says he *was not*. McGroarty says he *was;* Guinn says he *was not*. A hundred others are about equally divided. Some say that he was a Chinese, but insist that "he was left along the way." So the matter will probably never be settled.

At any rate, Chinaman or no Chinaman, the involuntary colonists enjoyed the Mission's hospitality for sixteen days, until all were rested and recovered from the smallpox, and then they prepared to found a city. Governor de Neve came down from Monterey to deliver the principal address. The numerous accounts of the founding of the pueblo differ somewhat as to minor details; hence I take the best from all of them.

It was a colorful procession that marched at sunrise, September 4, 1781, from the Angel Gabriel Mission. The Governor led the parade on horseback, followed by a detachment of cavalry. Next came several sandal-shod Franciscan priests, trudging along in their skull-caps and corded robes, attended by Christianized Digger Indian acolytes. The colonists followed; the men walking, the women on mule-back, the children bedded down in an ox-cart festooned with flowers and cool mosses. Next came the equipment wagons and the live stock: horses, mules, cows, goats, sheep, and oxen. A gang of Gabrielino neophytes, and some non-Catholic Indian *kibitzers*, brought up the rear.

Arriving in "Los Angeles" the procession marched slowly and impressively around the theoretical Plaza and then gathered in it. The Spanish flag was planted; a priest asked a blessing on this municipality about to be born. Candles were lighted, a *Te Deum* was sung, and the soldiers fired three volleys of musketry. On the outskirts of the clearing a group of scared Yangs, drawn to the scene by the noise, peeped through the underbrush, their painted faces mingling artistically with the grapevines and bright wild flowers. The Governor then delivered his formal address. Alas, no copy of this speech remains. "But we may well believe," one historian, Florence E. Winslow, assures us, "that it was full of hope, encouragement, and good, sound advice." At any rate, the Governor eventually concluded his harangue, the audience applauded, and the priests offered a benediction.

Whereupon the escort bade the pioneers a fond farewell and departed for the Angel Gabriel Mission, leaving the little group of bewildered *pobladores* alone in the desert, as Laurance L. Hill says, " a thousand miles from nowhere." Of course, it was not a thousand miles from nowhere, but it probably seemed that way to those First Families of Los Angeles, suddenly transplanted from the easy communal life of Sonora and Sinaloa into this lonely country, full of crazy Indians and wild beasts, so far from their former homes.

The setting sun catches them, huddled there in the bare " Plaza," in the middle of all their belongings, no roof over their heads; the mothers weeping, the fathers resting, the children screaming, the live stock setting up an unearthly racket. Down the river comes the sharp, gladsome, supernatural cry of the startled waterfowl, settling back on the bosom of the lordly Portiuncula.

The City of the Angels is on earth.

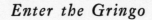

Enter the Gringo

The first Angelenos pitched right into the superb adobe mud beneath their feet and built themselves homes. And that was about the last work they ever did. For the Yangs were only a quarter of a mile down the river.

Now, the first Angelenos, as we have noted, were pretty low in the human scale, but compared to the neighboring Yangs, they were supermen. Today, thanks to the anthropologists, we know a good deal about the Yangs. These petit Asiatics nested on the ground. They subsisted mainly on acorns, coyotes, snakes, grasshoppers, and grub worms. When they ran, they galloped. They had no writing and no hieroglyphics; they sowed not, neither did they herd. A hundred unintelligible "ooh-ahs" comprised the whole vocabulary of the Shakspere among them. Their few simple artifacts, on exhibition today at the Southwest Museum, were all of the Stone Age!

So far as I can learn, the Yangs had only one thing in

common with eighteenth-century man, and that was a thirst for strong drink. Their weakness, as I have intimated, was *pishibata*. They made this liquid dynamite, says Nellie Van de Grift Sanchez, out of " powdered shells, wild tobacco juice and crushed wild cherries " — and probably they shook in a few dashes of rattlesnake bitters, for it worked on them, says Mrs. Sanchez, " like hasheesh." The degraded Yangs, of course, were no kin to our noble, one-hundred-per-cent American, buffalo-nickel Redskins. They were poor little fortysecond cousins of the Alaskan and Aleutian tribes, themselves no Junior Leaguers.

What happened, therefore, was what usually happens when a superior people is placed in proximity to an inferior race. It was not long before the godlike Angelenos had the Yangs working for them on a crop-share basis. They taught the little aborigines to herd cattle, tend flocks, and till the soil, to hew wood, draw water, and make awful brandy. This gave the first Angelenos more time to doze in the sun, get drunk themselves, fight roosters, and play the guitar. The Yangs, paid for their labor in raw brandy, were delighted with the new arrangement. For after their paralyzing *pishibata* the vilest grape distillation was to them as sound bourbon would be today to barbarians accustomed to bath-tub gin.

To increase the population, the angelic pueblo was officially converted, with the approval of Mexico City, into a combination penal colony, health resort, and old folks' home. New residents appeared forthwith. They were not material for the social register, but they were human. Did a northwestern Mexican offender, whose crime called for exile, appear before the Governor of Sinaloa for sentence? " Ah, well," sighed His

Excellency, "send him to El Pueblo de Nuestra Señora la Reina de los Angeles for five years." The same good fortune awaited military deserters from the California presidios. The sick were delivered into the pueblo by the ox-cart load; all the old Spanish Legion boys were pensioned to Los Angeles, to live forever. More adobe huts sprang up; an armed guard patrolled the town. Pretty soon a jail was built, the first public building. It was the only one for thirty-three years.

The first census, taken in 1790, revealed a population of 141 souls, nine of whom were nonogenarians, showing the salubrious nature of the climate. In fact — "If it were not for the invalids," said Governor Arrillaga in 1792, "Los Angeles would not amount to anything." Two years later his successor, Governor Borica, wrote to the Viceroy of Mexico: "To take a charitable view of these inhabitants, their absence for a couple of centuries, at a distance of a million leagues, would prove most beneficial to the province, and redound to the service of God and King." He pleaded with the Viceroy to send Los Angeles a ship-load of "healthy young women." But this request (subsequently repeated many times) was never granted.

The squalid little pueblo drifted along, slowly increasing in size. Several times the Franciscan fathers tried unsuccessfully to start a church in the town. Finally, in 1814, they did start one, by the simple expedient of donating to its construction seven barrels of brandy. The sleepy Angelenos suddenly leaped into action. The brandy was converted into labor, "drink by drink," says the historian Burdette, "with the enthusiastic co-operation of the populace." Thus the foundation of the Angel City's first House of God was built by the Demon

Rum. But only the foundation. The brandy ran out then, and no more of the edifice was built for six years. The San Gabriel priests, no Prohibitionists themselves, wrote sadly to the Governor that inebriety was "fast becoming a civic virtue."

When California changed from Spanish to New Spanish (Mexican) hands in 1822, Los Angeles got more population. Spain had robbed the grave and the gallows to inhabit the town; Mexico robbed the cradle. A shipload, not of healthy young women, but of foundlings, plucked from the orphan asylums of Mexico City, was sent round and dumped into the growing pueblo.

The countryside was filling up, too; the grandees were coming. The largest land grant ever issued in California was made out to Don Manuel Nietos in 1783. This ranch, starting just beyond the Los Angeles "city limits," was small compared to the five-million-acre parcels given out by the King of Spain elsewhere, even in much smaller countries (for example, in Porto Rico), but it was large enough for a gentleman to reside on without feeling cramped: it was three hundred and fifteen thousand acres. Similar vast estates around Los Angeles were bestowed upon Don Antonio Yorba, Don José Maria Verdugo, Don Juan José Dominquez, Don Francisco Reyes — the list could be continued for half a page. By 1825 these feudal barons, together with the Angel Gabriel Mission, owned all the land for leagues about. The whole country was one vast cattle ranch.

So between one thing and another, the convicts and the *pobladores*, the sick and the old, the peons and the priests, the orphans and the Dons, Los Angeles gradually became large enough to aspire to municipal government, and to hold its first election in 1826. The election was declared null and void by Governor Echeandía on the grounds that all the candidates were " vagabonds, drunkards, and worse," but ten years later, when the population of the town (counting the people on the neighboring ranches) was 2,500, Los Angeles became temporarily the seat of the provincial government. It was then that Don Leonardo Cata, the first Los Angeles booster, addressed the City Council as follows:

" Los Angeles now finds itself the capital of California. It should proceed to show its beauty, its splendor, and its magnificence in such a manner that when the traveler visits us he may say: 'I have seen the City of the Angels; I have seen the work of its sanitary commission, and all this demonstrates that it is a Mexican paradise! ' Alas, it is not so under present conditions, for the majority of its buildings present a gloomy and melancholy aspect, a dark and forbidding aspect; they resemble the catacombs of ancient Rome more than the habitations of a free people."

Spiritual life kept pace with material progress. There was an army of priests at San Gabriel, and everywhere you looked in Los Angeles you could see one. Now they had a church and a large, devout flock. An article in the *Century Magazine* for December 1883, entitled " Echoes in the City of the Angels," describes the religious atmosphere which prevailed about 1830:

" Looking forward to death, the greatest anxiety of these simple souls was to provide themselves with a priest's cast-off robe to be buried in. These were begged or bought as the greatest of treasures; kept in sight, or always at hand, to remind them of approaching death. When their last hour drew near, this robe was flung over their breasts, and they died happy, their stiffening fingers grasping its folds. The dead body was wrapped in it, and laid on the mud floor . . . till the time of burial. Around it, day and night, squatted, praying and singing, friends who wished not only to show their affection for the deceased, but to win indulgences for themselves; every prayer said thus, by the side of a corpse, having a special and specified value."

The town had another religious custom, less creepy. Every morning the oldest member of some household rose with the morning star and struck up a hymn at the top of his voice, usually beginning with a short shout: " Rejoice, O Mother of God! "

At the first note every person in the adobe mansion sat up in bed and joined in. From house to house the caroling spread until the whole town sang, accompanied by the protests of awakened live stock, the howls of dogs and cats, and the crowing of roosters. A translation of one of the most popular hymns thus sung is quoted in the *Century* article:

> Come, O sinners,
>   Come, and we will sing
> Tender hymns
>   To our refuge.
>
> Singers at dawn
>   From the heavens above,
> People all regions,
>   Gladly we too sing.
>
> Singing harmoniously,
>   Saying to Mary,
> O beautiful Queen,
>   Princess of Heaven:

Your beautiful head
  Crowned we see;
The stars are adorning
  Your beautiful hair;

Your eyebrows are arched,
  Your forehead serene,
Your face turned always
  Looks toward God. . . .

II

The first gringo ever to enter this priest-ridden Spanish-Mexican-Indian paradise was Cap'n Josh Shaler of Boston, skipper of the good ship *Lelia Byrd*. Returning home from the Hawaiian Islands with a scurvy-stricken crew, he anchored off the suicidal mud flats of San Pedro in 1805 and went ashore in search of fresh meat. Foreign ships were not permitted to land in California, and any foreigner caught there was supposed to be put to death. Nevertheless, Shaler landed unmolested and traded for cattle and hogs. At San Pedro he observed great piles of cow-hides and bulging bags of tallow, waiting for the San Blas (Lower California) ships; between Catalina Island and the mainland he saw many whales and sharks.

The *Lelia Byrd* departed, taking the good word back to New England, and a few years later Yankee brigs started anchoring off San Pedro with increasing frequency and boldness. Some hunted whales and sharks; others traded the Spaniards merchandise and manufactured goods for tallow and hides. The whales moved up and down the coast twice a year, keeping close to the shore. (As late as 1862 small whaling vessels working out of San Pedro were harpooning a whale a day.) The waters of San Pedro Bay itself were alive with sharks. One day no less than a hundred and three were speared, for the oil from their livers. All the ships bought their supplies in Los Angeles; the Yankee traders went ashore, and nobody was put to death. That was probably because they transacted their business and got out.

Research shows clearly that the Spanish law prohibiting this trade with foreigners was not taken seriously by the leading people of southern California. This foreign trade, indeed, was very welcome to the Angelenos and the great landowners; they obtained from it many civilizing things from the outside world. It was contraband, of course, but no one of consequence objected to the smuggling, least of all the priests, since much of the bootleg merchandise eventually made its way into the bosom of the Angel Gabriel Mission. This trade was at its height in 1835 (by that time the prohibition law had been repealed) when the brig *Pilgrim* anchored off San Pedro with Richard Henry Dana aboard serving as a common sailor. In his *Two Years Before the Mast* Dana says of San Pedro:

"I . . . learned, to my surprise, that the desolate-looking place we were in furnished more hides than any port on the coast. . . . About thirty miles in the interior was a fine plane country, filled with herds of cattle, in the centre of which was the Pueblo de los Angeles, — the largest town in California. . . .

"The agent . . . went up to visit the town and the neighboring mission; and in a few days, as the result of his labors, large ox-carts, and droves of mules, loaded with hides, were seen coming over the flat country. . . . We had to unload, and to load the carts again with our own goods; the lazy Indians, who came down with them, squatting on their hams, looking on, doing nothing, and when we asked them to help us, only shaking their heads, or drawling out ' no quiero.' "

Four fifths of these early traders were Americanos. None of them remained in the country, however, because they were not permitted to remain. The Spaniards excluded us, just as we exclude the Japanese and Chinese there today. The one-hundred-per-cent Españoles, indeed, felt towards my countrymen as many one-hundred-per-cent Americans feel today towards the Russians. They were willing to trade with us, but otherwise we were revolutionary gringos, spreading the insane propaganda of democracy on earth, and we constituted a Red, White, and Blue menace.

But " manifest destiny " — that is, the will of God — is not to be oppilated, or evaded, or avoided. In 1818 a privateer from Buenos Aires landed at Monterey, destroyed and burned the town, and then moved south and raided the great Ortega ranch near Santa Barbara. Two members of the pirate crew were captured by the indignant Spaniards and sent forthwith to the Angel Gabriel Mission to be executed. One was Joe Chapman, a Massachusetts Nordic who had been shanghaied in Honolulu; the other was Tom Fisher, a blackamoor escaped from Georgia slavery.

Sizing up their captors, who were reeking with Catholic superstition and Spanish vanity, the two Americans flattered the childlike Spaniards out of the idea of killing them. Instead, they were permitted to live, as convicts. Chapman thereupon proceeded to show the Spaniards a thing or two. He built the San Gabriel padres a water-run grist-mill, the first in California. Then he built them

THE PLAZA, THE CHURCH OF OUR LADY THE QUEEN OF THE ANGELS, AND "SONORA TOWN," IN 1869

a small schooner, for otter-hunting. Then he took a gang of Indian neophytes to Los Angeles and finished building the church which had been started with brandy in 1814, the Church of Our Lady the Queen of the Angels, which stands facing the ancient Plaza to this day. The building has been reconstructed several times, but Chapman's original timbers remain in it.

On the basis of these accomplishments, Chapman pleaded for his liberty. It was offered to him on the condition that he join the Holy Roman Church, renounce his American nationality, and swear everlasting allegiance to the King of Spain. He accepted eagerly, and thus he became a naturalized Spaniard. But his instincts were still American. Released from the chain-gang, so to speak, the first thing Joe did was to go right back up to the great Ortega ranch which he had helped to devastate, make friends with the family, and then woo and marry the beautiful Señorita Guadalupe Ortega, apple of her daddy's eye, fairest flower of the valley, and the richest heiress for leagues around! Historically this was one of the most important things that ever happened in California.

Papa Ortega bought the children a huge ranch near the Angel Gabriel Mission, and presto! the penniless ex-convict, Joe Chapman, became Don José, a grandee, and settled down to drink wine, praise God, and raise a large family. He had done all this and was living happily with his wife and children about him when the next Americano arrived in Los Angeles, in 1826.

Fisher was not so lucky; his color was against him. Nevertheless, he was set free and did pretty well. He became a dashing vaquero, lassoed wild steers, played the guitar, drank plenty of brandy, and dozed happily in the sun, dreaming, no doubt, of that Georgia hell from which he had escaped.

Gradually more Americanos came into the neighborhood; about one a year for the next eighteen years. When the Mexicans took over from the Spaniards in 1822, the " death to foreigners " law was abolished, but foreigners, nevertheless, were decidedly not welcome and were not permitted to remain in the country as such. To remain they had to do what Chapman did; that is, they had to become Mexican citizens and members of the Catholic Church. That was easy.

In 1826 the second gringo, Joe Pryor, arrived in Los Angeles from Santa Fe. He got in touch with Chapman at once, and he was hardly rested from his journey before he had joined the Church and had taken oath to be a good Mexican. Shortly thereafter he married into the rich Sepúlveda family, thereby becoming Don José and the owner of a huge orchard and vineyard. Pryor was followed by Jack Temple, a Reading, Massachusetts, merchant. Temple married Señorita Rafael Cota, and thereby came into possession of the title of Don Juan and the far-spreading Los Cerritos rancho, upon which now stands a part of Long Beach. Next came Abel Stearns, a Salem, Massachusetts, trader. He took for his bride the beautiful Doña Arcadia Bandini, became Don Abel and the owner of the great Los Alamitos rancho, a fraction of which is now the Bixby ranch. On Christmas Eve 1828 the brig *Danube* was wrecked off the San Pedro mud flats. One of the few survivors, Johann Groningen, a German, promptly married into the rich Feliz family and became Don Domingo and the gift-owner of vast acreage. Jonathan Warner, a Connecticut Yankee, arrived, married into the Pico family, became

Don Juan José, and acquired two great ranches, one near Los Angeles, the other near Santa Barbara. Bill Wolfskill, a trapper, appeared, married into the Lugo family, and thereby acquired a huge tract. Hugo Reid, a Scotchman, wandered in. He simply married the daughter of the chief of the Gabrielino Indians (who had been freed by the Mexicans), and took over the entire reservation, the vast Santa Anita rancho, later made famous by its subsequent owner, " Lucky " Baldwin. Ben Wilson blew in. He married the exquisite Señorita Ramona Yorba and thereby acquired the great San Pasqual ranch (upon the edge of which Pasadena was built), became Don Benito, and among other things named Mount Wilson for himself. The list could be extended for another page. . . .

So the gringos came: Yankees, Germans, Frenchmen, Scotchmen, Jews, Irishmen, Swedes; traders, merchants, miners, sailors, trappers, adventurers, what not. All joined the Holy Roman Church, all renounced allegiance to whatever country they belonged to, all " went Mexican," and all, or nearly all, grabbed off señoritas and the dowries that went with them. The Mexicans, of course, were not pleased. But there was nothing they could do. When a gringo came in and bald-facedly went through the motions of joining the Catholic Church, taking the oath of allegiance to Mexico, and otherwise adopting the country, the childlike Mexicans were helpless. Against such an insidious attack they had no prophylactic.

And what was happening around Los Angeles was happening everywhere else in California. Thus we learn the meaning of that vague phrase: " benevolent assimilation." Now we know how the Americans conquered

California. They married it. Chapman, not Frémont, was the real Pathfinder!

The Spanish costume worn by the native male gentry at this time, and quickly affected by the gringos, was quite colorful. We can see " Don Juan " Temple strolling through the dusty lanes of early Los Angeles. He wears a broad-brimmed sombrero, a silk shirt, a colored waistcoat, and a short jacket of figured calico. His legs are encased in long, bell-bottom pantaloons of velveteen, slashed at the side below the knee and laced with gilt cord. Behind him comes " Don Abel " Stearns. His costume is the same, except that Abel wears knee-breeches, white stockings, silken garters with ornamented tassels, and deerskin shoes. A crimson sash serves both gentlemen in lieu of suspenders. A short cloak of brocade, the *sarape*, is flung over the shoulders with ostentatious carelessness.

Surely there are few things in all history more comical than the spectacle of this growing gang of gringos, this motley collection of erstwhile vagabonds and fortune-hunters, wearing this hot Spanish costume, dozing in the sun, lapping up wine, going solemly to mass with their Spanish brides, and greeting each other gravely (though no doubt with many a wink), as " Don Otto," " Don Ole," " Don Bill," and " Don Jake." What an uproarious travesty on the high-toned word " Don," a title ordinarily conferred only upon grandees, aristocrats, and gentlemen! For years the innocent Mexicans took these frauds at their face value. Finally they woke up, and with a vengeance. About 1840, as Major Horace Bell recorded in his *Reminiscences of a Ranger*, " the genuine, Simon pure Dons began to deny emphatically that these gringos were ' Dons,' or even ' hidalgos,' a word used to describe a man who has a father, or is the son of somebody." But it was too late then.

III

After 1840 every American-Mexican around Los Angeles (as elsewhere in California) was a spy. They encouraged the Californios in their trick revolutions and took part in many of the battles, " fighting " on both sides. None was ever hurt. At the Battle of Providencia the American-Mexicans on the opposing sides got drunk together before the fight and watched it with great glee.

As early as 1842 the United States had decided to " acquire " California. On October 19 of that year Commander Ap Catesby Jones, in command of the man-o'-war *United States,* landed at Monterey, took over the town without firing a shot, and flew the Stars and Stripes over it. But that was a false start; we were not quite ready. The following day Jones withdrew his marines and lowered Old Glory. More, he went to Los Angeles and " apologized " to Governor Micheltorena for having momentarily captured Monterey. Micheltorena, delighted, gave him a banquet and presented " Articles of Constitution," which called for Americans to pay an indemnity. Jones read them solemnly, toasted Micheltorena, politely returned the " Articles," unsigned, and everybody was happy.

Finally, four years later, the time was ripe, and Commander Sloat announced that the United States was taking over the country. All the naturalized American-Mexicans, all the gringo " Dons," now renounced their allegiance to Mexico, became one-hundred-per-cent American patriots, and joined in the war against their benefactors. It was one of the most classic double-crosses of history.

Stockton landed at San Pedro with five hundred men and started the march to Los Angeles. The town was occupied by the Mexican Admiral-General Castro with fifteen hundred men. Castro politely sent a courier to warn Stockton that the City of the Angels would be his grave if he entered it. Stockton sent back word to have the bells of the Plaza church tolled at eight o'clock the next morning, as he would enter Los Angeles at that time. Castro thereupon breathed mighty oaths against the Americanos. He lined up his army in the Plaza, waved his sword towards San Pedro, and shouted: " All who wish to save Mexico, follow me! " His loyal army was with him to a man. Then — " About face! " ordered Castro, and marched to Mexico.

Stockton entered the City of the Angels, took possession of the town without firing a shot, and raised Old Glory above the adobe hovels at 4.00 p.m., August 13, 1846. The Americans, as I have said, had already married most of the surrounding country. What they had not married they stole a few years later.

Hell-Hole of the West

Los Angeles, a town of five thousand inhabitants, was the proud capital and chief metropolis of California when the United States swallowed that country. The hamlet of Yerba Buena (San Francisco) was nothing before 1848, and the other villages, save Monterey, were even less.

But the Gold Rush changed all that. A year after the first nugget was found in a mill-race of the Columbia River, the population of Los Angeles had fallen from 5,000 to 1,600. Six miserable northern villages, not including the roaring madhouse of San Francisco, had passed it in size and importance. Worse, in 1849 the Constitutional Convention met at Monterey to apply for admission to statehood, with the foregone conclusion that the seat of government would go north.

Los Angeles, therefore, opposed California's entrance into the Union. It advocated, instead, a division of California, with San Luis Obispo as the dividing line; the northern section to become the ". State of California," the southern part to become the " Territory of Colorado." This proposition was laughed aside, California was admitted to the Union in September 1850, Sacramento was made the State capital, and the Angel City became a county seat.

Once started, the effort of Los Angeles to break California into two parts has continued intermittently ever since, the last demand for separation occurring as late as 1924. The agitation for division almost succeeded in 1859. A bill calling for it was passed by the Legislature and was signed by Governor Latham, but Congress, fearful of creating another slave State, smothered it.

The Los Angeles *Star*, or *La Estrella de Los Ángeles*, the town's first newspaper, which made its appearance in 1851, printed half in English, half in Spanish, was flooded with letters demanding the separation. The following communication, printed on February 19, 1859, was typical:

" I am settled in the conviction that unless we succeed in being detached (as now we may if our Southern press will aid us), the time will soon come when our feeble voice will become eternally silenced by an unnatural, unhappy, unprofitable, damnable and irrevocable fusion with the great metropolis and Sodom of San Francisco."

The San Francisco *Herald*, commenting on the subject, spoke scornfully of the native Californians in the southern part of the State as a " degraded race." " A large proportion of them," said the *Herald*, " are so exceedingly dark complexioned that it requires an expert to detect the difference between them and the Indians, and they are but little removed from the black race."

This fact gave the early American elections in Los

Angeles considerable color. Since the people had been swallowed bodily by the United States, all were given the right of citizenship and the vote, except the Indians who remained obviously in the aboriginal state, like the Yangs. The Americans drew up the tickets, dividing the offices with popular Mexicans, retaining the key positions for themselves. There was much confusion. Nobody knew who was who; whether a man should be classified as an Indian, a mulatto, or a mestizo; whether a half-breed was named Pedro or Juan; whether an alleged citizen had been there five years or five days. Accordingly, Indians and half-breeds were rounded up indiscriminately and carried to the polls. One drink and one dollar were the price of a vote. There was terrific challenging, but with little success. After a " citizen " had been voted once, the Americans cut off his long hair, washed his face, and otherwise disguised him. Then they gave him another name, another drink, and another dollar and took him back and voted him again. And still again if they could get up another disguise.

There was great interest in these early elections, and for a very good reason. Los Angeles County, when it was first created, in 1850, comprised all of its present vast area, plus all of San Bernardino and Orange counties, plus parts of Riverside and Kern counties. It was a *county* larger than the combined *states* of Connecticut, Delaware, Maryland, Massachusetts, New Hampshire, New Jersey, and Rhode Island. The Americans were getting ready to divide up this huge domain; to defraud the Mexicans out of their land. And they did it very neatly.

In 1851 Congress passed that incomparable Act entitled: " A Bill to Settle Private Land Claims in California," appointing a Board of Land Commissioners to settle claims and prepare the way for granting patents to the owners. This bill actually prepared the way for the greatest land steal in history; compared to it Cromwell's confiscation of the land in Ireland was mere petty larceny. The American machinery worked beautifully; there was perfect team-work between commissioners, lawyers, district courts, the Attorney General, the Surveyor General, the Secretary of the Interior, speculators, squatters, and the Supreme Court of the United States. Said the *Star:* " If the title of this Act read ' An Act to Confiscate the Private Lands Belonging to the Inhabitants of California,' nobody would be deceived, and the authors would have the merit of candor and frankness."

The Mexican ranchers needed cash to fight in the American courts, and they had little difficulty in obtaining it from their conquerors. Gringo usurers, says Harris Newmark in his authoritative *Sixty Years in Southern California*, charged them " from two to twelve and a half per cent. a week; and this brought about the loss of many early estates. I recollect, for example, that the owner of several thousand acres of land borrowed two hundred dollars, at an interest charge of twelve and a half per cent. for each week, from a resident of Los Angeles whose family is still prominent in California; and that when principal and interest amounted to twenty-two thousand dollars, the lender foreclosed and thus ingloriously came into possession of a magnificent property."

At the same time land taxes were doubled and tripled. The result was inescapable. In 1848 gringos owned eight of the one hundred and three ranches immediately surrounding Los Angeles. Four years later they owned eighty of them; while six of the ten largest landowners in the huge county were Americanos. When the land grab was all over, not only did the Mexicans have no land; they were also up to their necks in debt. For example, Don Pio Pico of Los Angeles, the last Mexican Governor of California, finally had to pawn his medals to keep out of the poorhouse. By 1858 the two largest individual taxpayers were "Don" Abel Stearns, $186,000, and "Don" John Temple, $89,000.

II

The Gold Rush drained Los Angeles for two years. Then the backwash filled it up again. Murderers, horse-thieves, and highwaymen, escaping the nooses of the gold country, made Los Angeles headquarters, augmenting disappointed prospectors, ranchers, vineyardists, gamblers, politicians, invalids, and land speculators. Around the Plaza, infesting the adobe hovels, there grew up a crib district containing one of the worst collections of prostitutes ever assembled in Christendom. Gold was plentiful. The years '49–'50 exhausted the supply of beef cattle in the north; thereafter the supply was obtained from the southern "cow country," of which Los Angeles was the incontrovertible queen. For several years the sale of cattle brought two or three million dollars annually into southern California.

From 1850 to 1870 the City of the Angels was a bad place, perhaps the most disreputable of all American frontier towns. The number of individual murders is not known, but according to the records there were forty "legal" hangings and thirty-seven impromptu lynchings. Few have heard of the Vigilantes of Los Angeles, but, as the late Charles Dwight Willard pointed out in 1891, they lynched " four times the number credited to the famous Vigilance Committees of San Francisco." And the historian Guinn recorded: " In the first 25 years of American rule in Los Angeles thirty-five men were executed by vigilance committees; during the same period only eight were hanged by the vigilantes of San Francisco. The nineteen Chinese massacred by a mob are not included in the thirty-five."

Items like these are to be found in nearly every issue of the *Star:* " Last Sunday night was a brisk night for killings. Four men were shot and killed, and several wounded in shooting affrays. . . . A Yaqui Indian named Augustine Del Rio murdered a Mexican because he refused to drink more whiskey after he went to bed. . . . On Sunday, the better the day the better the deed, a dispute arose between Nicho Alepas and a negro named Governor Scholes, which resulted in the death of the former."

And like these, in one issue of the *Southern Californian,* the town's second newspaper, which appeared in 1854: " The verdict of the coroner's jury on the body of Seferino Ochoa returned that he came to his death by the discharge of a gun loaded with powder and balls. . . . A party of Salt Lake and Montana teamsters had a lively row on Monday night; several shots were fired, from the effects of which one man died. . . . A shooting affray occurred between Mr. T. Baldwin and Mr. Adam Linn. Mr. Baldwin was shot through the heart, but unloaded his pistol before he expired, dying without speaking. Mr. Linn was uninjured."

The town consisted of one hotel, La Bella Union, a dozen stores, a score of saloons and gambling-joints, a church, a jail, and a crib district, all grouped around the Plaza; and several hundred houses scattered here and there. All the buildings, says Burdette, were " of adobe, one story high and absolutely fire-proof "; parts of which, he might have added, washed away at every rain. In 1849 the crazy ex-Mexican village had been surveyed in the hope of laying it out in some sensible fashion, but when the streets were staked off in accordance with the new survey, houses were left stranded in the middle of the streets, and no one knew exactly where his property began or ended.

Graded streets and sidewalks were unknown; hence during the rainy season the streets were a mass of sticky adobe mud from six inches to two feet deep. During the dry season the mud turned to dust. There was no shade except that provided by projecting verandas and a few scattered trees. At night lanterns, suspended in front of saloons, furnished the only light in the town. As late as 1860 the *Star* was saying: " We think the city council should also take the hint and hang out lights at many corners. It might prevent commission of crimes which are perpetrated under cover of night."

The Plaza and the various roadways served as a dumping-ground for refuse and rubbish. If a man bought a suit of clothes, he threw the discarded garments into the street, where they remained until some tramp took possession of them. Dead horses and other animals lay in the streets for days at a time, until Indians cut up the carcasses for food. The town was a mecca for mongrel dogs, a subject of comment by every visitor. There were sixty or seventy on every ranch, and Los Angeles itself was overrun with these vicious beasts. When a stage arrived from San Francisco, it was followed by an army of half-starved dogs, barking, snarling, and fighting; when the stage drew up at La Bella Union, the brutes had to be dispelled with guns.

The streets were thronged day and night with pedestrians and horsemen. The three most respectable saloons and gambling-houses were the Montgomery, the Palace, and the El Dorado. From the Plaza it was only a step in one direction to the Calle de las Vírgenes (Street of the Maids), one end of which was known as Squaw Lane, and another in the opposite direction to the classic precincts of the Calle de los Negros, better known as Nigger Alley. This was a dreadful thoroughfare, forty feet wide, running one whole block, filled entirely with saloons, gambling-houses, dance-halls, and cribs. It was crowded night and day with people of many races, male and female, all rushing and crowding along from one joint to another, from bar to bar, from table to table.

There was a band in every joint, with harps, guitars, and other stringed instruments predominating. The *Star* recounts the untimely death of one popular musician as follows: " On Monday evening Mr. Charles Enken, a musician, known as Bass Viol Charlie, died very suddenly while engaged in playing on his favorite instrument at the La Polka Saloon. He arose from his seat and fell dead upon the floor." Orchestras of the primitive Mexican-Indian brand, says Bell, " sent forth discordant notes to mingle with the yells and cries and the jingle of gold, while several Mexican ' maromas ' were usually underway at once in uproarious confusion, the dope-crazed revellers making the night hideous with their howlings."

There were seven thousand Indians in the vicinity of Los Angeles, including about a thousand Yangs, interbred with other tribes. Emancipated by the Mexicans, forgotten during the Gold Rush, all these savages were now undergoing destruction. Vineyardists, ranchers, merchants, saloons, and gambling-houses used them for slaves and paid them in *aguardiente*, a terrific fire-water. Every Saturday evening, as soon as they were paid off, several thousand Indians met in the Calle de los Negros and in a near-by set of hovels known as Sonora Town and spent the night drinking, gambling, fighting, and raising hell in general. By late Sunday afternoon, when the show ended, Nigger Alley was a madhouse, filled with a mass of drunken, crazy Indians, male and female, of all ages, fighting, dancing, killing each other off with knives and clubs, and falling paralyzed drunk in the street. Every week-end three or four were murdered.

At sundown Sunday the town marshal unlocked the jail and let forth several squads of special Indian deputies, or *alcaldes*, whom he had kept locked up all day to keep sober. These aboriginal " peace officers," quickly getting drunk themselves, would whip, drive, carry, cart, and drag their fellow barbarians into a large cattle corral behind the Plaza. There they would sleep off their spree Sunday night. Monday morning, full of headaches, they were offered for sale as slaves for the week. One or two were always found dead in the corral Monday morning. The following item appears in the press with monotonous repetition: " The coroner's jury sat on the body of a dead Indian. The verdict was: ' Death from intoxication, or by a visitation from God.' "

The *Star* of March 12, 1859 prints this illuminating " Presentment of the Grand Jury, February Term ":

" The Grand Jury would respectfully call attention to a feature in our local government which calls loudly for reform. It refers to the Indian Alcalde system. The Indians thus selected and clothed with a brief and illegal authority are in no respect in advance of the mass of their degraded race; and the constantly recurring scenes enacted in our streets, wherein these miserable creatures of both sexes are dragged to jail by a crowd of equally miserable and often-times more intoxicated and beastly Indian officials, serves but to divest law of its majesty and render our thoroughfares, especially upon the Sabbath, unfit for the presence of decency.

"In this connection the Grand Jury would recommend that steps should be taken for the removal from the city of all vagrant Indians, male and female. Of the latter class, more especially, large numbers are daily and hourly encountered on every street and corner, in every conceivable state of intoxication, disease and misery, without any abode, and ekeing out a precarious existence from the proceeds of crime and licentiousness."

The hamlet of San Gabriel, now a thriving suburban community huddled around the ruined Mission, was also a popular place, with three saloons, all run by Americans. On Sundays they catered to five or six hundred customers. The Americans preferred whisky, the Mexicans and Indians brandy; the high-toned ladies of joy sipped "Angelica"; the hilarious squaws drank anything. Two monte games ran in each bar-room, there was cock-fighting and hoochy-koochy dancing in the rear, and horse-racing out in the road in front. The Indians, having learned one of the Americanos' favorite sports, hanged one of their race nearly every Sunday.

It was a miracle that everybody in Los Angeles didn't die of some plague. Until the seventies the town was criss-crossed with a network of *zanjas*, or open ditches, which served confusedly as runways for domestic water, irrigating canals, hog-wallows, swimming-holes, comfort stations, and laundries. There were eight ditches, all supplied by the *zanja madre* (mother ditch), which got its water from the contaminated river. For years the *Star* complained bitterly about citizens' throwing refuse into the water ditches, and on February 5, 1859 records that a child was drowned in the *zanja madre*. Naturally, smallpox epidemics hit the town every year. Only a few " nuts " submitted to vaccination, and sanitary measures were laughed at; everybody objected to isolation, and disinfecting was unknown. During these sieges the whole town was exposed; men and women loaded up with liquor; some left, many died.

The place was such a sink of iniquity that the four Protestant preachers, Methodist, Baptist, Presbyterian, and Episcopal, closed their churches in disgust in 1858 and abandoned Los Angeles to the Devil. A new Methodist divine shortly appeared on the scene and attempted to organize a general Protestant church. A brick building was started, but before it was well under way six Mexicans were lynched, the preacher left town, and the project petered out, leaving the Catholics as the sole survivors. The Presbyterian pastor, the Reverend James Woods, contributed to the press this sad benediction as he departed: " To preach week after week to empty benches is certainly not encouraging, but when in addition to that a minister has to contend against a torrent of vice and immorality which obliterates all traces of the Christian Sabbath; when he is compelled to endure the blasphemous denunciations of his divine mission, to live where society is disorganized, religion scoffed at, where violence runs riot, and even life itself is unsafe — such

condition of affairs may suit some men, but it is not cal-
culated for the peaceful labors of one who follows un-
obtrusively the foot-steps of the meek and lowly Savior."

The town's angelic name was too ridiculous for such
a hell-hole. Throughout the State Los Angeles became
known as Los Diablos, or The Devils, and letters thus
addressed had no difficulty in reaching their proper des-
tination. Colloquially, the town was simply called Los,
meaning " The " — perhaps implying " The *What Is
It?* " — which seems to have been appropriate, for during this period there was hardly any other name to give
Los Angeles except " the Hell-hole," and the " Pest-
house," as it was frequently called.

III

But everything was not so sordid. Throughout the
fifties we find the manufacturers of London Clubhouse
Gin running the following delightful advertisement in
the *Star:* " To persons travelling in these days of rapid
transit " — at that time it took eighty hours by stage to
go from Los Angeles to San Francisco, and seventy-two
hours to go from Los Angeles to Yuma, Arizona — " To
persons travelling in these days of rapid transit, who are
constantly changing their water as well as their climate;
who are drinking, indeed, a dozen kinds of water in every
twenty-four hours, and each draught containing some
property acting in chemical antagonism to the preceding
one, thereby causing an unnatural degree of excitement
to the stomach — it is positively and absolutely necessary
to use a counter-acting agent. From the fact that London Clubhouse Gin is prepared expressly to meet such
exigencies, and to act as we know it will act, as an anti-

dote, we confidently prescribe it as the very best article in the country."

Perhaps that is why everybody in Los Angeles didn't die of dysentery, smallpox, or some other disease.

Every Sunday there was horse-racing in the Calle de las Vírgenes. Folks for miles around came to enter their steeds, betting money, merchandise, land, and live stock. One of the most celebrated horse-races ever run in California was held in Los Angeles in 1852; a two-horse competition between Pio Pico's Sarco, the undefeated champion of the cow country, and José Sepúlveda's Black Swan, imported all the way from Australia to challenge him. The race was ballyhooed throughout the State; sportsmen from San Francisco to San Diego went to witness the contest. The official stakes were $25,000 in cash, 500 mares, 500 heifers, 500 calves, and 500 sheep; smaller fortunes were placed in side bets.

This race was not one of your ridiculous modern five-furlong sprints; these noble steeds raced *nine miles*, starting on San Pedro Street near the " city limits," and running four and a half miles to town and back again. The Pico entry took the lead. At the seven-mile pole, however, Black Swan, getting his second wind, shot past Sarco; and from then on, it was just a breeze for the Swan. Pico's nag had looked great in competition with the ordinary ranch horses, but against the Australian speed-demon he resembled a milk-wagon plug.

Cock-fights were held every day in the dusty lanes, facetiously called streets; fanciers strolling proudly round with their fighting roosters under their arms. The chief fights were always held on St. John's Day, a religious holiday. Then only the gamest and most ferocious cocks were matched, the combatants wearing not the ordinary ice-pick spurs, but double-edged steel contraptions which resembled safety-razor blades. These weapons were so deadly that frequently a rooster, jumping up at his adversary, cut his own throat. Feats of horsemanship also marked the pious observance of St. John's Day, and roosters (though not game roosters) also assisted in the most popular game, the *carrera del gallo*. The feathers were plucked from a live cock's neck, his neck was greased thoroughly, and he was then buried in the ground with only his head and neck exposed. A horseman got back sixty yards, starting at a given signal. The object of the game was to ride by at full speed, lean from the saddle, seize the rooster by the neck, and pull him squawking from the ground, a most difficult feat.

There were bull-fights every week, and several at Christmas and New Year's. The " Plaza de Toros " was a cattle corral at the end of Nigger Alley, the same one used for the Indians. Said one historian: " There were tiers of elevated seats for the elite who cared to pay and witness the slaughter in comfort; the rabble had the privilege of peeping through the fence. Before the fight a canvas enclosure accommodated the bull and the bull-fighters, a rag partition dividing the belligerents, on the theory that familiarity breeds contempt." A Mexican string band played brave, solemn music. Each fight was advertised by placards proclaiming the exceptional ferocity of the bull and the skill of the toreador who, in every case, was " direct from Mexico City." Usually he was a humble cow-hand on a near-by ranch, but on the day of the bull-fight, at least, he was a grand toreador. Entering the ring to a burst of applause, he always made a speech before risking his life. Straining forward on tip-toe, he addressed the audience, pointing out that he was very brave, that he had much honor, that it was far better to die than to live with a taint on one's honor, and usually ending with the modest assertion: "I am the bravest man in the world, all of which you will have due proof of when you see me encounter the most ferocious bull in California."

The most ferocious bull in California often turned out to be such a tame old bull that he had to be converted into a walking pincushion before even a red flag bothered him. Sometimes the crowd, hissing fiercely, jumped into the arena of blood and sand, opened the gate, and ran the bull out of the ring, twisting his tail. At other times the amateur toreador made so many false stabs and broke off so many swords in the poor animal that the Master of the Arena finally pushed him aside and walked up and killed the dazed brute with a knife. On such occasions the disgraced toreador leaped the fence and took to his heels.

Bear-hunting was another sport; the woods were full of bears. The crowds rode out around the hills until one was found; then four horsemen were selected to get him. One lassoed the bear, and when the enraged brute started after him or began biting or tearing the *reata*, a second horseman lassoed him. These hunters, mostly Mexican vaqueros, were so expert with a lariat that they could rope a bear by the paw, just as they could rope a wild mustang by any leg. When the four had the bear helpless, in a spread-eagle position, a brave rode forward and dispatched him with a lance. Sometimes, however, Bruin was brought in alive, for a fight with a bull. The animals were starved and taunted before the combat, and the Angelenos took other precautions against a "no contest." Before letting the maddened beasts at each other, they chained one of the bull's forelegs to one of the bear's hind legs, thus assuring a slaughter. If the animals showed any reluctance to fight, they were goaded to battle. These fights were very popular, especially with the ladies, whose feminine yells and screeches of joy enlivened the occasions, lending a softening note to the butchery. The last bear and bull fights were held in Los Angeles in 1860. The *Star* of December 18, 1859 describes one at some length.

As early as 1852 the population no longer sang hymns in bed at dawn; the Americans objected to the noise. The town, nevertheless, was full of religion. Sweet-toned bells tolled morning and evening at the Church of Our Lady the Queen of the Angels, calling supplicants, dogs, and beggars. Each year the Corpus Christi festival was held in the Plaza, which was first " carefully cleared of debris and dead cats." Altars, decorated with silks, satins, and jewelry, were erected around the square, a priest presiding at each altar. Carrying banners and flowers and robed in white, the celebrants marched round, pausing for formal worship at each altar. The progress around the Plaza took a couple of hours; twelve men, each carrying a huge burning candle, represented the twelve Apostles.

The Feast of the Holy Week, however, was the main religious celebration in the Angel City, ending crescendo fortissimo on the seventh day with a public execution of Judas Iscariot. A gibbet was erected in the Plaza early in the week. On Saturday afternoon a life-size effigy of Judas was mounted on an ox-cart, driven through the streets, and finally brought to the gallows, where the populace assembled. One after another a dozen Mexican orators leaped to the scaffold and violently denounced the traitor, shaking their fists in his face and slapping him about. They accused Judas not only of betraying the Savior, but also of rustling horses, stealing chickens, cheating at cards; of being a gringo, and, worst of all, of being a Jew. They had an idea, it seems, that Christ was a Mexican. All this time the crowd was working itself up to the fever pitch. Finally a squad of Mexican soldiers, the drums beating, marched up to the gallows, the commander gave the order, and a volley riddled Judas. This was the signal for a general fusillade from the crowd, which immediately let go with shot-guns, revolvers, and empty whisky-bottles. Meanwhile the band played furiously, and the mob, drunk on both liquor and religious fanaticism, yelled, shot, and hooted in triumphant glee as Judas was sent to the Devil until next year. In 1854, by special arrangement, the firing squad which executed Judas in the Plaza was composed entirely of Americanos and was commanded with great honor by Captain W. W. Twist of Santa Barbara. My countrymen acquitted themselves admirably, blowing the despicable Iscariot properly to hell, to the drunken roars of a patriotic assemblage.

IV

But the chief sport, of course, was real lynching. It is not my intention to give much space to these sordid affairs. One was in sight on October 13, 1854, when Dave Brown, a gambler, killed a popular citizen, Mr. Pinckey Clifford. Fortunately, Mayor Stephen G. Foster, a Yale graduate and a scholar, met the mob and persuaded it to disperse. How? If, the Mayor said, after a fair trial, the court did not sentence Brown to hang, then he himself would lead the crowd to lynch him. Thus assured that the victim could not escape, the mob went into watchful waiting. Brown was tried and sentenced to hang on January 12, 1855, the same day, it happened, that one Felipe Alvitre was to pay the same penalty. Two days before the fatal day, however, the Supreme Court granted Brown a stay of execution. No relief was provided for Alvitre. The populace, thus cheated of a " double-header," was somewhat disappointed, but at all events it had the pleasure of one hanging. Soon after breakfast Alvitre was strung up on Gallows Hill, a knoll behind the jail, in a pouring rain, before a great crowd, including many women. At the first attempt the rope broke. The executioners sprang forward, lifted the body, knotted the rope together, and once more drew aloft the writhing form, to the delight of the mob.

This taste of blood proved too much for the patience of the Angelenos. From the top of a beer-keg one orator after another made eloquent appeals for the immediate lynching of Brown. The oratory continued all the forenoon and was resumed after the heavy midday meal. Finally the crowd began to move towards the jail. Mayor Foster thereupon mounted the beer-keg, publicly resigned his office, and placed himself at the head of the mob. The jailer was " overpowered," Brown was dragged out across Spring Street, a rope was placed about his neck and thrown over the cross-beam of a corral gateway. Juan Gonzales, a horse-thief, volunteered to act as chief hangman, or first man on the rope. When all was ready, Brown was asked if he had any last words. The condemned man said he objected most emphatically to being executed by " a lot of greasers."

All those who held the rope with Gonzales were Mexicans. Accordingly, a half-dozen race-proud Americanos sprang forward and did the deed.

Bill Workman, editor of the *Southern Californian*, had endeavored to speed up the lynching-bee so that his account of it would reach the steamer then at San Pedro before it left for San Francisco. But oratory held back the proceedings. So he wrote in advance a lurid report, giving every detail, even to the " confession " of the condemned man on the improvised gallows, and slapped it on the press. Several hours before the tragic event took place the *Southern Californian*, containing his account of the hanging, was on its way to San Francisco and was also on sale in Los Angeles. During the lynching many of the mob had Workman's report of it in their hands, comparing his description with the actual event. There were some bitter complaints of inaccuracy. After the hanging Foster immediately resumed the office of mayor.

A short time later a hundred Angelenos, under the leadership of Henry Crabb, a Stockton lawyer, set out from Los Angeles to conquer Mexico. The filibustering expedition got as far as Sonita, a little town across the border from Yuma, Arizona, where they blew up a church. That, apparently, was a great mistake, for the American patriots were quickly surrounded and then annihilated by a mob of infuriated Mexicans. Those who were not killed in the battle were captured, tied to trees, and executed. Of the hundred Americanos, only one was spared, a fifteen-year-old boy. Crabb's head was cut off and sent back to the Angel City in mescal.

A report then spread through Los Angeles that the Mexican population was preparing to slaughter every gringo in the town. The Americanos were seized with terror. All their women were rounded up and placed in Armory Hall, while the men went out to patrol the streets and hills. Before sundown four men, including a German and a Pole, were killed by a small group of Mexicans on the outskirts of the town's far-flung city limits. Sheriff Barton set out with five deputies to capture the murderers. They met the Mexicans in Santiago Canyon, where the Sheriff and three of his deputies were killed, the other two escaping back to Los Angeles. The town was placed under martial law, one company of soldiers was rushed to it from Fort Tejon, another from San Diego, and the State Legislature voted funds at once to finance posses. The result was a general round-up of forty-two Mexicans, many dragged from their houses in Los Angeles.

Then the real fun began. The Vigilantes gathered on the veranda of the Montgomery Saloon, elected a chairman, and held court. The procedure, as described by Newmark, was simple. The Chair called out the name of a prisoner, announced that he was held on suspicion of murder, and then asked: " What is your pleasure? " The pleasure was: " Hang him! " The Chair then put the question: " Gentlemen, you have heard the motion. All those in favor of hanging So-and-So will signify by saying: ' Ay.' " And the citizens roared: " Ay! " Having thus expressed their will, the assemblage retired for a drink and then marched to the jail, " overpowered " the jailer, and took So-and-So up to Gallows Hill and dispatched him. Then they returned for another drink and another " trial."

Of the forty-two Mexicans taken prisoner, eleven were thus hanged, until even the bloodthirsty Angelenos grew weary of the sport. The last man lynched was a twenty-year-old boy, Juan Flores. He was executed, says Newmark (an eyewitness), "in sight of such a throng that it is hardly too much to say that practically every man, woman and child in the town was present, not to mention many people drawn by curiosity from various parts of the State who had flocked into the town."

On October 12, 1871, a few days after the beginning of the great Chicago fire, the *Star* printed one of the most caustic editorials ever addressed to a community by its press. "Three days ago," said the editor, "the press of this City called upon the public generally to meet at a stated hour last evening, at the County Court-room, to do something towards alleviating the sufferings of the destitute thousands in Chicago. The calamity which has overtaken that unfortunate city has aroused the sympathy of the world, and the heart and pulse of civilized humanity voluntarily respond, extending assistance in deeds as well as words. From all parts of the globe, where the name of Chicago is known, liberal donations flow into a common treasury. We had hoped to be able to add the name of Los Angeles among the list, as having done its duty.

"But in whatever else Los Angeles may excel, her charity is a dishonorable exception. Her bowels are absolute strangers to sympathy, when called upon to practically demonstrate it. At the place of meeting, instead of seeing the multitude, we were astonished to find but three persons, viz: Governor Downey, John Jones, and a gentleman from Riverside, who is on a visit here. Anything more disgraceful than this apathy on the part of her inhabitants Los Angeles could not be guilty of. For her selfishness, she justly deserves the fearful fate that has befallen the helpless one that now lies stricken in the dust. Let her bow her head in shame. Chicago, our response to your appeal is: 'Starve! What do we care?'"

The lash drew blood. Always over Los Angeles, from the earliest days, in the sunshine hung a constant shadow: the fear of a devastating earthquake. Within a week more than two thousand dollars was raised and sent to Chicago.

Six days later war broke out in Chinatown. "In the course of the years," says Newmark, "Nigger Alley had come to be more and more occupied by the Chinese. One whole side of it was given over to their opium dens, shops, laundries, and residences. There, also, their religious rites were celebrated in the joss house, some of the hideously painted gods being visible from the street." A Chinaman with two revolvers ran out into the street and, firing wildly at a countryman, accidentally killed a white man. Other shots from Chinese barricaded behind iron shutters wounded a number of bystanders.

In less than ten minutes Nigger Alley was surrounded by a frenzied mob of more than a thousand bloodthirsty Angelenos, armed with pistols, guns, knives, and ropes. A Chinese armed with a hatchet ran out of a house and tried to escape across Los Angeles Street. He was caught, rushed to a corral gate, and strung up. The mob, wild for blood, then rushed into the adobe buildings and dragged forth and slaughtered every Chinese they could lay hands on. The New York *Times* reprinted from the San Francisco *Bulletin* a two-thousand-word account of this massacre. I quote a few extracts:

"One of the most horrible tragedies that ever disgraced any civilized community. . . . The denizens of

ABOVE: THE CALLE DE LOS NEGROS,
WHERE THE CHINESE MASSACRE STARTED

BELOW: AN IMPROMPTU HANGING
AT THE FOOT OF GALLOWS HILL, WHERE THE
FEDERAL BUILDING NOW STANDS

Nigger Alley are cosmopolitan, consist of the dregs of society, some of the greatest desperadoes on the Pacific Coast. Murderers, horsethieves, highwaymen, burglars . . . make this their rendezvous. In this place also the Chinese congregate, monopolizing about two-thirds of an entire block. . . . The streets rattled with a deafening din. . . . The entire block was surrounded by an unbroken link of human devils, thirsting for revenge. Curses and loud denunciations of the whole ' heathen ' crew arose on all sides. . . . The yelling and cursing was frightful to hear. . . .

" Trembling, moaning, wounded Chinese were hauled from their hiding places; ropes quickly encircled their necks; they were dragged to the nearest improvised gallows. Three thus suffered in a cluster, to the end of a water spout. A large wagon close by had four victims hanging from its sides. . . . Three others dangled from an awning. . . . Five more were taken to the gateway and lynched. . . . Hellish proceedings. . . . A little urchin, not over ten years old, was as active as anyone in doing the hanging. His childish voice sounded strange at that place, as he called aloud for more victims; a stranger and sadder sight still to see him lay his hands to the rope and help to haul them up. In the background a woman was looking on. . . . She loudly congratulated the lynchers on their diabolical work, and encouraged them to continue. . . .

" Looting. . . . Every nook, corner, chest, trunk, and drawer in Chinatown was carefully ransacked. Even the victims executed were robbed. The Chinese Doctor had his garments stripped from off his person while hanging; others had their pockets cut out with knives, which entered into and fearfully lacerated the flesh, the lynchers having neither time nor patience to rifle them in the usual way! . . . $7,000 was extracted from a box in the Chinese store."

The Chinese massacre succeeded the Chicago fire as a topic of national news. Nineteen Chinese were lynched, or, rather, strangled to death after being stabbed and beaten. It was estimated that forty thousand dollars in cash was stolen by the mob, not to mention much costly jewelry and other valuables. This was Los Angeles's first appearance on the front pages of the nation's newspapers. The great majority of Americans, of course, had never heard of the town before, and the incongruity of its angelic name and such a slaughter created much cynical comment. Newspapers throughout the country printed editorials, some beginning with the caption: " Los Angeles or Los Diablos? " One hundred and fifty men were indicted by the Grand Jury, and six were convicted and sentenced to the penitentiary. A few days later, I hardly need to say, they were released on a " technicality." Chinese throughout the country held lamentation services for the Los Angeles victims; four Chinese priests went down from San Francisco to conduct the funeral services. Later the United States paid China a large indemnity.

This quieted the City of the Angels down. There were several more lynchings during the next few years, but the bad days were over. A new era had already begun to dawn for California, an era of miracles for Los Angeles.

PART TWO

On the Wings of Iron Horses

*W*hat are the prospects for Los Angeles as the sixties draw to a close? Here is a sleepy little Spanish-American town of six thousand population, dozing in the sun on the farthest frontier of America. It is not a seaport; neither does it have any natural resources. It nestles in a precarious valley which is hospitable to agriculture only by reason of artificial irrigation. The great cattle industry, the backbone of the country, has been ruined by drought. About the countryside are flocks of lean sheep, scattered orchards, many dusty vineyards. From a commercial standpoint the only things worth mention- ing are wine-making and brandy-making. What little surplus Los Angeles County produces goes by wagon- train to San Francisco, to Salt Lake City, to the Arizona mining-towns; or else by ox-cart to San Pedro, where it is transferred into lighters and carried out to the San Francisco steamers, anchored outside the mud flats.

Trade comes in in the same way. The town does not seem to have much of a future.

Nevertheless, Los Angeles is hopeful, as all of California is hopeful, for at last the dream of twenty years is coming true. The transcontinental railroad is about to be completed. No longer will California be isolated. No longer will people who are desirous of going there from the East — and they are many — be forced to take one of those three awful journeys: either (1) overland by covered wagon or stage, (2) by water all the way round Cape Horn, or (3) by water to Panama, across that fevered isthmus by stage, and thence upward again by ship. The plans of the Central Pacific and Southern Pacific railroads, soon to merge, constitute the main, the vital topic of conversation up and down the Pacific coast. As soon as the transcontinental line is completed between San Francisco and Chicago, the railroad proposes to cross the Pacific stem of that elongated, unfinished T, with a line running up and down the coast, thus linking the entire State of California with the nation.

In anticipation of this great event Los Angeles County embarked upon its first official business venture. It built a jerk-line railroad from Los Angeles to San Pedro (the natural terminus of any railroad running south), for the purpose of selling it later to the Southern Pacific at a handsome profit. This little road, twenty miles long, was finished in 1869; the last cross-tie, presented by Wells, Fargo & Company, was of polished laurel. A trick locomotive came by steamer round the Horn; it was named " Gabriel," in honor of the archangel. Evidently " Gabriel " traveled very slowly, for the *News* in an editorial headed: "Horse Flesh vs Railways," said: "Stages of Tomlinson & Company, with passengers from the steamer came into the city 31 minutes ahead of stages connecting with the railroad 4½ miles from the city. Railway communication may be the cheapest but it appears horse flesh is much the fastest."

About the same time, May 1869, the great transcontinental railroad was completed at Promontory, Utah. All eyes in California now turned to the Southern Pacific. South of San Francisco the State stretched like a broken finger for six hundred miles to the Mexican border, hemmed in by mountain, desert, and sea. No town in all that vast domain had a rail outlet. Great agricultural valleys, hundreds of little towns, waited eagerly for the railroad to extend its lines through the Golden State. The Southern Pacific thus held California in the hollow of its hand. It was in a position to " make or break " any community; to control the destinies of every town, every section of California, for years to come, if not permanently.

It proceeded, naturally, to make the most of its position. Slowly, invitingly, tantalizingly, the Southern Pacific pushed its tracks down through the rich San Joaquin Valley, one of the greatest agricultural sections on earth. Approaching a town, it paused to inquire how much that community was prepared to offer for a railroad. Or, rather, the railroad asked for " co-operation " — so many sections of land, so many acres for a depot, so much right of way, so much actual cash. There was no appeal. If a town declined to meet the Southern Pacific's " suggestions," the railroad laid its tracks round that town twenty, forty, sixty miles away, put up a depot in a bare field, and started a little community of its own. Soon the town which had refused to meet the railroad's " requests " found itself out of luck, disintegrating, the surrounding farmers hauling to the railroad station, sheep-herders taking their flocks there for shearing, stores going up there — a new town supplanting the old one as the center of the section. Virtually all the large San Joaquin Valley towns of today (Modesto, Merced, Fresno, etc.) were founded and plotted by the railroad's construction company. Its land agents took charge, and the lots were offered for sale at auction. In vain communities pleaded, wheat-growers raged, orchardists beat their breasts. There was no appeal. The Southern Pacific crawled through the San Joaquin Valley like a steel thousand-legged worm, extending itself towards a town invitingly, contracting itself threateningly, putting forward spur tracks, drawing them back, moving its tentacles in and out. It was Frank Norris's " Octopus," and how beautifully it functioned!

Communities which refused to " listen to reason " withered and died. Only two municipalities, Bakersfield and Visalia, successfully defied the Iron Horse. The Southern Pacific passed them up, dispassionately and without hesitation, but their positions were so favored that eventually the railroad had to go to them. Thirty times that many towns shriveled and died, bitterly, bankrupt, all without sense, and most without honor. For if the Southern Pacific Railroad was an Octopus, then the little towns which howled and fought for its services were so many jackals, cutting each other's throats. In their efforts to get a railroad, there is nothing in American history to surpass the performance of these California towns in municipal throat-cutting, doublecrossing, backbiting, and neighborly hating. To believe that the small-town bankers, two-by-four merchants, and greedy wheat-farmers of the various competitive sections of San Joaquin Valley were moved by sentiments, motives, or actions more noble than those of Leland Stanford, Charlie Crocker, Mark Hopkins, and Collis P. Huntington — the prehensile " Big Four " of the Southern Pacific — is to believe in fairies. They were all trying to profit as much as possible.

When the Southern Pacific reached the Tehachapi Mountains, it made its demands upon Los Angeles. It merely wanted, in addition to the usual right of way and the alternate land sections, sixty acres in the middle of the town for a depot, the railroad which the county had built to San Pedro, and a cash sum representing five per cent of the county's total assessed valuation! Otherwise its tracks would go sixty-five miles east to San Bernardino, and thence later across the continent — the southern route. Los Angeles called to high Heaven to witness this " hold-up," yelling bloody murder, but the Southern Pacific was adamant. After cursing the railroad for a year, the county put the matter to a vote, on November 5, 1872. The Southern Pacific got what it wanted. It had been a right smart piece of business for the county to build that little road to San Pedro, with the confident expectation of selling it to the Southern Pacific at a handsome profit; it was excruciatingly painful to have to turn it over to the Octopus as a gift, laurel cross-tie, " Gabriel," and all. The cash subsidy, moreover, was $750,000.

The building of this line to Los Angeles was marked by two pieces of marvellous, costly construction. Rising from the floor of the San Joaquin Valley, the Southern Pacific surmounted the Tehachapi Pass by a line of track that swerved back and forth up a mountain side, through eighteen tunnels, and finally looped over itself. While one army of Chinese laborers moved over this mountain, another force, working up from the south, pierced the San Fernando Mountains with a seven-thousand-foot tunnel. Four years later, on September 6, 1876, the two tracks met at a little place called Lang, forty miles north of Los Angeles.

That was a momentous day for Los Angeles. Three hundred and fifty Angelenos went forward in two flag-draped special trains to witness the " Wedding of the Rails "; a delegation of forty came down from San Francisco, including Crocker, president of the Southern Pacific. The completion of this line did not mean much to San Francisco; it meant life to Los Angeles. People from over the countryside rode horseback to the scene, or drove in teams, taking their families. When the ceremonies were ready to start, nearly a thousand persons were present.

There remained fifteen hundred feet of track to be laid down before the gap in the railroad was closed. The road-bed was graded, and the ties were all in place, ready for the last rails. As a grand finale a track-laying contest was staged by the opposing forces of Chinese laborers. Seven hundred and fifty on a side, they started at the drop of a hat; eight and a half minutes later the rails met. A Los Angeles jeweler stepped forward and presented Crocker with a golden spike and a silver hammer. The president of the Southern Pacific drove the final spike, surrounded by the silent, bare-headed throng, while the fifteen hundred proud Chinese coolies stood dumbly in the sun, sweat pouring from beneath their crazy hats, their picks and shovels held at " present arms." The crowd burst into cheers, and both trains headed for the Angel City for a celebration at Buffum's Saloon.

II

Let us glance at Los Angeles as the first iron horse reaches it. Laurance L. Hill, a local writer, has fashioned a romantic and colorful little picture: " Mingling along the unkept streets are ox-drawn carretas, diminutive American-built horse-cars, dusty covered wagons, pack trains, family surreys, droves of slab-sided steers and ragged sheep, and unnumbered dogs without pedigree. Guided in some mysterious manner by a single jerk-line, come 10, 16 and sometimes 20 animal teams, dragging huge freighters, with their trailers. Easy-sitting caballeros, with silver-studded saddles and huge spurs, ride spirited California-bred horses; for no one thinks of walking a block while horse-flesh stands at each well-chewed hitching-rack. Red-berried peppers droop over the squat, unpainted adobe houses of ' Sonoratown,' and spear-pointed century plants overlook crumbling walls. Green vineyards and sweet-scented orange orchards spread out over the level land. Set back in velvety lawns, and surrounded by blazing flowers from many climes, hospitable homes in the carved and turreted style of the Ulysses S. Grant period of architecture, range northward from the cultivated fields toward the Plaza."

Men take their siestas in the balmy air, doze on verandas; the place is a picture of lazy, easy-going activity. " Two dissimilar nationalities," wrote Clara Spalding Brown at the time, " two distinct cultures, are represented; one by the quaint dilapidated *adobes* of ' Sonora Town,' the other by the un-paved streets and wooden houses of the Gringo section. A step from the practical, ambitious, horse-car world of the *Americanos* is the dreamy air of Old Mexico." Los Angeles is not really an American town; the Mexicans are dominated, but not swallowed; the gringos rule, but they are outnumbered. " Mexican women glide about everywhere; the soft Spanish speech is heard on all sides. Long-robed priests hurry to and fro; the jangling bells of the Church of Our Lady the Queen of the Angels ring out morning and evening." Orange-venders, sellers of firewood (the roots of the manzanita), drive up and down in antiquated carts. There are no paved streets, the dust is thick; when it rains, animals and vehicles sink knee-deep into a mixture of adobe mud and offal. The " sidewalks," consisting mostly of planks or gravel, are little better.

The Plaza, to quote Mrs. Brown again, " shifted slightly from the original location, is a dismal and dusty place, with a feeble fountain in the center, the Square surrounded by a row of tall Monterey cypresses, shorn and clipped in the shape of huge cones. Idlers bask in the sunshine on the fountain's stone rim, or lie face down in the triangles of shade made by the cypress trees. All over the town foliage is sheared and compressed into unnatural and distorted shapes, which gives the place a foreign look, in keeping with its buildings, population, and crooked streets." Houses are scattered out on both sides of the river and into the hills near by. There are gas street-lamps (fed from tanks), four hotels, and one three-story sky-scraper.

In Buffum's Saloon the coming of the railroad is celebrated with oratory and wine. This is the most elegant of the town's one hundred and ten drinking-places, the social center, the headquarters of the volunteer fire-department.

LOS ANGELES

WHEN THE SANTE FE RAILROAD ARRIVED IN 1885

" This happy consummation," said the *Express*, " will be celebrated in a much more signal manner than the banquet this evening. Its fitting celebration will be the filling up of the ample domain of Los Angeles County with prosperous homes. Rapid settlement and enhancement of values, a hopeful and vigorous life in our young and growing community, will be a permanent and ever fructifying celebration. . . ."

Alas, the immediate results did not live up to the *Express's* rhetoric. During the next few years a good many people came into California, but most of them stopped before they got to southern California; the Sacramento and San Joaquin valleys caught their eyes and held them. Between 1875 and 1880 Los Angeles, indeed, went from bad to worse. Droughts and floods hurt everything. There were no oranges to speak of; the only thing in the whole Gargantuan county that could be produced in sufficient quantity to be shipped in carload lots was wine. The year before the railroad arrived, the national bank panic hit the town — the panic which spread all over the United States after the Jay Cooke failure and the " Black Friday." The three banks in Los Angeles closed; two forever. A dozen merchants went bankrupt. A Board of Trade had been established in 1873 and had started out briskly, but with these failures it died. Tourists did not come; trade did not pick up.

The Octopus tightened its hold. Over its jerk-line railroad from San Pedro, the gift of the county, a distance of twenty-two miles, the Southern Pacific charged a passenger fare of two dollars and a half each way, with freight rates proportionately high. In desperation a group of merchants acquired a steamer and started a freight service of their own to San Francisco, loading and unloading the merchandise at tide-water, and carting it to and from Los Angeles. This infuriated Leland Stanford. The Southern Pacific, he said, would spend a million dollars if necessary to kill " that miserable competition." Bitterly the merchants sold their boat to the railroad; the Angelenos cursed the ground the Southern Pacific ran on. Finally the town council made a gesture of defying the Octopus. Crocker appeared before the council in a fury, threatening to " make grass grow in Los Angeles streets."

A group of Oregon capitalists sized up the situation and entered the picture. They built a jerk-line from Los Angeles to Santa Monica, a pleasure beach, and ran a freight pier out into the ocean. This competition was welcomed by the Angelenos. Santa Monica was twenty-five miles closer to San Francisco than San Pedro; ships saved half a day by going there. Trade went to the new line. The Southern Pacific tolerated this competition until June 1877. Then it bought up the little railroad, stopped running trains to Santa Monica, and tore down the pier. Times were hard; money was close. Smallpox raged. In 1877 drought destroyed the sheep-raising industry.

Arizona was the lively place. The Tombstone mines were making things hum; there was much activity at Tucson. The 1880 census gave Tucson a population of 6,994; Los Angeles, 11,311. Wise men predicted that in another five years the Arizona town would be twice the size of Los Angeles.

In the spring of 1881 the Bixby family, then owning most of the great Los Cerritos rancho, subdivided ten thousand acres fronting on the ocean, on the present site of the city of Long Beach. They called the subdivision the "American Colony," advertised it in the East, and offered parcels of ten and twenty acres for sale as fruit ranches. Thirty-six lots were sold, and six houses were built. A hard winter followed, with heavy floods. People did not come; buyers defaulted in their payments. The enterprise was a failure; and so were many Angelenos.

But things, nevertheless, are looking up, developing slowly, taking shape. This vast, sunshiny, semi-tropic country of southern California, lying between the purple mountains and the azure sea, with its mild genial climate and a soil capable of growing almost anything on earth, given water, has not been exactly standing still for a century. Numberless varieties of flowers and shrubs have been brought into it. Around farm-houses honeysuckle, heliotropes, geraniums, callas, and roses bloom; not occasionally, but all the year round. Palm and pepper and eucalyptus trees (the latter brought in from Australia in 1858) begin to take some of the curse off the primitive highways. Here and there, dotting the chaparral and sagebrush, there are growing patches of productive beauty: orange groves, fig, lemon, and almond orchards.

Watered artificially (or naturally when there is a good season of rain), bathed in the sunshine that sends things leaping from the soil, this country has a vital power of come-back from every blighting caprice of Nature. Time and time again it is inundated or burned up; but always it blooms again. It may be bare one year, if there is a drought, and washed out the next year, if there is a flood, but the following year wheat and corn grow in the fields, fat cattle and sheep graze in the pasture-lands. The country has a natural, seductive charm. Gold-green orange trees, with white, waxy, heavily perfumed blossoms, smile here in the sun; up yonder gaunt pines walk like sentinels on the crest of the snow-covered Sierra Madres; over there are the natural beaches of the blue Pacific.

It is, in fact, a Valley of Promise. All that this uncultivated country needs is water and work, the power of money and men, to transform it into something approximating the traditional conception of the Garden of Eden or the Promised Land. Do I seem to grow lyrical? Then I resort to the bare statistics. Observe what is growing in this sunshiny county named after the angels of heaven, in the year of Our Lord 1882 — and note particularly the exotic, the nostalgic, the appealing nature of this produce. Of *bearing* trees it has 450,125 orange, 48,350 lemon, 38,175 peach, 64,380 apple, 4,000 olive, 3,100 quince, 23,640 pear, 33,000 walnut, 8,335 plum, 3,000 almond, and 10,225 fig. The same year the county produces 11,700,000 bushels of wheat, 1,267,500 bushels of corn, 28,250 tons of hay, 7,000 tons of potatoes, 220,000 pounds of butter, 855,-450 pounds of cheese, 3,550,670 pounds of wool, 275,-000 pounds of honey, 3,100,000 gallons of wine, and 145,000 gallons of brandy. It has 11,440 acres of bearing grapes, and 4,800,000 new vines. There are six wineries in the county, one of them the largest in the world.

This county of which the little town of The Angels is the center is huge, and its orchards and vineyards are separated by leagues of bare desert land. All in all, it has perhaps an unprepossessing worm's-eye view. But when its bearing spots are drawn together, the picture is unquestionably that of a pastoral land of milk and honey, of sheep and vineyards, of orange and almond, of fig and olive trees. It has something appealing, alluring; and the world is about to hear of it.

III

In 1882 Helen Hunt Jackson, exploring the Southwest in search of literary materials for a study of the mission Indians, arrived in Los Angeles, and wrote first a series of widely read sentimental articles about the San Gabriel and San Fernando valleys for Eastern magazines and then her novel *Ramona*.

The same year, in the prime age of forty-four, a man who was destined to become the dominant and dominating figure of southern California for the next thirty-five years drifted into the town and became editor of the *Times*, a struggling weekly. He was Harrison Gray Otis, a high-powered, emotional patriot from Ohio, a former editor of the *Grand Army Journal*. He immediately acquired " a deep and abiding faith " in the country and started out to share that faith. Otis was pretty well known in the East. He started boosting his adopted land to the skies and sending copies of his papers east, as well as writing many letters to Civil War veterans urging them to come out to this new country.

In 1883 the Southern Pacific Railroad completed its southern route to the East and began advertising southern California as a rich field for home-seekers and pioneers, where valuable land could be acquired for almost nothing. Inside the next year about five thousand newcomers arrived in Los Angeles County, bringing the population of the town, which had declined, back up to about eleven thousand.

In 1884, at the International Exposition at New Orleans, oranges from southern California took first prize from Florida, which had hitherto reigned supreme in the production of that fruit. This made a profound impression in horticultural circles and caused many Easterners to prick up their ears. Indeed, it was an eye-opener to many people in southern California and brought about a great planting of citrus trees.

About the same time, Charles Nordhoff, a New York newspaper man, went through southern California and wrote first a series of delightful articles and then a lyrical, romantic book about the section. He told of the gentle climate, praising it mightily as fine medicine for tuberculosis, or consumption, as the disease was then generally known. He told of the unsurpassed natural beauties of the section, noted the splendid agricultural possibilities, pointed out that land was dirt cheap, and concluded by advising one and all to come early and avoid the rush. His book *California: For Health, Pleasure and Residence* was published by Harper's and had a wide sale throughout the United States and Canada. Los Angeles historians to this day give this volume more credit for sending people to southern California than anything else ever written about the section.

The New York *Times* and other newspapers began running regular articles from Los Angeles, and a series of sketches about the town and the surrounding country appeared in the *Century* and other magazines.

All of this disconnected propaganda was complimentary, and, moreover, it fell on extremely fertile ground, for the word " California " was still magic anyway and had been so since the Gold Rush. Thousands of people had a great desire to see that fabulous country. Times were bad in the East. " Go west, young man, go west," was in the air. Civil War veterans, men like Otis in their early forties, were looking for a place to make a new start before it was too late. The psychology and the time were ripe for a new land-rush; the signs and portents were in the air, and speculators, bankers, and real-estate operators sensed it.

Over the hills and through the valleys a new Iron Horse — a competitor for the Southern Pacific — was galloping west. The Atchison, Topeka & Santa Fe Railroad's first train snorted into Los Angeles, the end of the line, in the fall of 1885. Just two weeks later the two competing railroads suddenly started running newspaper display advertisements, announcing reduced rates from Missisippi Valley points to Los Angeles, each endeavoring to underbid the other. At the same time Eastern lines cut fares to Mississippi River points.

The response to this was almost instantaneous. New land! Low fares. The railroads were opening up a new country! All over the United States groups of smart people started west to get in on the ground floor. Citizens of New York, Indiana, Ohio, and Illinois moved more quickly and in greater numbers than anybody else. These were not Middle Western farmers. They were home-seekers, city families questing for open country, clerks, adventurers, war veterans, merchants, misfits, promoters, speculators, what not — mostly, perhaps, the type of people who take their money and go to booms, in the hope of making more.

Were the Southern Pacific and the Santa Fe railroads bitterly competing, or did they have a tacit agreement to cut rates to the bone and open up southern California, as well as the intervening country? Both railroads are evasive about the matter, even today. No doubt they had an "understanding." They never made public the matter to their stockholders, but the owners and directors of both railroads owned thousands of acres of land in southern California and were interested in many proposed development enterprises. They desired, naturally, to create communities on vacant lands traversed by their tracks, to increase the value of their own private property, and to produce freight and passenger traffic along their lines. But whether the two railroads were moved to "cut-throat competition" by "bad feeling" and "commercial jealousy," or whether that idea, which they carefully fostered, was just a little joke between them, the fact remains that they were the patron saints of the modern City of the Angels.

Ten days after the Santa Fe reached Los Angeles, driving the last (golden) spike at Cajon Pass on November 9, 1885, it reduced the straight fare from Mississippi Valley points to Los Angeles from $100 to $95, and the round-trip fare from $150 to $140. The Southern Pacific met this cut and went its upstart competitor one better — and the greatest railroad "rate war" ever seen in America was on. Fares continued to be cut, first by one road and then by the other, a matter of five or ten dollars at a time. Business started to pick up; people began packing their trunks. One road cut the round-trip fare to $130; the other retaliated by dropping it to $125. The newspaper ads were kept going. Land! Cheap land, in sunny California! The one-way fare went down to $85. Personally conducted tours were organized, starting at Chicago and St. Louis. Freight rates went down proportionately; for example, the rate on salt from New York was sixty cents a ton; coal was transported from Chicago for a dollar a ton.

"Eighty dollars to Los Angeles from anywhere west of the Missouri!" shouted the Santa Fe. "Seventy!" yelled the Southern Pacific. "Sixty!" screamed the Santa Fe. "Fifty!" roared the Southern Pacific. Starting in dribbles, the movement to southern California gained volume rapidly as the fares went down, and shortly thereafter, when transportation was offered practically free, it assumed the proportions of a mad rush.

"Forty dollars to Los Angeles!" Down, down went the rates. The Angelenos were no longer cursing the Iron Horse; they were petting him. The Santa Fe was the pride of the countryside. The hated Southern Pacific had suddenly become a benefactor — a left-handed one perhaps, but nevertheless a benefactor. Nice Octopus, good Octopus! "Twenty-five dollars to Los Angeles!"

Prospective passengers, now excited and bewildered, dashed from one railroad office back to the other, and then to the first one again, as the bidding for trade developed into a farce. For several weeks one could buy a ticket from any Mississippi Valley point to the City of the Angels for $15; for one week it was $5 — and at the very peak of the "bitter, cut-throat competition," for one day, in the spring of 1886, the fare was $1. "Kansas City to Los Angeles for a dollar!" This, obviously, was not a "rate war." It was a "come-on" proposition, a lure for suckers, a ballyhoo for a circus. The crowds rushed to it, first scores, then hundreds, then thousands —

Boom! Boom!

A flood of humanity poured into southern California. Some, coming in over the northern lines of the Southern Pacific, stopped in central California, but the cry was: " Los Angeles! " Once started, the mob rush took care of itself. People from San Francisco, Washington, Oregon, British Columbia, caught the fever and joined in the stampede. Some went to settle, some to invest, more to gamble and speculate. Many had real money and were able to command more. Regular trains were divided into three sections; special excursions entered the amazed town of Los Angeles at the rate of five a day.

The advance guard took possession of all the empty houses, and those who followed began to build. Hotels and rooming houses filled to overflowing; the demand for quarters could not be met. Tent colonies sprang up. The native Angelenos, both American and Mexican, were thoroughly bewildered. A miracle had suddenly happened. Everybody wanted to buy land; many had cash to pay for it. The price of " choice " property in the startled town jumped from a hundred dollars a front foot to two hundred, then to three hundred, four hundred, five hundred. Newcomers began sending back enthusiastic letters; they founded " the Southern California Immigration Society." A short time later the society went to pieces in the midst of the furor, its members overwhelmed and appalled by the rush.

The city fathers, inspired, started spending money to spruce up the town. New buildings, new homes, new developments, meant new sources of taxation. They employed horses and men to create Eastlake Park (later changed to Lincoln Park), and set crews of laborers to work with pick and shovel to rescue the long-neglected Plaza from its primitive state. The Plaza loafers, stirred from their siestas in the patches of shade, rubbed their eyes, complained, and wondered. The oncoming hundreds who now poured off every train from the East saw signs of life and endeavor, where the first arrivals had to use their imaginations.

A group of forward-lookers got together and decided that the ancient horse-cars must go off the spotty dirt street which they called Broadway. Old fogies contended that the joggling horse-cars were fast enough, but young bloods voted them down. The tracks were torn up; cable-cars were installed. These shiny new contraptions scooted along fast over the unpaved streets, lending life to the scene; the moving cable whirred and crackled in its buried slot — here was the sound and clatter of Progress. The aroused population, envisioning great things ahead, elected as Mayor the progressive go-getter Billy Workman. He set right to work and carried the town along with him. The growing city's treasury had money to spend; the horde of visitors who were coming from the East were not to be greeted with mud roads for streets. Mayor Billy thought of a unique way to shame the sluggards into action. One rainy night men worked late and mysteriously in the principal streets. The next morning it was discovered that the thoroughfares were decorated with mounds of mud resembling graves, with imitation tombstones above them bearing such inscriptions as:

" Beware of Quicksand! "

" Fare for Ferrying Across, 25 cents! "

" No Duck Hunting Allowed in This Pond! "

" Boats Leave this Landing Every Half Hour! "

" Requiescat in Pace! "

That did the trick. Scores of workmen were set to paving the streets. Main Street, Spring Street, Broadway, and Hill Street were shortly transformed from rutty, dusty lanes (mud holes when it rained) into slick new thoroughfares. The promoters now had a new talking point, the new citizens something else to write home about. They wrote. Letters mailed in Los Angeles increased from 2,083 a month to 21,333. Long lines of coaches dumped people into the town every day and hurried back east for more. Every stick of available lumber went into the hasty construction of small hotels and rooming houses; freight steamships rushed lumber down from the north. The Southern Pacific could not handle the freight unloaded at San Pedro; caravans of teams and wagons plied back and forth, bringing cut lumber and logs for the booming town. There was great demand for laborers, plasterers, road-makers, carpen-

SOME OF THE FIRST ARRIVALS

OF THE GREAT BOOM

ters; they poured in from the north. Builders worked night and day constructing flimsy houses, many of them thrown together with still unseasoned lumber.

Some came to settle down and grow up in this new country; home-seekers, men and women with young children, invalids, tuberculous folk in search of a cure, Civil War veterans, *bona fide* pioneers. But the great majority who swarmed into the town at this time came, not to settle down and build up, but to make a quick fortune in real-estate speculation. Many of them had learned the game, with all its tactics and tricks, in the smaller frenetic booms which had previously swept through the Middle West. Now in the warm, seductive southern California climate, their enthusiasm and ardor were boundless. Transient merchants rushed into the town and set up stores. Everybody was selling land to everybody else. Salesmen met each train; new arrivals were rushed off to barren subdivisions before they had a chance to admire the scenery. Within a few months real-estate prices rose more than three hundred per cent. An acre of ground that cost fifty dollars was divided into five lots selling for three hundred dollars each. City lots around the Plaza jumped to a thousand dollars a front foot.

The general intoxication soon took on the proportions of a gorgeous spree. The little Spanish-American town, dozing in the sun but a few months ago, was a madhouse. Native Angelenos who had sold their lots at the beginning for ten times their value paid speculators' prices and bought them back, to sell them again at still dizzier figures. Lunchroom waitresses, hotel bellboys, splurged their wages and tips on tracts and lots, sold them the next day, made more money than they had ever seen before, and plunged the profits into new speculations. Policemen on their beats stopped to sell a stranger a lot or buy one.

By the fall of 1886 the boom was going full blast. Architects, teamsters, dentists, mechanics, were promoting subdivisions. Men and women who could not write their own names or read their own glowing prospectuses were real-estate brokers. They set up " offices " all over the town and even out in the cactus and wild mustard. Merchants did business in the streets. Every store, almost every residence, rented space for real-estate offices. Corners of twelve-by-ten fruit-stands were sub-let at a rental of a hundred dollars a month. Hundreds of operators, perhaps thousands, carried their " offices " in their hats.

Humanity enveloped Los Angeles like a tidal wave. In 1884 the population was 12,000; thirty months later the town claimed 100,000 permanent residents. Two weeks after one city directory was published, another was issued containing five thousand additional names. The annual freight carried by Wells, Fargo & Company alone jumped from 300,000 to 7,000,000 pounds. The *recorded* real-estate transfers (and half of them were not recorded) mounted from virtually nothing to eight, nine, ten, eleven, twelve millions of dollars a month, reaching nearly thirteen million dollars in July 1887. Everybody in southern California was living, not on the fringes, but in the actual realm of real-estate lunacy.

Long lines of buyers stood for twenty-four, forty-eight, even seventy-two hours in front of real-estate offices waiting for some particularly well-ballyhooed subdivision to be thrown open so that they could plank down their money for a piece of land. Some men made a business of standing in line and then selling their places, frequently for as high as five hundred dollars. The standee, in turn, then bought a lot with his money. The most feverish buyers kept three and four substitutes in line, visiting them every few hours, apprehensive lest they sell their places. No one was so poor that he couldn't buy one lot at least. They were " available " from fifty dollars up, payable in monthly installments of five dollars. Cooks, dish-washers, scrub-women, ditch-diggers, bought lots on time and sold them immediately to the incoming thousands pouring in with ready money. Having " turned one deal," they became promoters themselves.

Owners of undeveloped plots within five miles of the courthouse were hunted down on the street, in their houses or " offices " — even while they sat in church pondering their sins — and besought to sell their holdings forthwith. Agents hired hackmen, hotel employees, porters, to put them in touch with prospective buyers. Sales were made on the curbstone, in saloon bars, at restaurant tables. The big speculators carried rolls of bills, waving them under the noses of reluctant owners. Others, having no money at all, comparatively speaking, scraped together a few hundred dollars for an option, acquired the services of surveyors and graders by deeding to them part of the unowned land, stood off the printer for running off handbills and pamphlets, held a sale, made a stake, and then repeated the process on a grander scale.

Groves of oranges, lemons, and pears in the heart of the town and on the outskirts were hacked down so that the land could be subdivided into development tracts. Vineyards were torn up and transferred into streets.

The boom continued unabated throughout 1886, grew wilder during the spring of '87, and hit the top during June, July, and August of that year, when the recorded real-estate transfers for the three-month period amounted to thirty-five million dollars. The total for that year was a hundred million.

II

Outside the " city limits " the real craze held sway. Raw, desert land, purchased for twenty dollars an acre, was cut up into " choice villa " tracts and sold at eight hundred dollars an acre.

The promoters' swiftest road to fortune lay in the " town site." From Los Angeles to the San Bernardino county line, a distance of thirty-six miles, twenty-five " towns " were laid out. Since they averaged more than a mile square, the entire distance was a series of theoretical municipalities. To lead their flocks into these barren pastures, to launch a subdivision where the coyotes howled and tarantulas and centipedes made whoopee, the promoters bought full-page ads in the town's three newspapers. Editors demanded and got cash in hand for these ads. The newspapers, especially the *Times,* reaped a golden harvest. Circulations doubled, quadrupled. Advertising rates went up with them. Machinery, printers, copy-writers, were rushed in. Here is a full page announcement:

Boom!   Boom!

ARCADIA

Boom!   Boom!

Another one begins:

HE OR SHE
That Hesitates is Lost
An axiom that holds good in real estate, as well as in
affairs of the heart.
Selah!

Another:

Halt! Halt! Halt!
Speculators and Homeseekers, Attention!
$80,000 — Eighty Thousand Dollars — $80,000
Sold in a Day at Marvellous
McGarry Tract

A whole newspaper page advertises a new " town " with a single word:

RAMIREZ!

Page after page, day after day, they appeared:

> " Catch on before the whole country rushes to Ferndale! Every man who wishes a home in Paradise should locate in this, the loveliest district in the whole of Southern California."

Copy-writers grew delirious in describing the " Lily Langtry " tract at " Vernon."

> " Go wing thy flight from star to star
> From world to luminous world, as far
> As the Universe spreads its flaming wall —
> One winter at Vernon is worth them all!"

A man named Monroe started " Monrovia," by buying a piece of land and building himself a house. On May 17, 1886, after appropriate propaganda had been exerted, an excursion was run to this almost barren piece of mesa land sloping down from the Sierra Madres, jammed with buyers. Five-acre tracts sold at two hundred and fifty dollars the acre; lots measuring fifty by a hundred and fifty feet went with a rush at a hundred dollars — thirty dollars down, the balance in six months.

Another promoter started " Glendora," naming it after his wife, and at the first day's sale auctioned off three hundred lots. Placards placed around the bare land informed prospects.

" This is where the orange groves are loveliest! "
" This is where the grapes are most luxuriant! "
" This is where the vegetation is grandest! "
" This is where the flowers are prettiest! "

A group of Quakers from Indiana, Iowa, and Illinois started the town of Whittier, selling four hundred thousand dollars' worth of lots in three days. One newspaper said of it editorially: " Whittier is the coming place! It will dwarf Monrovia and eclipse Pasadena. Nothing can stop it! The Quakers are coming in from all over the United States! " The accompanying advertisement read:

WHITTIER! WHITTIER! WHITTIER!
Queen of the Foothills and Crown of the San Gabriel Valley!

For every advertisement the newspapers threw in a " news story " to go with it. Some poet tore off this full-page announcement:

THIS IS PURE GOLD! ! !
SANTA ANA,
The Metropolis of Southern California's Fairest Valley!
Chief Among Ten Thousand, or the One
Altogether Lovely!
Beautiful! Busy! Bustling! Booming! It
Can't be Beat!
The town now has the biggest kind of a
big, big boom.
A Great Big Boom! And you
Can Accumulate ducats by Investing!

Eighty thousand dollars changed hands in two hours when the sale opened. At " Fullerton," ninety-two thousand dollars swapped owners in half a day.

Another read:

TUSTIN
The Beautiful
Unexcelled in charm and loveliness
An Earthly Eden Unsurpassed in
Wealth of Flower and Foliage.
However, Imagination Cannot Conceive It:
It must be Seen to be Realized!

They ran out of names. One tract was called " Azusa " — taking its name patriotically from the first and last letters of the alphabet, plus U. S. A. It is a pretty little community today, with a big banner across its main street, wishing one and all: " Welcome to Azusa."

Grand Railroad Excursion and Genuine
AUCTION SALE!
No Chenanekin! !
Thursday, June 7, 1887.
Beautiful Palomares, Pomona Valley!
Lunch, Coffee, Lemonade, and Ice Water Free!
Full Band of Music!

BOOM! BOOM!

Under the caption, " Veni, Vidi, Vici! " a full-page advertisement announced that an excursion, " Led by Bartlett's Seventh Infantry Band," would open up

Magnificent Monte Vista!
The Gem of the Mountains!
The Queen of the Valley!

Towns sprang up like mushrooms: Alosta, Gladstone, Glendora, Beaumont, Arcadia, Raymond, Glendale, Burbank, Lamar, Rosecrans, Bethune, Mondonville, Olivewood, Oleander, Lordsburg, Happy Valley, Mc-Coy (advertised as " The Real McCoy! "), Busy Vista, Broad Acres, Ivanhoe, Alta Vista, Nadeau, Bonita, San Dimas, Ballona, Southside, Ontario, Walleria, Ocean Spray — a hundred more. The promoter who started Gladstone announced proudly: "A deed to one lot has been sent to the Prime Minister of England! " Gladstone sold like hot cakes, whereupon another master mind started St. James, advertising it as "extremely English." A hundred vehicles and five hundred persons were engaged in taking care of the mob which rushed to St. James when it opened; they bought forty thousand dollars' worth of lots in thirty minutes.

Another promoter ran private trains to Santa Monica, where he sold " villa lots " and five-acre farms, ten per cent down, and the " Balance in six, twelve, and eighteen months." His advertisement read as follows:

HO, FOR THE BEACH!
Tomorrow! Tomorrow!
Grand Auction Sale at
Santa Monica
350 — Acres — 350

One of the Grandest Panoramic Views the Human Eye ever Rested upon, including Ballona, Lake and Harbor, with its out-going and incoming Vessels, the Grand Old Pacific, the handsome new Hotel Arcadia, while in the Distance may be seen Los Angeles, the Pride of All, and the Coming City of Two Hundred Thousand People!

Lots at one hundred and fifty dollars and upward were offered and sold at "Peerless Long Beach." "This," said the promoter, "is not a new settlement, but a prosperous town of 2,000 people. The hotel will be doubled in size, with a billiard room for ladies, streets will be sprinkled, and a bathhouse, with hot and cold water, will be built."

Real money was spent. All in all, about a score of towns came into being, fifteen of which started right off with big, brand-new hotels if nothing else. These quickly-erected hostelries were the chief selling points of real-estate brokers — they were to accommodate the droves of new home-seekers and buyers which the brokers and their customers both believed would come.

Maps and literature glorified the about-to-be-opened agricultural tracts. The promoters promised everything. The land would grow anything, and beneath the surface there was probably iron ore and oil, perhaps silver and gold. Brass bands rode through the streets in cable-cars, hay-wagons, and carriages, followed by fantastic parades a block long, with signs and banners announcing a new location. Martial music filled the air. Elephants and giraffes, lions and tigers, human freaks (the remnant of a stranded circus), were used as magnets. The blarings and blastings lasted all through the day and into the night. Hordes of prospects were loaded into buses and wagons and, preceded by the animals, the freaks, and the music, escorted out to where the virgin lots lay in the sun, marked off with American flags.

Here were long groaning tables, laden with free lunch — anybody could come and eat all he wished. Lots were raffled off, drawn by lottery, offered on wheels of fortune. Free music, free entertainment, free rides, and free food; it was the hobo's heaven. Sharpers and swindlers, gamblers and touts, prostitutes and evangelists, patent-medicine venders and pickpockets bore down from the East and from the North along the coast, eager to share in the carnival spirit and the flow of loose money. The banks lent money freely on five-day notes at usurious rates, cleaning up.

Calmer heads (those who had already made a fortune) began to look on with alarm. The boom was going great guns for business and population, but it was getting completely out of hand. New York and San Francisco bankers, backing the local Shylocks, began to get worried. The *Times* ripped and roared, sending copies back east. Los Angeles had no time nor place, shouted Otis, for " dudes, loafers, paupers; those who expect to astonish the natives, those afraid to pull off their coats, cheap politicians, business scrubs, inepecunious clerks, lawyers, *and doctors.*"

No warning had any effect on the boom-crazed population. If more cautious prospects wanted a bit of assurance that the surburban land was worth the sky-rocket prices, the promoters were lavish with promises, and some of them backed them up. A new tourist hotel was to be erected here; there was the site of a manufacturing plant. Did some practical man want water on the land? The Los Angeles (Portiuncula) River and other streams were diverted, and artesian veins were tapped. " Town sites " were laid out with a cartload of surveyors' stakes and a series of American flags; maps called for streets up mountains, across gulches, and through ravines. Lots changed hands several times a day. Tired salesmen were roused at night to show their wares by lantern-light.

Ten, twenty, thirty miles out into the desert ran the bands, the free-lunch wagons, the circus animals, and the land-hungry suckers. One broker guaranteed in his prospectus that a railroad would run through his tract. Before the eager parade reached his land, he bought and hurriedly laid down on the ground a carload of fence posts in lieu of railroad ties. Few of the prospects knew the difference. " Towns " sprang up overnight along the existing railroad lines and branches. A man with five hundred dollars could get an option on a tract, lay out a " town," work up enthusiasm for it, and sell off his lots at six hundred dollars each; one third down, the balance in easy payments. Land eighteen miles from Los Angeles which had sold for a dollar an acre was snapped up at a thousand dollars an acre. " There were enough subdivisions," says Newmark, " to accommodate ten million people; enough syndicates to manage the affairs of a nation."

Fifty thousand dollars' worth of lots were sold on a mountain top where to this day few human feet have ever ventured. Land advertised as having " water privileges " was land under water, or dry creek beds; " villa sites " possessing " scenic attractions " consisted of precipices, ravines, and chasms. Enormous amounts of money changed hands. The assessment figures for the county rose from $32,000,000 to $63,000,000.

The wonder is that the galloping boomers stopped their amazing labor at fifteen hotels and twenty-odd towns. The lid was off, certainly, and hotels and towns could be brought into being as by Aladdin's magical lamp. At the lunatic peak Philip D. Armour, that eminent captain of industry and financial magnate, declared: " This is merely preliminary to a boom that will outclass the present activity as thunder to the crack of a hickory nut! "

Prognosticator Armour's prediction must have been made for the suckers. A month later, at any rate, the boom collapsed.

Tapping the Middle West

The boom exploded in the summer of 1888 when the banks suddenly stopped lending money on all but real estate located in the heart of the town, and then *only on the basis of the ancient values!* The result was precisely the same as if a pin had been stuck into a balloon. Everybody unloaded — or tried to. The president of a bank and the owner of a daily paper fled to Mexico. The most popular preacher in town departed, carrying with him the savings of many widows. Paper " millionaires " went bankrupt, a dozen men committed suicide. Banks worked overtime foreclosing, lawyers were swamped, courts were overwhelmed with litigation, the jail was taxed to capacity. The influx of population suddenly stopped.

The mass psychology of failure spread even faster than the propaganda of success. For thirty months people and money had been pouring into Los Angeles; now they took their money and departed for San Francisco, Oregon, Washington, the East — at the rate of a hundred a day. Fear of panic seized the town. Houses were left vacant, the railroads ran empty trains in and full trains out. " Swift as the rise had been," wrote Willard, " the descent was even more rapid."

Everything went wrong at once. The climate, which had been on its best behavior for two years, suddenly became cantankerous, bringing floods, heat, and windstorms. There were two slight earthquakes, the first felt in many years. The " town sites " returned to normalcy, with jack-rabbits cavorting among the real-estate flags, and coyotes howling in the " streets." The assessment figures for the county, having risen from $32,000,000 to $63,000,000, dropped back to $20,000,000 — or $12,-000,000 below what they had been before the boom.

Most of the agricultural land was in the hands of speculators, clerks, school-teachers, dentists, plumbers, and others who had been " stuck " with it. They knew nothing about farming and cared less. Neglected, the land went to utter ruin; fruit trees were dried up and covered with scales; the soil was tangled with weeds. Many vineyards and orchards had been chopped up. *The newspapers carried over three pages of taxes listed on property whose owners were unknown.*

Scattered about the countryside were a dozen great tourist hotels with nobody in them, the flowers dead, weeds growing up, tattered red, white, and blue bunting flapping pathetically in the breeze. Right in Los Angeles was the massive stone foundation of the great " Tenth Street Hotel," a magnificent edifice which was to have risen at a cost of a million dollars. The stone foundation was laid at the corner of Main and Tenth streets at a cost of eighty thousand dollars, and there it languished, a ghastly reminder when the bubble burst.

The people who remained in Los Angeles may be roughly grouped into several classes: merchants, *bona fide* home-seekers, small agriculturists, sick people, old people, tramps, Civil War veterans, men who had grown rich out of the boom and built themselves permanent homes, and people who had been left " stuck " with the land. The other thousands who made up the hundred thousand population were leaving at the rate of three thousand a month.

II

In this dark hour the shade of Felipe de Neve, the first realtor, came to the rescue through the medium of the Santa Fe Railroad. " Procure me villagers, *pobladores*," Señor Neve had said. " Get farmers, permanent settlers," the Santa Fe said. The Santa Fe saw that this country, intrinsically, was the same as it had been before the boom. The sunshine was still there, the soil was still there, the country was still there, the potentialities were unchanged. Convinced that the future of the section lay, not in real-estate booms, but in the gradual development of its one great natural, or unnatural resource, agriculture, the officials of the Santa Fe Railroad proposed to the desperate business men and bankers of Los Angeles that they make a frank, expensive, concerted, immediate effort to lure into the section a host of steady, industrious, intelligent dirt farmers from the Middle West. That proposal was made in practically so many words.

Obviously, the executives of the Santa Fe Railroad were intelligent men. They sensed what we have already noted; that here potentially was the " Garden of Eden," with a powerful appeal, æsthetic and religious, not for wiseacres and city slickers, but for good, plain, middle-class, God-fearing American men and women. Here was a happy land for people who were living unhappily on bleak farms, on lonely ranches, in harsh climates; the sick and the old, craving warmth and sunshine. There was Pasadena, fifteen miles away; a growing, permanent little community which had been founded, not by real-estate sharks, but by a group of respectable Hoosiers from Indianapolis who had deliberately come to southern California in 1873 to escape harsh winter, to find a place, according to their own documents, " where life was easy." Neither the boom nor the aftermath had affected them much; they were growing oranges, living happily, praising the Lord, and taking it easy in the sunshine. . . .

That was the substance of the Santa Fe's argument; the business men with vision grasped it; those with imagination believed, and carried the skeptics with them. No one grasped the point quicker or whooped it up louder than Otis. Indeed, he had known that this was " God's country " from the beginning. On his motion, in the fall of 1888, the business men formed themselves into that organization which must be known all over the world now — The Los Angeles Chamber of Commerce. Heroic measures were necessary. The Santa Fe's general proposal was received with great enthusiasm, and a definite project was launched at once. The Southern Pacific also contributed an idea. If Los Angeles ever hoped to be a great city, it would have to have a decent harbor at San Pedro; money could be got out of Congress through the Rivers and Harbors Bill; Leland Stanford, now president of the road, was also a United States Senator from California; he would push it. The business men embraced that thought; that, too, became a definite objective, a cardinal point in the new commerce body's creed. Then they went into action.

While local writers were put to work preparing literature, the Chamber of Commerce rented a hall in the center of the town and started a " permanent exhibition " of southern California products. Notices appeared in the newspapers urging horticulturists and farmers to send in specimens of their prize produce — the largest and best oranges, figs, potatoes, etc. Organizers went from farm to farm, from town to town. Everybody was willing — nay, eager — to help; they started sending in the prize exhibits. All this produce was carried free of charge by the railroads. The Southern Pacific and Santa Fe sent instructions to all agents to accept and transport free of charge all produce addressed to: " The Chamber of Commerce, Los Angeles."

The first literature was now prepared and ready to go out. Each of the town's three newspapers, led by the *Times*, had printed " special editions " pointing out the incomparable glories of southern California. . . . Let me set the date. The business of luring the Middle Western farmers to paradise began in December 1888. In that month ten thousand copies of the special edition newspapers were tenderly wrapped and mailed with a prayer to as many unknown people throughout the Middle West — many of the names obtained from professional " sucker lists." The " special editions " were followed almost immediately by ten thousand copies of the Chamber of Commerce's first piece of literature, a pamphlet of thirty-six exquisite pages, rhetorically entitled: *Facts and Figures about Los Angeles City and County*. This was a masterpiece of colorful rhetoric, linking together oranges, lemons, sunshine, angels, the Creator, mountains, sea, cheap land, and profits of a thousand dollars an acre. It gave the population of Los Angeles as eighty-five thousand. Two years later, when the national census was taken, the figure had shrunk forty per cent. This early brochure was the forerunner of forty books and pamphlets which were published inside the next two years with a circulation of more than a million copies.

The next step was now ready; the choice produce was coming into Los Angeles from all over southern California in a steady flow. The city thereupon " carried the message to Garcia " by opening a permanent exhibit of this prize produce (and prize literature) in Chicago. The Santa Fe donated the space in Chicago, and Los Angeles pledged ten thousand dollars to keep the exhibit going for the first year. All materials for this display were carried free of charge by the Santa Fe; each week the produce in the Chamber of Commerce headquarters was picked over, and the best of it was selected and rushed to the Windy City. Not as freight. Each week the Santa Fe provided a baggage-car for it, and the fresh stuff was rushed across the continent on its fastest passenger train! The exhibit was an instantaneous success. The rooms in Chicago were filled with visitors all day. Orators pointed to the produce, handed out literature, and discoursed on the beauties and opportunities of the " Land of Heart's Desire," the title of one document. More than seventy-five thousand copies of a booster book of a hundred and thirty-six pages, entitled *The Land of Sunshine*, were handed out, and fifty thousand copies of a smaller, " follow-up " booklet. Both were the products of Harry Ellington Brook, an editorial writer on the *Times*. This exhibit lasted three years, culminating in a grand finale at the World's Fair, and sent a multitude of people, mostly from the Middle West, to southern California. The historian of the Los Angeles Chamber of Commerce says: " This exhibit alone, in bringing in population and money, was worth a million dollars a year, and also was of incalculable indirect benefit thereafter."

Fifty thousand copies of a hundred-and-twelve-page booklet called *Southern California* were issued. Copies were sent through the mails to the editors of eight thousand publications throughout the United States. Each book was accompanied by a printed notice saying that a copy would be sent to " any friend." About three thousand newspapers published the notice free of charge, giving the book an advertisement in a circulation of about two million. The pamphlet was requested from every part of the country, with the result that the entire fifty thousand copies were " intelligently placed."

Other pamphlets of twenty-five thousand and fifty thousand copies, of " general interest," were sent hither and yon. Special pamphlets were published for the Atlanta Exposition (twenty-five thousand copies) and for the one at Omaha (fifty thousand copies). A sales brochure was even prepared for circulation in the Klondike, and ten thousand copies were scattered in that frozen country to emphasize southern California's balmy climate in a place where the contrast would be most keenly felt. A hundred thousand copies of a booklet called *The Land of Promise* were distributed, plus thousands of leaflets and circulars dealing with irrigation, fruit-growing, etc. One of the most widely distributed books was entitled *How We Grow!* showing photographs of twenty Los Angeles business blocks " in process of construction, all taken on the same day." By 1901 it was estimated that this literature aggregated two million pieces, and that it had been examined by one adult out of every five in the United States.

An Orange Carnival was started in Chicago and entertained more than a hundred thousand visitors in 1890. Complimentary tickets, good for the opening night only, were printed in Los Angeles, and all newspapers in southern California announced that anyone who had " friends " in Chicago could get tickets. A circular describing the show and relating some facts about the orange industry was issued with the tickets. Twenty thousand tickets, accompanied by the circulars, were sent by people in southern California to " friends " in Chicago. The result was that on the opening night the streets about the exposition building in Chicago were so packed with people and vehicles that riot squads had to be called out, and thousands were unable to get into the building. The Chicago papers described the scene vividly the following day. It was estimated that ten million people examined the southern California exhibits at the World's Fair and learned of the wonders of the climate.

In 1892 three hundred members of the National Editorial Association visited Los Angeles. They were supplied with all kinds of pamphlets and statistics, and in addition each editor was given a so-called news story, fifteen hundred words in length, written in the first person. Few of the editors bothered to rewrite it, simply signing and sending it to their papers. It appeared practically unchanged, over their signatures, in two hundred and fifty Eastern papers. The " writers " showed particular enthusiasm over the climate and dwelt upon it at great length, their " stories " announcing that " the day was bright and beautiful, neither too warm nor too cold," and that southern California had the most delightful climate in the world. On that particular day, " neither too warm nor too cold," the thermometers registered one hundred; it was the hottest April day Los Angeles had experienced in twenty-nine years! The unfortunate editors were nearly melted and went about saying: " If it's like this in April, what must it be in July and August? " Perhaps they were too hot to read the hand-outs before placing them in the mail.

Los Angeles County spent thirty thousand dollars on a Columbian Fair exhibit, plus eight thousand dollars raised by private subscription. Twenty-five thousand dollars was raised by subscription to construct a building and place an exhibit at the Mid-Winter Fair in Chicago, immediately after the World's Fair closed. At Omaha the exhibit cost seventy-five hundred dollars, and a hundred and twenty-five thousand pieces of literature were handed out to visitors. Displays were made at religious conventions all over the country, the sunshiny climate, the nature of the produce, and the name of the town having a definite theological value. In 1901 a great exhibit was sent to the Paris Exposition; similar exhibits were sent to the exposition at Guatemala in 1898, to the one at Hamburg the same year, and to countless pure-food shows and horticultural and agricultural fairs.

In 1890 the population of Los Angeles was 50,000; by 1900 it was 102,000 again, and this time the people who comprised it had come to stay. This extraordinary increase shows how successfully the sales project was carried out. Advertising was of all kinds: distribution of printed matter, space in magazines and newspapers, and, most important of all, the sending of large exhibits to the great fairs of the country. At the Mid-Winter Fair in San Francisco in 1894, the Cotton Exposition in Atlanta in 1896, the Trans-Mississippi Exposition at Omaha in 1898, and the Pan American Exposition at Buffalo in 1901, Los Angeles had exhibits that attracted wide attention. It also had numerous displays elsewhere in America and in Europe. As early as 1901 the Chamber of Commerce was advertising in national magazines and receiving a hundred letters of inquiry a day.

A book entitled *California of the South*, written by two of the town's leading boosters, was published by D. Appleton & Company and contributed to the good work. Various writers were subsidized by the city and the railroads. Newmark says: " Charles Dudley Warner . . . the distinguished American author . . . who was editor of Harper's Magazine, came ostensibly in the service of the Harpers, that firm later issuing his appreciative and well-illustrated volume, *Our Italy*, in which he suggested certain comparisons between Southern California and Southern Europe, but the Santa Fe Railroad Company, then particularly desirous of attracting Easterners to the Coast, really sent out the author, footing most if not all of the bills. Mrs. Custer, widow of the General, was another guest of the Santa Fe; and she also wrote about Southern California for periodicals in the East."

Some people may remember the " California on Wheels." This was a train loaded with the choicest agricultural products of the entire State, which did a two-year barn-storming act all through the Middle West and parts of the South. It visited every town of importance in the Middle West, and more than a million people passed through its doors. The train traveled free over all the lines of the Santa Fe and the Southern Pacific. A State project to begin with, the people of northern California soon lost interest, and during the last year it was a southern California enterprise entirely. It was accompanied by a brass band, a battery of Los Angeles " come-on " men, and tons of literature prepared by the Los Angeles newspapers and the Chamber of Commerce.

Either by the grace of God or owing to the perception of the Santa Fe, or perhaps both, the " California on Wheels " was timed with psychological perfection. At the beginning of the last decade of the nineteenth century, following twenty years of the most relentless soil-robbing ever known in America, literally thousands of people throughout the prairie lands simultaneously reached the limits of physical endurance, the gates of senility and financial independence. They were ready for the Promised Land.

And the Promised Land, as represented by the " California on Wheels," was ready for them. Here, before wide bucolic eyes, was the semi-tropic evidence; the oranges and lemons, the figs and olives, the fruits and nuts. There were the portraits of palm trees, purple mountains, and sapphire seas. There were the orators with their promise of cheap land certain to produce crops similar to the prize exhibits at a profit of " from $500 to $1,000 an acre." They told of a climate of everlasting June, guaranteed to restore the bloom of youth to tired bodies which a lifetime of hard work had brought close to bliss eternal. And, finally, there was the reading. Ah, the reading! The pot of gold beyond the drab horizon! The magic sunshine city of the Lord, discovered by His own angels! The thing was quickly done. It was done beyond the fondest dreams of Los Angeles. The Middle Western farmer sold or leased the old homestead and turned his weather-beaten face west to paradise. The business man quickly followed suit and headed for the new El Dorado. Lastly, the farm-hand himself begged, borrowed, or stole the price of a ticket to the rainbow's end.

III

Two things were stressed by all the orators and writers, subsidized and otherwise, and that was " escape from the elements," and " the value of the climate as a cure for tuberculosis." " These people," said the official Los Angeles Chamber of Commerce historian, " now came as a class, a people of means who sought a place to live where they could be free from the insistent struggle with the elements. Frequently there was some member of the family who was not in good health, or who had tuberculosis, a disease generally called at that time consumption; and the papers were full of consumption cures. These people bought property and built pretty homes and planted shade trees, rose gardens, and lawns. The possibilities of southern California as a health resort had been noted by many newspaper correspondents and magazine writers who had visited the country.

" Nordhoff's book set forth in glorious terms the benefits that the mild climate wrought in cases of consumption. This volume had a wide circulation all through the eastern states, and many thousands of people affected with that disease were brought to Southern California. Most of these were far advanced toward death. The invalids who were too far gone for recovery died, but those with whom the disease had merely secured a foothold were, as a rule, saved, and they wrote home advising other invalids to come to Southern California."

So they came, too, the old and the tired, the sick and the weak, and with them, or soon after them, came the army of preachers, faith-healers, and medical quacks.

There is no question that many of these good people believed that they were being released from bondage; that they were being ushered into the actual biblical " Promised Land." When they reached southern California, the great empty hotels, and houses, were there for them; bearing orchards and vineyards could be bought for taxes; artesian wells, bored at much time and expense by others, spouted water out of the ground; towns with clean new vacant buildings were waiting to be occupied. These people, mainly Methodists and Baptists, knew their Bible; they remembered what Moses had said to the children of Israel: " And it shall be, when Jehovah thy God shall bring thee into the land of milk and honey which he sware unto thy fathers, to Abraham, to Isaac, and to Jacob, to give thee great and goodly cities which thou buildedst not, and houses full of all good things which thou filledst not, and cisterns hewn out which thou hewedst not, vineyards and olive trees which thou plantedst not; and thou shall eat and be full; then beware lest thou forget Jehovah, who brought thee forth out of the land of Egypt, out of the house of bondage " (Deuteronomy vi, 10–12). They did not forget; they have never forgotten.

A special effort was made to get religious colonies into the section; all kinds of attractive offers were made, and successfully. Surely, the great boom hotel at "Lordsburg" was not to remain unoccupied! One of the first things the boosters did was to spruce it up, and the following year, 1889, the great frame building, and all the unsold lots around it, were practically given to a colony of Dunkards, brought in from everywhere. The Dunkards puzzled over what to do with the huge building for almost a year. In the meantime the magazine the *Southern Californian* set itself up inside the empty, resounding walls of the structure, and the editor was moved to publish this proud and extraordinary boast:

"The largest, most elaborate and costly building occupied as a printing office south of San Francisco in this State is that of 'The *Southern Californian*,' at Lordsburg in this valley. The building cost $90,000; it occupies an acre of ground, is four stories high, and has 126 rooms. It is one of the most complete buildings in this region, being furnished with plate-glass windows, electric bells, a $1,600 elevator, oak and cherry stairways, hardwood floors, marble mantels, oak doors, bathrooms, wide hallways, and wide piazzas."

Perhaps the perusal of this enchanting account enabled the Dunkards to take heart and make some sort of use of their bargain. Late in 1890 they hit upon the idea of establishing a denominational school in the old hotel, and it became, after a long period of precarious existence, La Verne College. A few years ago the college moved into a new building, and the old hotel was then destroyed by fire, as a spectacular feature for a movie.

The old boom hotel at Claremont recently inspired George W. Savage, editor of the Claremont *Courier*, to do some research work concerning it and similar ambitious undertakings of those crazy days. Carpenters were scarce, even at four and five dollars a day, and men and boys who could hardly drive a nail straight worked with flimsy material to throw the big hostelries together. Mr. Savage learned, he wrote, that the Claremont Hotel — three stories and a tower — was raised from its foundations without the benefit of a single spike — " only small nails held the building together." This hotel was put up before the first house graced the town. When the boom collapsed, it, too, became the seat of an institution of the higher learning — Pomona College.

The Seventh Day Adventists, arriving in the land of dreams, followed the example of the Dunkards and took over a large hotel which reposed on a hill between Redlands and San Bernardino; this was all the boom left of the projected town of Mound City. Under the Adventists' skillful hands this hotel became the Loma Linda Sanitarium — one of the best-known in California.

There were some brick hotels among the mushroom hostelries, notably at Orange and at Alesandro. The latter is still standing, its sagging windows boarded up; and few travelers who pass on the road to San Jacinto recognize this ramshackle ruin as a subdivision's pride of the halcyon years. Boom hotels went up at Upland and Pomona, at Auburndale, on the banks of the Santa Ana; at Rincon, now known as Prado, and at Corona, which had, in its heyday, " one of the finest hotels east of Los Angeles." This hotel, which covered an entire block, was built by a Sioux City, Iowa, banker. When the lean days came, he handed it as a doubtful gift to his mother-in-law! A merciful fire ended its forlorn career. The great Inn at San Dimas became the " Margaret and Mary Home for Orphans."

So Los Angeles grew, and has continued to grow, steadily. Every year since 1890 the Middle West has bred and raised a host of new residents for Los Angeles. Five per cent of the city's population today is native born; eighty per cent has come from the farms and villages of the cow, corn, and wheat belts within the last twenty-seven years. This annual emigration is a definite and significant phenomenon of American life. It reached its greatest height between 1910 and 1915, rose high again in 1923-4, and even the " depression " winter of 1932 was lucrative, with Iowa, Texas, and Minnesota furnishing the largest quotas. With rhythmic regularity the Middle West gives till it hurts.

The corn-belt press howls bitterly against this movement which each year relieves the " bread-basket of the United States " of a portion of its youth and of those to whom time, toil, and frugality have brought a modicum of financial independence. The corn-belt press alleges that Los Angeles has the civic ethics of a burglar. It declares that if the common decencies existing between human beings were applied to municipalities, there is not a cow-pasture in the Middle West which could not successfully sue the City of the Angels for alienation of affections. The obvious and reiterated answer to such sentimental nonsense is that Los Angeles is a city favored of God, and that consequently any means of increasing its eminence are justified in His eyes.

The Middle Western editors, however, are wholly unreasonable. They bring forth statistics, upon which they base blistering epithets in the hope of stemming the tide. Thus, a few years ago, when Los Angeles had fewer

wage-earners and fewer industries than any municipality of equal population in America, the metropolis
became known throughout the Middle West as "the
City of No Legitimate Business." Today it is referred
to by the Iowa-Kansas press as "the City of the Living
Dead," a sardonic sobriquet derived from the fact that
the span of life in Los Angeles is longer than in any
other large city. Some of these editors splash an extremely wicked pen. In 1928, for example, one outraged Minnesota editor dubbed the City of the Angels
"the Suicide City," for the reason that Los Angeles
at that time had the highest suicide rate in the United
States. The palm has since gone to San Francisco.

But they may as well howl against the moon. Each
year, as sure as the icy hand of winter descends upon the
prairie lands, an army of pilgrims fares forth to join sisters and brothers, uncles and cousins, in the new Eden.
Most of them have more relatives in Los Angeles than
they have at home. Many folks from the "Stop-Bathing-
with-the-First-Frost-on-the-Pond Belt" (Oklahoma,
Kansas, Iowa, the Dakotas, Minnesota, Wisconsin)
simply visualize Los Angeles as the Golden Dream City
of the Western Sea; the gorgeous Midway between the
gaunt cornlands of this world and the pearly gates of
the next. So they come by the thousands each year, settle
down in the salmon-hued bungalows, praise God, raise
peonies, and start playing for the next batch of pilgrims.
They are good American citizens, Christian people,
church-goers, mostly Fundamentalist Baptists and
Methodists. And the first sermon they hear upon arriving in paradise — never to forget — still is from Deuteronomy: "The children of Israel led out of Egypt
into the Promised Land."

Quickly the rural newcomers catch the contagious spirit of Los Angeles. For, as the largest Chamber of Commerce on earth points out with faulty but effective logic, the more people that come to Los Angeles, the more money the present inhabitants will be able to make. Quickly the newcomers get into the game — the game of selling Los Angeles, or any part of it, including the ground underfoot, the car in the garage, or the roof overhead.

Now the Angelenos love their city with a great passion. They believe and know that Los Angeles is a city favored of God. Since four fifths of them are comparative strangers, however, this emotion is naturally not the love a person might feel for old ways, faces, places, and things. It is rather the deep affection a man might entertain for a rich wife or a growing business.

Huntington — The Harbor Fight

*T*he Angel City's great campaign to acquire population from the Middle West was accompanied by an equally ambitious project — the effort to get a harbor built at San Pedro. For, as the Southern Pacific had pointed out (and as the boom had clearly demonstrated), Los Angeles, a town twenty miles from the ocean, could never expect to become a great metropolis without a harbor. At San Pedro, there since the days of the Spaniards, the town had a " port," to be sure, but what a port! It was, in fact, a suicidal, exposed death-trap; the fear of mariners, the graveyard of countless ships; probably one of the worst places in the world for a seagoing vessel to approach. Dana described it as follows when he saw it in 1835: ". . . doubling a high sandy point, we let go our anchor at a distance of three or three and a half miles from shore. It was like a vessel bound to St. John's, Newfoundland, coming to anchor on the Grand Banks; for the shore, being low, appeared to be at a greater distance than it actually was, and we thought we might as well have stayed at Santa Barbara, and sent our [small] boat down for the hides. . . . What brought us into such a place, we could not conceive. No sooner had we come to anchor than the slip-rope, and the other preparations for southeasters, were got ready; and there was reason enough for it, for we lay exposed to every wind that could blow, except the northerly winds, and they came over a flat country with a rake of more than a league of water. . . . The boat was lowered, and . . . as we drew in, we found the tide low, and the rocks and stones, covered with kelp and seaweed, lying bare for the distance of nearly an eighth of a mile. Leaving the boat, and picking our way barefooted over these, we came to what is called the landing-place, at high-water mark."

But Dana did not do full justice to this " port," and it looked somewhat different and even more terrifying in 1888 when the Chamber of Commerce decided to do something about it. There was a shallow pocket in the coast-line, guarded by a long, slim island, running parallel with the coast. This island was divided in the center by three thousand feet of mud flats, partly submerged even at low tide, so that there were really two islands. On mariners' charts one of them was called Deadman's Island; the other, Rattlesnake Island. Between the two islands and the mainland was a sort of harbor, a narrow channel two miles long and thirty-five yards wide. The water here was from six to ten feet deep; the entrance was blocked by a sand-bar where the water was only eighteen inches deep at low tide. All ships of any size, therefore, had to anchor out in the ocean, exposed, as Dana said, " to almost every wind that blows," and receive freight and send it ashore by lighters. Even steam-

LOS ANGELES HARBOR IN 1873,
GUARDED BY DEAD MAN'S ISLAND

ers had to stop out there, where small boats met them to transfer passengers.

Naturally, all ships evaded the place if possible. During the boom commerce at San Pedro, even under such difficulties, had increased fourfold, but fifty times that much tonnage, destined for Los Angeles, had gone on to San Francisco and then come back four hundred miles by train. And as it was during the boom, so it was destined to be always unless something was done about it. Nearly all water shipments originating in southern California went first to the northern metropolis by train. Worse, all the Eastern goods destined for far Pacific countries, which reached the west coast via the southern rail routes, went (and would continue to go) right by Los Angeles on to the water outlet at San Francisco.

So it was clear that Los Angeles, if it ever expected to be anything, would have to have a deep-water harbor; and the city, once it realized that fact, solemnly dedicated itself to the task of getting one — the taxpayers of the United States to pay for it. " The matter had been mentioned before," wrote Willard, " but only as a vague and distant futurity, like the building of the Nicaragua Canal, or the redemption of the Mojave desert."

Well, the Nicaragua Canal itself was now a possibility, and what a bright one! (At the time it was thought that a canal might be built through Nicaragua, not Panama.) The nautical experts pointed out that even if Los Angeles had a decent harbor, the most convenient course for sailing vessels coming round the Horn was to go out into the mid Pacific and strike the trade-winds to make the port of San Francisco. " But," they said, " when the Canal is built, commerce will be transported mainly by steam vessels of moderate draft, which will move up along the coast and seek the nearest favorable and available port from which their freight can reach its market."

Everybody got together on the harbor project, the Southern Pacific, the Santa Fe, the newspapers, the general business and banking interests, under the determined leadership of the lusty Chamber of Commerce. The Southern Pacific Railroad was the real leader in the ballyhoo. Its president, Leland Stanford, did a tremendous amount of missionary work at Washington, while the Los Angeles Chamber of Commerce kept the idea alive at home.

" A favorite method employed by Los Angeles to work up interest," says Willard, " was to seize upon any Senator, Congressman, or influential man who happened to be on the Pacific Coast and convey him to San Pedro by special train." The lay-out at San Pedro was dismal enough, but the guest was overwhelmed with statistics, charts were spread under his eyes, and otherwise every effort was made to " sell " him the idea that Congress ought to appropriate the money for Los Angeles to build itself a harbor. If the visitor approved or committed himself to the scheme, he was wined and dined, and the newspapers gave him handsome write-ups. The idea somehow got round, not that Los Angeles wanted to create a harbor, but that it already had a busy, though somewhat inconvenient harbor and only wanted an appropriation to make some improvements. The wish was father to the thought, and soon the Angelenos were believing it themselves. Stanford finally got six members of the Senate Commerce Committee to go out to Los Angeles and look over the ground.

They were Senators Frye of Maine, Dawes of Massachusetts, Platt of Connecticut, Davis of Minnesota, Morgan of Alabama, and Turpie of Indiana. Escorted by Stanford on a special Southern Pacific train and accompanied by an excited crowd of Los Angeles citizens, experts, economists, orators, and engineers, the Senatorial party arrived at San Pedro on a sunshiny morning in 1889, alighted from the train, and walked down a little hill to a place where tables had been set up on the ground.

With gusto the Chamber of Commerce spokesman unrolled a vari-colored chart, placed it on the table in front of the Senators, and made a formal speech, explaining the plan for a great artificial deep-water harbor.

The Senators looked, listened, smiled pleasantly, asked a few questions, and said nothing. That is, all of them except Senator Frye, the chairman of the committee. The grouchy old Senator from Maine looked out over the mud flats in front of him; he stared back at the dingy swamp land behind him. He saw some bare sunburnt hills, and a few small boats out in the water. He twisted his walrus mustache and squinted his eyes.

"Why," he demanded harshly, "where are all the ships? I was given to understand that there was something of a harbor here! I was given to understand that a great deal of traffic was carried on!"

The Chamber of Commerce orator, disconcerted, started in to explain that — well, there would be a lot of ships just as soon as Los Angeles got a big harbor. Senator Frye turned to the map.

"'Rattlesnake Island'!" he read aloud. "'Deadman's Island'! I should think it would scare a mariner half to death to come into such a place!"

Somebody suggested that the names of the islands

could be changed. Senator Frye perused the map in dead silence for perhaps two minutes, and then he looked up.

" Gentlemen," he said, " as near as I can make out, you propose to ask the Government to create a harbor for you, almost out of whole cloth. The Lord has not given you much to start with, that is certain. It will cost four or five millions of dollars to build, you say. Well, is your whole country worth that much? "

There was much expostulation; everybody started to talk at once. But the Senator from Maine was no longer interested.

" Now," he concluded, " it seems that you have made a big mistake in the location of your city. You should have put it at some point where a harbor already exists, instead of calling upon the United States Government to give you something which Nature has refused " — and having dropped this wet blanket upon the proposed project, the Senator stamped his way up the hill to the special train, followed by the crowd. It was a gloomy, indignant group that rode back to the City of the Angels.

" My remarks," said Senator Frye in an interview the following day, " were intended to be of a somewhat jocular nature."

II

Los Angeles was stopped momentarily, but only momentarily. The following year Congress appropriated five thousand dollars to pay for looking into the matter of building a deep-water harbor somewhere in the vicinity of Los Angeles, " between Points Dume and Capistrano," and appointed three army engineers to do the work.

Thereupon something else began agitating Los Angeles. Would a great artificial harbor, if the Government ever actually built one, be placed at San Pedro? There was no assurance that it would; the army engineers might select any place between the two points. The Chamber of Commerce officially laughed that idea aside, but, nevertheless, real-estate operators, land speculators, and other deep thinkers got busy. One group of capitalists decided that the ideal spot for a port was a little beach town named Redondo, twelve and a half miles closer to San Francisco than San Pedro and closer to Los Angeles by a few miles. They formed the Redondo Railway Company, constructed a short wharf over a submarine canyon (where there was deep water, and fairly safe anchorage except when great storms prevailed), and built a narrow-gauge railway to Los Angeles. The Santa Fe Railroad also decided that Redondo was the likely spot and constructed a second wharf there. Presently considerable freight began to flow into this new port. It was two hours closer to San Francisco than San Pedro; moreover, ships were not compelled to use the slow and expensive method of delivering their cargoes by lighters.

Another group of capitalists, satisfied that any harbor, if built, would go where the Southern Pacific wanted it to go, organized the Terminal Railroad, built a jerk-line road to San Pedro, acquired terminal facilities, and constructed wharves on the western shore of Rattlesnake Island. Soon it was sharing some of the business there with the Southern Pacific.

It may be imagined that this new double competition did not please the Octopus; its line to San Pedro began to lose money.

The army board came in 1891, examined the coast-line

around Los Angeles, and reported to Congress that San Pedro was the most desirable place to build an artificial harbor. The following year Senator Felton of California prepared to ask Congress for two hundred and fifty thousand dollars to begin the preliminary work. Then it was that Collis P. Huntington (who had recently kicked Stanford out of the presidency of the Southern Pacific and taken over the reins himself) played his first card. While the Senate Commerce Committee was considering Felton's request, William Hood, chief engineer of the Southern Pacific, sent a telegram to the Senate Commerce Committee, warning it not to make an appropriation for San Pedro! The ground there, he said, was rocky, unsafe, and unusable. The Southern Pacific, he said, had encountered such difficulty in driving piles for construction of a private wharf that it had been compelled to give up the work and was now preparing to put up a pier at Santa Monica instead!

The two hundred and fifty thousand dollars was summarily thrown out of the bill then being drawn up. Senator Felton was astounded. Senator Frye announced calmly that Santa Monica appeared to be the best place for a harbor near Los Angeles, if any. That, shouted Felton, was absurd! Why, the Southern Pacific had torn up a pier at Santa Monica several years before! Well, responded Frye, maybe it had more information now. It was strange indeed, he continued, that the Southern Pacific Railroad, which was already at San Pedro, would give up its work there and start building a pier at Santa Monica. That made no difference, the excited Felton pointed out; an army board had already recommended San Pedro. Yes, replied Frye, but a great railroad, on the spot, was now warning Congress that the army engineers had made a mistake. Finally the confused Felton appealed to the committee to ask Congress to appoint another board to settle the matter definitely. Frye quickly agreed to this, and so the Rivers and Harbors Bill which passed Congress in 1892 carried the following strangely worded provision written by Frye:

" The Secretary of War is hereby authorized and directed to appoint a board of five engineering officers of the United States Army, whose duty it shall be to make a careful and critical examination for a proposed deep-water harbor at San Pedro or Santa Monica Bays, and to report which is the more eligible location for such a harbor in depth, width, and capacity to accommodate the largest ocean-going vessels, and the *commercial and naval necessities of the country,* together with an estimate of the cost of the same."

Thus Huntington at one stroke placed the proposed project among the " commercial and naval *necessities* of the country," killed the proposed San Pedro appropriation, set up Santa Monica as a competitive spot, and also, by the terms of the bill, excluded consideration of any other spot. Why?

Among the little spur lines which the Southern Pacific was building out in various directions from Los Angeles — to " open up the country " — was one to Ocean Park, a little beach resort two miles south of Santa Monica. To get to the beach at Ocean Park the railroad had to tunnel under a high cliff, which brought the tracks to the ocean front, perhaps eighty yards from the sea. Now, this huge cliff runs from Ocean Park to beyond Santa Monica, right along the sea, a steep, sheer, perpendicular precipice, part of which today is called Pacific Palisades. Below the cliff runs a narrow stretch of firm land and then the sandy beach. The cliff at Ocean Park is about seventy feet high; as it runs north, it increases in height to about a hundred and eighty feet. The Southern Pacific bought this narrow right of way between the cliff and the sea and ran its tracks along it for a distance of about eight miles. Then Huntington announced his plans. There was to be no harbor, either at Redondo or at San Pedro, he said. The harbor was to be built at Santa Monica, at a point which he designated as " Port Los Angeles," in front of his railroad. The Southern Pacific would build a million-dollar pier, running out into the water forty-three hundred feet, the Southern Pacific tracks would run out to the end of it, and the Government would appropriate money to build a great harbor there.

It was quickly discovered that friends of Huntington, or Huntington personally, had bought up all the land around this narrow strip of railroad and on both ends of it, so that no other road could come in. The Santa Fe couldn't terminate on a cliff even if it could buy the land from Huntington or his friends; it couldn't build directly under the cliff because the Southern Pacific tracks were already there, on both sides of the unborn " Port Los Angeles "; and even if it tunneled beneath the cliff, it couldn't get to the sea at this point without crossing the Southern Pacific tracks. And between the S. P. tracks and the sea was only a hundred feet of sandy beach, suicidal for any railroad to build on.

Whereas Redondo was twelve and a half miles closer to San Francisco than San Pedro, Santa Monica, bear in mind, was twelve and a half miles closer than Redondo. Where ships landing at Redondo from San Francisco were saving three hours over San Pedro, at Santa Monica they could save three hours over Redondo and half a day over San Pedro. In other words, what Huntington proposed to do at one fell swoop was to kill the competition of the Santa Fe and Redondo railroads at Redondo, and the competition of the Terminal Railroad at San Pedro, and in addition get the great harbor directly in front of his tracks at Santa Monica, where no other railroad could possibly reach it! Los Angeles went wild. So did the Terminal Railroad, the Redondo Railroad, the Santa Fe Railroad, the Chamber of Commerce, the real-estate owners, and the land speculators. There was a rush to get land near Santa Monica.

When the second board of five army engineers, known as the Craighill Board, reached Los Angeles and held a public meeting at the Chamber of Commerce on September 8, 1892, the town was ready for it. The Huntington and Santa Monica crowd was there; the Terminal Railroad and San Pedro crowd was there; the Redondo Railroad and Santa Fe Railway crowd was there. Present also in great numbers were business men, merchants, bankers, speculators, and promoters, who had bought land in one place or the other, guessing which way the cat would jump. It was a hot meeting.

William Hood, the chief engineer of the Southern Pacific, was examined in part as follows:

Mr. Gibbon: " As I understand you, this land here, extending from the canyon, is the private property of Mr. Huntington, the president of the company? "

Mr. Hood: "I say it is my opinion that it is. I don't know the details, but I understand it to be so; and you might as well assume it."

" That is land with a very high bluff? "

" Yes, sir."

" And your company owns or controls all this property here. That represents a frontage of how much? "

" It is about two thousand feet, more or less."

" What we are getting at just now is the length of the usable land for railroad purposes, the breadth, rather, between those aligning bluffs and tide water."

" I think other roads could go parallel with ours, outside the right of way, for about seventy-five or eighty feet, and hold it, as we propose to hold it, with rock."

" But you cut off all access here. It is necessary to cut across your track to get across here."

" It would be; but there is room here."

" And there is no possible approach from this side, because that is all bluff? "

" That would be very difficult."

The Southern Pacific attorney thereupon addressed the board, pointing out the engineering facts as follows:

" We stand upon our manhood and our rights! We stand upon the bottom of truth and justice and commercial economy, and the best interests of the people of southern California; and that is a platform that will stand, when all these miserable insinuations, with their authors, are buried in oblivion."

III

The board's report was filed with Congress on October 27, 1892. It was devastating to Santa Monica and Redondo and concluded that San Pedro was the logical spot. The Chamber of Commerce sent two lobbyists to Washington to ask that the money be donated at once. Bills were introduced, but they got no farther than Frye and the Senate Commerce Committee. Senator John P. Jones of Nevada, who owned a great deal of land about Santa Monica, was also a member of the Commerce Committee. Huntington had the way blocked. The Southern Pacific was stalling for time, and successfully, as it pushed completion of its long wharf at Santa Monica. Freight coming south was now stopping there, instead of at Redondo or San Pedro, saving from three hours to half a day's time. The *Herald* and the *Express* began to support Santa Monica. The more influential *Times* was for San Pedro.

One day in 1894, when the Southern Pacific's long wharf was completed, Huntington appeared at the Los Angeles Chamber of Commerce and told the secretary to round up the officers; he had something to tell them. The board of directors was hurriedly assembled.

"You people," Huntington said, "are making a big mistake in supporting this San Pedro appropriation. The Rivers and Harbors Committee of the House will never report in favor of that place — not in a thousand years. I know them all and have talked with them about the matter. The same is true of the Senate Committee on Commerce. The chairman of that committee, Senator Frye, says that he will never consent to the expenditure of one dollar for an outside harbor at San Pedro."

"But, Mr. Huntington, will Congress appropriate money for an improvement against the advice of its engineers?"

"It has done so on numerous occasions," replied Huntington. "Congress is all-powerful in the matter of appropriations and can do as it sees fit. It can appoint a board with instructions to find in favor of Santa Monica if it chooses to do so.

"Now, I propose to be frank with you people," the

president of the Southern Pacific continued. " I do not find it to my advantage to have this harbor built at San Pedro. I shall be compelled to oppose all efforts that you or others make to secure appropriations for that site. On the other hand, the Santa Monica location will suit me perfectly. If you folks will get in and work for that, you will find me on your side — and I think I have some little influence at Washington — as much as some other people, perhaps."

The commerce men hemmed and hawed. Finally Huntington brought his fist down on the desk and rose to his feet, his face flushed with anger.

" Well," he said, " I don't know for sure that I can get this money for Santa Monica. I think I can. But I know damned well that you will never get a cent for that other place! "

A moment later he was smiling pleasantly as he invited the chamber's board of directors to go down to Santa Monica the next day in his private car and inspect his wharf. They did, and Huntington entertained them with a sumptuous luncheon, served wine, and proved to be a delightful host. But the chamber men pointed out that their organization was committed to San Pedro. Huntington smiled and said nothing. A few days later he played another ace in the hole.

For eighteen months J. M. Crawley, the Southern Pacific's local agent, had been secretly circulating a petition asking that the harbor be built at Santa Monica instead of San Pedro. On March 7, 1894, about a week after the Santa Monica luncheon, he appeared before the Chamber of Commerce and presented this document. It carried the signatures of eighty-three of the town's leading business men, particularly those engaged in wholesale trade and importing, representing capital of more than ten million dollars. All the signers were members of the Chamber of Commerce!

" The men who sign this document," said Crawley, " are all active members of your organization, their names are fairly representative of the mercantile element of your community. Now I ask, also as a member of this organization and as representing a corporation which is largely interested in the welfare of southern California, that you act as this petition suggests, and resolve in favor of appropriations for Santa Monica."

This stumped the business men. The commerce chamber had always been officially for San Pedro. No other place had ever been considered by it. Now there was a division in its own ranks. What to do?

A secret meeting was called. Some members asked the chamber to stick by San Pedro, others asked it to switch in favor of Santa Monica. One prominent citizen, L. N. Breed, suggested that the city demand money from Congress to build harbors at both places! Mr. Breed, I hardly need to say, was a banker. Alas, a reporter for the *Express* smuggled himself into this secret meeting as an assistant clerk. The next day the *Express* broke the news to Los Angeles that the members of the Chamber of Commerce, whose organization was officially and ostensibly committed for San Pedro, were, in reality, as definitely divided as so many dogs over a bone.

In the face of a storm of criticism, the Chamber of Commerce called an open election of all of its members to vote on the question of what it was for. The election was set a week hence. In the interim the *Times* thundered for San Pedro. The *Express* and *Herald* yelled for Santa Monica. The Terminal Railroad distributed pamphlets all over the town demanding San Pedro. The Santa Fe demanded San Pedro. Every mail brought showers of circulars and letters to the commerce men. The election was by ballot and was conducted by the secret " Australian " method. It lasted all day of April 7, 1894. There were several fist fights. The returns showed:

| San Pedro | 328 |
| Santa Monica | 131 |

The chamber passed resolutions and sent three more lobbyists to Washington. Two months later they appeared before the Senate Commerce Committee, denounced Huntington, stated a long rigmarole case, and requested vaguely that some money be appropriated for building the harbor at San Pedro. The following day Huntington appeared before the same committee. He wasted no time trying to make a case. He attacked nobody. He simply asked that Congress appropriate *four million dollars* to build him a private breakwater and harbor at Santa Monica!

Huntington's bald request, accompanied by the howls of Los Angeles, attracted the attention of the Eastern press. " The county records of Los Angeles," said the New York *World* of June 26, 1894, " show that the property adjoining the exclusive waterfront of the Southern Pacific is divided into eight holdings. The title to parcels one, two and eight are in the names of Senator John P. Jones and Arcadia B. Baker. They constitute three-quarters of all the lands situated as described. All the remainder of the land, with the exception of a few feet at the mouth of the Santa Monica canyon, is in the name of Frank H. Davis, representing Mr. Huntington. It will be seen that Mr. Huntington's Santa Monica enterprise throughout its entire extent is as exclusive as though it were surrounded by a Chinese wall."

The St. Louis *Globe-Democrat's* Washington correspondent wrote: " The harbor contest at Los Angeles waxes warmer. C. P. Huntington was seen going the rounds of the hotels today, and although it was Sunday, he made no halt in buttonholing Senators. Four days ago there was a decided majority in the Commerce Committee in favor of San Pedro, but since the arrival of Mr. Huntington at the capital it is now a matter of great doubt where the majority will be found. . . . Ordinarily Mr. Huntington is philosophical and composed. Today he was ' rattled ' as no one remembers to have seen him, in his many visits to the capital."

A telegram from J. W. Reinhart, president of the Atchison, Topeka & Santa Fe Railroad read: " Atchison is too much interested with its $500,000,000 of property, to permit it to be held out of Pacific Ocean business by the Southern Pacific, whose prayer, if granted, would shut out Atchison and create absolute monopoly. Atchison is the only railway line, other than the Southern Pacific, reaching southern California. If the appropriation goes to Huntington, it throttles all chances of competition, besides permanently injuring the growth of California and adjacent States and Territories."

A group of the Chamber of Commerce men who favored San Pedro drew up a violent petition for the commerce body to send out. The chamber refused to do it, whereupon the San Pedro advocates formed the " Free Harbor League," got out its petition, and asked the chamber men to send it to any " friends " in the 53rd Congress. A third of the six hundred members did so. The document's concluding paragraphs read:

" The whole matter resolves itself into a question of how long a crafty corporation can defraud the people of their right to a free harbor. . . . The people of this section . . . refuse to submit to the commercial enthrallment which has so long retarded the growth and dwarfed the energies of San Francisco and Oakland. The presence of a competing railroad into Los Angeles has been thus far a protection against the encroachment of the Southern Pacific monopoly; but this will avail us but little if our waterfront is to be placed in their hands. We appeal . . . that those who are stealthily carrying forward this great wrong may be called to an open accounting, that the rights of the people may not be sacrificed to . . . the steady encroachment of a despotic corporation."

The Santa Monica crowd got wind of what was going on, and it, too, started petitioning " friends " in Congress. Since " two-thirds of all the business men in Southern California had moved there after reaching maturity in other States," the members of the 53rd Congress were pretty well covered.

The matter reached the open Senate on May 8, 1896. Senator White of California spoke two days in favor of San Pedro, and others spoke nearly as long. Senator Berry of Arkansas said: " I do not believe there is a man throughout the whole United States, save and except Mr. Huntington, who would have had the assurance, in the face of the reports of the army officers, to have come to the Congress of the United States and asked them to give him four million dollars in money to build a breakwater to serve his private interests. It is much better that no deep-water harbor should ever be had, better far that the money should be utterly and

SANTA MONICA,

WHERE COLLIS P. HUNTINGTON ASKED CONGRESS TO BUILD

HIM A FOUR-MILLION-DOLLAR HARBOR

absolutely thrown to the winds, than that we should make thousands of people believe that the appropriation was made, not in the public interests, but in order to promote the private interests of individuals."

Senator Frye spoke for a day in favor of giving the money to Santa Monica. " Oh, it is too paltry," he said, " to undertake to stop any legislation with that cheap demagogical cry that because Huntington has done it, no help can be given to Huntington. . . . He employs seventy-five thousand men . . . Mr. Huntington is not bulling the stock markets, nor bearing them. He is not cornering wheat or flour. He is engaged in enormous enterprises, the results of which are building up the commerce of this republic, and in all his enterprises he is successful."

The debate occupied the entire time of the Senate for five days. The Washington correspondents, Van Alstine, Bierce, Brown, Wellman, McLeod, and others, filed reams of copy, most of them taking the San Pedro side, a few the side of Santa Monica.

Congress finally voted an original appropriation of $2,900,000 to build Los Angeles an artificial harbor at San Pedro.

There was great rejoicing in the Angel City. The *Times'* wild-cat whistle (which the paper blows whenever great news comes) shrieked with joy. There were bands, banners, impromptu parades through the streets. Huntington was licked! The old boy was importuned to " make some graceful act of a good loser." Wouldn't he say that the railroad accepted the decision with good feeling? Huntington said nothing; neither then nor ever.

Three years later, on April 26-7, 1899, the city celebrated the " Free Harbor Jubilee." They had a great gathering at San Pedro, with a barbecue, flowers, and speeches; twenty thousand persons attended. The Southern Pacific refused to participate in the ceremonies and declined to make any subscription to the fund, although many of the twenty thousand rode to San Pedro on the Southern Pacific trains. The great crowd assembled near Point Fermin, where the first barge of stone, brought from Catalina Island, lay ready for dumping. In the White House President McKinley touched a button; it was supposed to set machinery in motion to fill air chambers in the barge, causing it to roll over on one side and dump the stone into the water. Unfortunately, the mechanism of the barge failed to work, and after an embarrassing delay the rocks were finally pushed off by hand. That symbolized Los Angeles' whole effort to get a harbor — no part of the long fight was easy; no step worked out as planned.

IV

Thus Collis P. Huntington — the Southern Pacific Railroad — was licked, for the first time in California. It hurt the old pirate and hastened his death. Today there remains a ghost of his dream at Santa Monica. The million-dollar Southern Pacific steamship pier is gone, but the jetty, which runs fifty feet out into the ocean, is still there. Beside it stands the Lighthouse, a cheap " swim and dine " restaurant, where public bathers buy pop and hot dogs. For a long time the Southern Pacific continued to run trains to its " port "; then Henry E. Huntington ran his interurban street-cars over the tracks; finally they, too, were stopped. Now there is nothing. The lovely Santa Monica water-front is a pleasure beach, as Nature, no doubt, intended it to be.

Beneath the cliff there is a string of rusty rails, half buried in the sand.

On the other hand, Los Angeles today has its great, busy, artificial harbor at San Pedro; to date it has cost nineteen million dollars. It stands as a magnificent monument to municipal enterprise, and to the common knavery of business men and statesmen; and it has probably done more than anything else to make Los Angeles the chief metropolis of California.

But let us move on to more amusing things.

Oil, Oranges, Iowa

By 1891 the sales campaign throughout the Middle West was showing definite returns in southern California. The *bona fide* dirt farmers who were lured to the " Land of Heart's Desire " began almost at once to make the soil productive again. Growing things in southern California — after years of toiling from daylight to darkness in the corn and wheat belts, plowing all day in the hot sun of summer, milking cows and feeding stock in icy barns on cold, wintry nights — growing oranges, olives, figs, and grapes was child's play. They went at it in a businesslike, competent, efficient manner. Bearing orchards, suffering from neglect, were cleaned out, the trees were pruned, the scales were disinfected and scraped away. Vineyards were cleared of weeds and put into order, the soil was pulverized and fertilized. Water was diverted from the Los Angeles (Portiuncula) and other rivers for irrigation purposes; artesian wells were bored from which the water spouted.

New vines were set out to bear in three years; new orange groves were planted to bring forth golden fruit in ten or twelve years. There was no rush; these people had been patient all their lives; they recognized paradise when they saw it; they were there to stay.

One of the biggest problems Los Angeles had was getting industry and manufacturing establishments. The town had few pay-rolls, and nearly everything the people used was brought from the East or North. Manufacturers were offered bonuses in land, stock subscriptions, and actual cash to come to southern California, but with little success. There were no raw materials, no fuel, and no markets. There was no oil for commercial purposes, and coal cost five times what it did in the East. But here again the Lord was with the City of the Angels.

In 1891 two prospectors, E. L. Doheny and C. A. Canfield, decided that there was oil under the town, and accordingly they acquired oil leases on a considerable amount of residence property. On November 4, working themselves with pick and shovel, they started sinking a crude shaft in the front yard of a private home at the corner of Patton and West State streets. Three months later, at a depth of a hundred and sixty feet, they struck a flow of " black gold," which caused great excitement. At once everybody started digging wells, in vacant lots, in orchards, in their front yards. " In some blocks," recorded William A. Spaulding, " there was a well for almost every lot." Within a few months the oil craze was in full bloom, companies were formed, printers were kept busy printing stock certificates. Amateur oil-hunters dug pits, blasted with dynamite, and otherwise tore up the earth; explosions shook the town, black oil sprayed houses, flower-beds, and Angelenos.

No wonder they were excited. Here was an industry! A natural resource!

Machinery was rushed in. " Black, uncouth derricks," said Hill, " sprang up among the ornamental shrubbery, gigantic steel-shod mules dragged loads of casing across the velvety lawns; the newly paved streets of the Boom were crushed and rutted by the wheels of ponderous tanks, often with trailers, drawn by eight, twelve, sixteen mules, four abreast." Housewives worked to the tune of the steam drill, shouting to make themselves heard; falling over cable and piping in their gardens and chicken-yards, wading in black, greasy pools. Oil splashed and dripped from the houses. A total of fourteen hundred wells were sunk, many of them in the heart of the town. A Mrs. Emma A. Summers, one of the real-estate operators of the boom days, put down a well in the shadow of the courthouse, on Court Street near Temple; the well produced so lavishly that Mrs. Summers soon became one of the largest individual operators in crude oil. Twenty-five years later the lady was still known as the " Oil Queen " of southern California.

This was the beginning of the career which ultimately made E. L. Doheny a multimillionaire. For the next four years he devoted his entire attention to the development and production of oil in the Angel City, acquiring outright, or a controlling interest in, sixty-nine wells. Subsequently extending his operations over a continent, Doheny became one of the petroleum kings of the nation. A patriotic, devout, and generous man, Mr. Doheny has long been one of the leading lights of Los Angeles. He built a Catholic church, helped to bring grand opera to Los Angeles, and donated to all worthy causes. Pretty streets and gorgeous subdivisions bear his name today. Alas, a few years ago, when Paul Y. Anderson of the St. Louis *Post-Dispatch*, and Senator Tom Walsh of Montana, blew the lid off Teapot Dome, Mr. Doheny had some difficulty in keeping out of a Federal penitentiary. The matter was somewhat vague, but American jurisprudence rose to the occasion. Albert B. Fall, former Secretary of the Interior, was convicted and sentenced to the penitentiary for accepting a hundred-thousand-dollar bribe from Doheny, but Doheny was acquitted of giving the bribe to Fall.

In any event, the discovery of oil, cheap fuel in Los Angeles, took a great deal off the city's mind and enabled it to make a successful bid for a few small industries. The population increased. Eventually the city's local oil boom played out, and one by one most of the fourteen hundred oil derricks came down. " The saturated soil was dug under, the lawns were remade, flowers bloomed, and repainted houses smiled once more in the sunshine." Some of the wells, however, are still flowing.

Thirty years after the discovery of oil in Los Angeles, southern California became one of the leading oil centers of the nation, when the great Signal Hill field was tapped at Long Beach.

II

Iowa farmers, especially, are associated with Los Angeles and southern California, and for a good reason. In 1905 the Southern Pacific Railroad advised the newly formed and struggling California Fruit Growers' Exchange, a co-operative with headquarters in

Los Angeles, that every dollar the Exchange would spend in advertising, the railroad would match. Accordingly, the Exchange put up ten thousand dollars and went to work.

Iowa was selected as the experimenting ground for this campaign, with Des Moines as the center. Prize fruit went forward to every town in that State in a special bannered train, accompanied by orators and literature. Page ads were run in the Iowa papers urging the people to come down and see the glorious California fruit, raised at a profit of a thousand dollars an acre. The whole State of Iowa was decorated with placards showing a little girl, " Miss California," feeding an orange to a little barefoot boy, " Master Iowa." At every Iowa town the managers of the tour wired back to Los Angeles, announcing the arrival of the " Fruit Special," and this information was blazed throughout southern California. The purpose of the campaign was twofold: first, to sell more oranges in Iowa, and secondly, to bring more Iowans to southern California.

Prizes were offered throughout southern California for the best articles and poems which could be used in advertising California oranges and lemons, the newspapers donating free space generously. The poetry contest, in particular, brought forward thousands of inspiring verses, glorifying the orange, the climate, the sunshine, mother love, home, country, flag, and God. The first prize was awarded to Miss Gertrude Hobby, of the rising town of Ontario, California, for the following poem:

Should You Ask Me — I Should Tell You

Should you ask me, whence these stories,
Whence these legends and traditions,
With the odor of the roses,
With the brightness of the sunshine,
With the rushing of great rivers,
Leaping headlong from the Mountains?
I should answer, *I should tell you,*
From the richest land 'neath Heaven,
From the snow-capped hills of purple,
From the broad and fertile valleys,
Where the orange and the lemon
Grow amidst the peace and plenty.
This they say — the happy dwellers,
In that land of flowers and gold —
That the orange is the symbol
Of their health and wealth untold.
All the brightness of the sunshine,
All the sweetness of the flowers,
All the glow of hidden gold fields,
All the dew from healing herbs,
Are by cunning nature blended
In this fruit of golden hue.
If long life you would be having,
Knowing naught of human ills,
Daily eat at least one orange,
Brought from California's groves.

The slogan " Oranges for Health — California for Wealth " was billboarded throughout Iowa by the railroad. The Southern Pacific also employed a prominent lecturer to tour the larger cities, expatiating on the many advantages of southern California. At the same time the Exchange, to identify and popularize its product, shipped the fruit in boxes imprinted with "California Fruit Growers' Exchange," advertising widely in the Iowa newspapers: "Ask for California Oranges in this Style Box."

Naturally a great deal of thought was given to the matter of selecting a good trade-mark, and after much deliberation the word "SUNKIST" was selected. This created another problem. The Exchange's oranges could be identified as the simon-pure "Sunkist" by stamping wrappers with the word, but how to keep the wrappers on the fruit? Accordingly, all Iowa orange-eaters, and later the nation's orange-eaters, were offered a premium — one beautiful "orange spoon" (to eat the oranges with) for twelve wrappers and twelve cents. That solved it. "When 'SUNKIST' was thoroughly established in consumer consciousness," says the Exchange, "the offer was abandoned."

Although slightly less than seven thousand dollars was expended by the Exchange in the native State of Chiropractic the first season, many times that amount of advertising was obtained, there and elsewhere. Jobbers used space adjacent to Exchange advertising, thereby magnifying its effectiveness, and newspapers throughout the United States " showed their faith in the power of advertising by co-operating most heartily, increasing the advertising many-fold."

Sales before and after the Iowa campaign were carefully checked the first year. They showed that while the Exchange had increased its orange business 17.7 per cent throughout the nation, the State of Iowa showed a *50-per-cent increase* in orange consumption! Consequently, in 1908, " The Executive Committee recommended that as the results of the advertising during the

ORANGE GROVES
IN SAN GABRIEL VALLEY

past season have proved to be beneficial, materially increasing the consumption of citrus fruits, and believing that we can increase the sales in other territories by a continuance of the advertising, therefore we declare the policy of this Board be to continue advertising and that not to exceed $25,000 to be expended this season." Six million stickers reading " SUNKIST ORANGES " and one million reading " SUNKIST LEMONS " were ordered in the fall of 1908 to be pasted upon the regular labels of Exchange shippers.

The district covered by this advertising was gradually expanded. In 1908-9 states adjoining Iowa were covered; in 1909-10 " Sunkist " advertising was used in the entire country from the Pacific to the Atlantic. Larger sums were expended until advertising on a national scale was effected, branching into " constructive work " with consumers, jobbers, and the retail trade. " Sunkist " electrical juice-extractors, and glass reamers now play an important part in increasing sales demand. " Oranges," says the Exchange historian correctly, " have long since ceased to be a luxury, to be bought by the rich alone, or only on festive occasions, and are now a staple, rightfully considered an essential in the everyday diet."

It appears that all kinds of experts were experting. Some genius discovered that American children could be induced to take castor oil in orange juice without calling in the police. This increased the nation-wide sale of oranges by six. The Exchange's best friend, however, was the unhanged optimist who discovered the " Orange Blossom cocktail." As a result of this atrocity it is estimated that at least nine million oranges are sold every year in Hollywood alone.

Was the second part of the campaign — the effort to bring more Iowans to southern California — a success? The last Iowa picnic in Los Angeles was attended by a hundred and ten thousand persons, a few thousand less than the entire population of Des Moines.

PART THREE

Hatred in the Sunshine

*I*t seems somehow absurd, but it is nevertheless a fact, that for forty years the smiling, booming, sunshine City of the Angels has been the bloodiest arena in the Western world for Capital and Labor.

This notorious conflict began, mildly enough, in the spring of 1890, when the four Los Angeles daily newspapers, the *Times*, the *Herald*, the *Tribune*, and the *Express*, all union shops, threatened their typographers with a twenty-per-cent wage cut, in the hope of forcing a ten-per-cent reduction. The local typographical union replied with an ultimatum, refusing to discuss any wage cut, and demanding, instead, a signed agreement, to run for one year, at the existing wage scale. The owners of the papers were given twenty-four hours to sign. They refused to do so, and the typographers walked out. A day later they went back to work on the *Tribune*, three days later they returned to the *Express*, three months later they went back to the *Herald*. The demand for an agreement was withdrawn; the controversy between the three papers and the union men was settled amicably. But not with the *Times*. Otis announced that the union men, having walked out of his plant, could never again darken his doorway.

Otis at this time was already the dominant, outstanding figure in southern California. He had arrived in Los Angeles, as I have said, in 1882 and become editor of the *Times*. When the boom was just starting, he acquired control of the paper, then a struggling weekly, and a few months later wealth descended upon him. Otis was a large, aggressive man, with a loud voice, a walrus mustache, a goatee, and a warlike demeanor. The military bee buzzed in his bonnet. He called his home in Los Angeles " The Bivouac "; and when the boom was at its height, he built a new plant for the *Times* which resembled a medieval fortress, with battlements, sentry-boxes, and other grim, challenging features, surmounted by a screaming American eagle. Otis was a natural warrior and something of a student of military tactics. He was not a man to be crossed.

His chief assistant was his son-in-law. " When the *Times* was four years old," said the magazine *Time* recently, " it acquired a new circulation hustler, one Harry Chandler, who three years before at the age of eighteen had quit Dartmouth and journeyed west to cure himself of tuberculosis. In storybook fashion, young Chandler did his job so well that he attracted the General's eye, got a promotion, married the General's daughter."

The *Times* employed what non-union workers it could find at hand, and brought in others from Kansas City. These " scabs " and the union printers came to words at once, and then to blows. Other local unions declared sympathy with the strike. Otis, in turn, through the columns of his paper, attacked first the union printers and then all closed-shop unionism. The San Francisco Typographical Union endorsed the strike and subscribed funds to bring the *Times* back " into line." Soon the powerful International Typographical Union followed suit and sent money to Los Angeles. Capitalistic organizations in California and in the East endorsed Otis's stand.

The unions not only boycotted the *Times*, but tried to boycott everybody who did business with the paper. Local merchants received visits from union delegates urging them not to advertise in a " scab " sheet and threatening them with the loss of the labor trade. A good many merchants withdrew their advertising from the paper. Literature denouncing it was thrown into stores, left at homes, and handed out on the sidewalks. Pickets walked up and down in front of stores which advertised in the *Times*, warning the public to keep out. The unions also conducted a house-to-house canvass against the newspaper. Most of this work was done by women, who urged housewives not to buy from certain stores and to cease subscription to the *Times*.

Otis thereupon went to work on the merchants as viciously as the unions. Those who stopped advertising in the *Times* were " cowards and cravens." Stores also received visits from delegates of the paper. The Los Angeles merchants were thus caught between the Devil and the deep sea — bedamned if they did, and bedamned if they didn't — and the whole town was quickly drawn into a fight which had started between one newspaper and one union.

While the first phase of the contest was at its height, there was a local railway strike, resulting in a compromise after sixteen days. Otis gave the railway strikers hell then — and again in 1893, when the local mechanics of the Santa Fe Railroad struck. The following year, when the great national railroad strike, or " Debs Rebellion," paralyzed the whole country, Los Angeles and southern California were hard hit. Only a few trains moved for many days. Hundreds of carloads of the spring fruit crop, a bumper one after two bad years, rotted on the tracks. The *Times* burst forth into a terrific attack upon the railway unions, attributing the national tie-up to " their organized despotism " and " robber rule." These epithets were in a new place; hitherto they had always been applied to the owners of the railroads.

On June 27, 1894 Los Angeles was cut off from the world; not a train moved. There was rioting on the streets, and since the *Times*, a public print, was now the avowed enemy of all union labor, the fighting centered at its plant. Strikers, union sympathizers, gathered round the *Times* Building, assaulted carriers and route men, tore their papers into bits, and cluttered up the streets with them. Union sluggers hit " scabs "; paid strike-breakers attacked union men. Every day for a week there were bloody street-fights. On July 2 six companies of the First Regiment, U. S. Infantry, were rushed to Los Angeles to maintain order.

Otis was gaining ground. He and his friends thereupon brought together the city's merchants, bankers, and business men and a few manufacturers and welded them into a union of employers — a militant union against unionism — the Merchants and Manufacturers Association, or "M. and M." It became powerful at once. Employers who were hesitant about breaking with Labor were threatened, browbeaten, and terrorized into it. The banks, naturally, were with Otis, or, rather, anti-Labor. Any employer of labor who was reluctant about joining this open-shop association was apt to find himself cut off from customers and credit alike.

As soon as this organization was on its feet, and while many business men were still on the fence, an employer-union organizer was brought from Denver to organize a local branch of the Citizens' Alliance, a national open-shop organization. "Los Angeles," said the *Times*, "proved a fertile field." Within a few weeks the organizer had six thousand paying members. As soon as the Citizens' Alliance was going strong the M. and M. absorbed it. Now the business men, or nearly all of them, were in the organized non-union-labor fold. Now they openly took their stand, paid their own union dues, and listened to their own walking delegates.

Simultaneously all the local union-labor men were welded into one organization. There was already a Los Angeles Council of Labor, but it was ineffective and split by dissension. In 1903 the American Federation of Labor began to take official notice of Otis; he was beginning to loom as a definite west-coast threat. What was needed in Los Angeles to combat the M. and M. was a strong central organization. Accordingly, Patrick H. "Pinhead" McCarthy, a San Francisco labor boss and politician (later Mayor of San Francisco), went down to Los Angeles and organized a new Central Labor Council, along the lines of the powerful and successful San

Francisco union-labor governing body. The new organization represented every labor union in Los Angeles.

II

Thus it was organized Capital against organized Labor, dog eat dog. There was a laundry strike, a brewery strike, a bakers' strike. The unions got the worst of them. In 1903 the local butchers struck. They circularized the city with a printed list of " fair " and " unfair " meat-dealers, the former to be patronized by the friends of union labor, the latter to be boycotted. The " unfair " meat-dealers immediately got most of the trade — perhaps because the capitalists could afford more and better steaks and lamb chops than the workingmen — whereupon the Sentous Meat Packing Company, one of the packers satisfactory to the unions, brought suit to enjoin the Labor Council from including its name on the " fair " list!

" As a sound business measure," said the *Times*, " the Sentous Company demanded to be boycotted, but the union officials avoided the process servers and continued to handicap the Sentous plant with their unprofitable approval."

The odds were in Otis's favor, and he was lucky. His circulation grew as Los Angeles started to reap the fruits of its after-boom campaign, and Otis boasted that his fight against the unions was responsible for it. But such was not the case; the circulations of all the papers increased. The population of Los Angeles rose from 50,-395 in 1890, when the fight started, to 102,479 in 1900. The influx of Middle Western population, indeed, is probably all that saved the *Times* from going under. If

Los Angeles had been a town with established industries, enjoying a moderate, normal growth, it is probable that the *Times* could not have weathered the storm,
then or later. The newcomers, arriving in paradise as a
result of the Chamber of Commerce ballyhoo, were not
interested in unions, or the *Times*, or in any Capital-
Labor fight. They were interested in real estate, in thaw-
ing out, in growing oranges " at a profit of $1000 an
acre "; in getting ahead in this new country. Mostly
farmers, which is to say the greatest of all individualists,
even the poorest of them were not what is known as
" class conscious." They refused to join any boycott
against the *Times* or any merchants, and if some of them
did, others were coming in every day.

In 1907 the International Typographical Union
charged that the *Times* had " unlimited financial backing " from the American Manufacturers' Association and
other capitalist organizations, and that these powerful
interests had deliberately made Los Angeles the focal
point of a nation-wide war against union labor in an
effort to break unionism throughout the country. Otis
denied that he had " unlimited financial backing " from
anybody; but his denial appears to have rested solely on
the single word " unlimited." When the American Federation of Labor held its convention in Norfolk, Virginia, in 1907, the Typographical Union appealed to it
for help on the grounds that the struggle in Los Angeles
had become national in scope. The A. F. of L. gave its
support, and advanced money. It also passed a secret
resolution which called for " a war fund for use in attacking the Los Angeles *Times*."

The same year the unions got a local mouthpiece of
their own by buying out the *News* and changing its

name to the *Citizen*. The paper was well supported from the start, particularly by Pasadena merchants, which plutocratic town, strangely enough, has always been rather friendly towards union labor. The opposing journals, the *Times* and the *Citizen*, then began to swap epithets. "Walrus," "Tin Soldier," "Passion Incendiary," "Character Assassin," the *Citizen* called Otis. "Grafters," "Sluggers," "Gas-pipe Ruffians," "Industrial Assassins," Otis called the union men. The following year Alfred Holman, editor of the San Francisco *Argonaut*, wrote: "The *Times* never lost its temper. But there was something approaching a spirit of religious fervor in its arguments against unionism, day after day, year after year."

Starting their second offensive, the unions concentrated on a single store, Hamburger's, the largest department store in the city, and the largest advertiser in the *Times*. Everything that was being used in the general boycott was perpetrated on Hamburger's, and a great deal more. Men, women, and children went into the store and made purchases; when their packages were wrapped up and they were reaching for their money, they asked pleasantly, as if by afterthought: "By the way, you don't advertise in the *Times* do you?" The reply was "Yes." The customer said: "Then I can't buy your goods," left the wrapped packages on the counter, and walked out. Large shipments of furniture and other bulky and expensive merchandise were ordered sent out, and then returned with the same information. Fake orders were given over the telephone, asking merchandise to be sent to the homes of people who had ordered nothing. The store, the quality of its merchandise, its business methods, its treatment of employees, the names of its owners, and finally their race, which was Jewish, were attacked in every possible way, in print and by word of mouth.

Hamburger's fought back. It increased its advertising in the *Times* and called the boycott against the store an "insane idea." At the height of the boycott the store put on a huge sale, advertising: "*At Extremely Low Prices: A Large Supply of Strictly Non-Union-Made Clothing, Scab Overalls, and Women's Apparel.*"

Secretly the *Times* and the store set spies to work to learn the names and addresses of the buyers. The reports revealed that many of them were union men, and, more particularly, female members of their families. Alas, feminine loyalty to the "cause" fell in the face of a bargain! The *Times* printed the facts and laughed. The unions were furious.

The American Federation of Labor started a national under-cover boycott against the *Times*. Throughout the country local unions were instructed to have their members write personal letters to the *Times'* national advertisers, warning them that unless they stopped advertising in this paper their product would no longer be used by organized Labor. A number of national advertisers did drop their accounts with the *Times*, after receiving literally thousands of such letters. "These frightened advertisers," said the *Times*, "wrote directly to the paper to cancel their advertising, although their accounts had been placed by agencies." Lists of *Times* advertisers, together with form letters, were supplied by the A. F. of L. to unions throughout the country, and thousands of working people wrote or signed them.

One of the *Times'* advertisers was the maker of "Bishop's pills," a quack patent medicine "for men only." Or, as the *Times*, always a lover of quackery, called it, " a proprietary medicine made at Salt Lake City for the exclusive use of men." Among the boycotters of the *Times* were six hundred good sisters of the Ladies' Garment Workers' Union of Memphis, Tennessee. These ladies sat down and laboriously wrote letters to this advertiser, telling him in no uncertain terms that they were going to quit using his product if he didn't stop advertising in the Los Angeles *Times*! Worse, the letters were simply addressed to " Bishop, Salt Lake City, Utah "; hence the whole six hundred epistles were received by the astounded Bishop of the Mormon Church! It was an excellent little freak-feature story, and as such was published in front-page boxes by newspapers throughout the country. The unions were speechless with rage. Old Otis — he was now seventy — cackled with glee.

While the unions were attacking Hamburger's, the Merchants and Manufacturers Association was playing no favorites; it was assaulting all local business firms. The San Francisco *Bulletin* described its procedure as follows:

" The Merchants and Manufacturers Association has one confession of faith, one creed: ' We will employ no union man.' The M. & M. also has one command: ' You shall employ no union man.' The penalty for disobedience to this command is financial coercion, boycott, and ruin. ' You hire union men and we'll put you out of business,' says the M. & M., and the employer knows that the oracle speaks. ' You declare an eight-hour day, and we'll stop your credit at the banks,' and the M. & M. does what it says.

" The M. & M. sandwich man does not walk up and

down the streets. He walks boldly into the front door, or puts his ultimatum on paper. The merchant who disobeys the M. & M. command runs into something which robs him of his business, hampers him in securing raw materials for manufacture, holds up his payment for work when it has been completed, and frightens him out of his power of speech to rebel."

Specifically, the unions' boycott against Hamburger's was matched by the M. and M.'s boycott against the McCan Mechanical Works, one of the largest foundries in southern California. David C. McCan, its owner, a rich man, informed both the walking delegates of the M. and M. and the labor unions that nobody could tell him whom he should employ, neither organized Capital nor organized Labor. " I employ," said McCan, " both union and non-union men. I intend to hire whom I please, when I please, and to ask no questions other than whether the man is competent to do the work. I will work them nine hours instead of ten if I choose " (ten hours was then the standard day for foundry workers), " and eight instead of nine if I want to." He soon felt the hand of the M. and M. at his throat. Sending out a letter to firms which needed his line of manufacturing, he received many letters refusing to do business with him. He published them. All said the same thing: " The position taken by you on the labor situation will not warrant us in placing any business with you."

The M. and M. imported one Seneca Beach from Oregon to form an open-shop printing organization. The union humorists wrote many letters to Mr. Beach, substituting an " f " for the " c " in his first name. Felix J. Zeehandelaar, secretary of the M. and M., was addressed as " Zeehandeliar." There was strike after strike;

carpenters, plasterers, plumbers, laundry workers, brewery workers. During the brewery strike the unions plastered the town with large black-type placards reading: " DON'T DRINK SCAB BEER. MADE BY [four firms], UNFAIR TO ORGANIZED LABOR." This request was tastefully set around a huge red skull and cross-bones, the symbol of poison. Each side threatened the brewers with prohibition.

III

The warfare continued with growing bitterness. In the spring of 1910 the San Francisco union labor leaders took command in Los Angeles. Some of them were McCarthy, O. A. Tveitmoe, Anton Johannsen, Tom Mooney, and A. J. Gallagher. San Francisco was the strongest union city in America. David Warren Ryder, writing in the *American Mercury,* said that after 1908 in San Francisco: " Not a hammer was lifted, or a brick laid, or a pipe fitted, or wall plastered or painted or papered without the sanction of the unions. Let an employer large or small discharge a drunken, insubordinate or incompetent workman without the union's consent, and he found himself the next day facing a strike, and compelled to reinstate the discharged workman and pay him and his fellows for the time they were out. The power of the unions was absolute, and for years they were able to exact the utmost obedience to their complex and extravagant rules and regulations."

In *Dynamite,* that superb story of class violence in America, Louis Adamic said: " The unions were a thorn in the side of San Francisco business. Labor costs there were higher than anywhere else on the Coast, and San Francisco found it difficult to compete with Portland,

Seattle, and particularly, Los Angeles. The wages were nearly 30 per cent higher in San Francisco than in Los Angeles. San Francisco was falling down, especially in ship-building; even repair work under the system of competitive bidding went elsewhere. Not only did new capital fear to come to San Francisco, but old capital was drawing out." This state of affairs was intolerable to both Capital and Labor in San Francisco; Labor fearing the menace of low wages in Los Angeles, and San Francisco employers protesting against paying higher wages than their competitors in the South. It was up to the unions, they said, either to lower wages in San Francisco, or to raise them in Los Angeles.

Accordingly, the Structural Iron Workers were sent into the fray. These were tough, hard-bitten men, comprising the most powerful and most feared union in America. Los Angeles employers were notified that the local union ironworkers would be called out in every plant in the city on June 1, 1910 unless a new wage scale was put into effect. The scale was not put into effect, and the strike was called. Three hundred ironworkers went out on the first call, and twelve hundred on the second. Violence started almost at once. Los Angeles, throughout the summer and into the fall, was full of employer organizers, union organizers, " scabs," and San Francisco labor gorillas. Strike-breakers were imported from the Middle West. Half a dozen strikes were going on at the same time. Union pickets marched round and round factories in single file, in sight of non-union workers inside. Union " entertainment committees " slugged non-union workers, strike-breaking thugs beat up union men. There were many street-fights, with brickbats, stones, clubs, and black-jacks. The police were neutral until the Los Angeles City Council passed its famous non-picketing ordinance; this automatically threw the police into the fight against the strikers. The court injunction also made its appearance, perhaps for the first time in America. The Superior Court granted seven separate injunctions restraining the strikers from demonstrating.

No attention was paid to these injunctions. The picket lines were doubled. " Pinhead " McCarthy announced that Los Angeles would be unionized this time, completely, once and forever. Tveitmoe, Johannsen, and Gallagher toured the State raising funds. The M. and M. did likewise. Jails and police courts were filled to overflowing with picketers; they openly fought the cops. More than three hundred strikers were arrested and sentenced to a fifty-dollar fine or fifty days in jail. At first the fines were paid by the unions, and the men went back on the picket lines. Then the picketers began demanding jury trials. Most of these were acquitted, revealing a significant new note; a great part of the public was in sympathy with the strikers. Violence spread to Long Beach, where the fighting was marked by even more brutality. The temper of strikers and strike-breakers alike daily grew more threatening, the attacks by both sides more murderous. Scores of arrests were made for assault and battery. Several men were convicted of felonious assault and sentenced to San Quentin.

The employers were panicky. Otis had a small cannon mounted on his automobile and went dashing about like a general at the front. The *Times* carried frantic editorials.

" Friends of industrial freedom," it said, " must stand together and back the employers who are at present being assailed by the henchmen of the corrupt San Francisco labor bosses. All decent people must rally around the flag of industrial liberty in this crisis, when the welfare of the whole city is at stake. If the San Francisco gorillas succeed, then the brilliant future of Los Angeles will end, business will stagnate; Los Angeles will be another San Francisco — dead! "

While a dozen strikes were at their highest point of intensity, a political item derogatory to Hiram Johnson's father was sent to all newspapers in the State. Every editor in California ignored it except Otis. He published it with trimmings. Senator Johnson rushed to Los Angeles enraged, and before a huge crowd at the Simpson Auditorium he paid his compliments to Otis, in part as follows:

". . . But we have nothing so vile, nothing so low, nothing so debased, nothing so infamous in San Francisco as Harrison Gray Otis. He sits there in senile dementia, with gangrened heart and rotting brain, grimacing at every reform, chattering impotently at all things that are decent; frothing, fuming, violently gibbering, going down to his grave in snarling infamy. This man Otis is the one blot on the banner of southern California; he is the bar sinister upon your escutcheon; my friends, he is the one thing that all California looks at when in looking at southern California they see anything that is disgraceful, depraved, corrupt, crooked and putrescent — that is Harrison Gray Otis."

In midsummer the police reported excitedly that " unexploded bombs " had been found at the two biggest building jobs in the city, the Hall of Records and the Alexandria Hotel. One of the " bombs " turned out to be a gas-pipe filled with street manure, with a rusty dollar watch tied to it, the joke of a bright newspaper reporter. It was charged by union sympathizers that the other had been " planted " by the non-union forces, or police, in an effort to win sympathy for the employers and turn the public against the strikers. At any rate, the news threw terror into Los Angeles.

A few days later a non-union worker was killed by the fall of a hoisting derrick on the Alexandria Hotel job. As his fellow workers carried his body out of the excavation, they engaged in a fight with union pickets, and a riot followed. During the fighting the dead man was dropped into the street, and his body was trampled and cut. In ninety-six-point type the *Times* shrieked at the union men: " CORPSE DEFACERS! "

On September 3 the *Times* said: " It is full time to deal with these labor-union wolves in such prompt and drastic fashion as will induce them to transfer their law-lessness to some other locality, for the danger of toler-ating them in Los Angeles is great and immediate. . . . Their instincts are criminal, and they are ready for arson, riot, robbery, and murder! "

On the other hand, Brann, the Iconoclast, said of Otis: " I can but wonder what will become of the *Times* edi-tor when the breath leaves his feculent body and death stops the rattling of his abortive brain, for he is unfit for Heaven and too foul for Hell! "

They were all seeing red now. Underdogs and over-dogs, they were all becoming mad dogs.

Dynamite or Gas?

*A*t one o'clock on the morning of October 1, 1910 the *Times'* mechanical force was busy, as usual, getting the paper to press. Forms were being closed up, stereotyped, and sent down to the press room. An hour later the presses would hum, turning out the morning paper. The news of the day was " in "; most of the editorial force had gone home, leaving the usual skeleton crew on duty. Altogether there were about a hundred employees in the grim four- and six-story building, which covered nearly half a block.

At seven minutes past one the building rocked with a series of explosions. The roars shook the city. The first explosion was heard for ten miles; it was followed by five more in rapid succession. Metal flew out in all directions like shrapnel; ink, exploding in barrels, shot up in geysers; huge rolls of news-print paper went hurtling through the air, bursting as they went. Machinery crashed, floors gave way, walls fell. In less than four minutes the building was a mass of flame on three floors.

Crowds, police, reached the scene before the last explosion. Customers and employees from the surrounding all-night restaurants, guests of the cheap hotels in the neighborhood, men and women rushed from their homes near by. Fire-bells rang, police whistles shrieked, people yelled and screamed. The police station was only half a block away, hence police reporters got there in time to be eyewitnesses of the catastrophe.

Through the smoke and flame men could be seen rushing round to the windows on the third floor. Spectators could hear the cries of distress, the groans of mangled and crippled men, imprisoned by the flames, about to be cremated alive. Apparently the exit doors had jammed. Some were jumping through flames from windows three and four stories up, breaking their legs and heads. Would-be rescuers, approaching the stairs, were driven back by heat, smoke, and flames.

Policemen came running from headquarters carrying a short ladder. It was inadequate, but at least it saved the life of one man. Charles Lovelace, the State editor, reached a window, jumped upon it, and escaped with a broken leg. Fire apparatus arrived. Nets were jerked out, but by that time it was impossible to approach the reddening walls. The *Times* Building was a fiery furnace. Those inside were doomed.

Twenty men lost their lives: the assistant night editor, assistant telegraph editor, a telegraph-operator, Harry Chandler's secretary, nine linotype-operators, three printers, one machinist, one compositor, one pressman, one apprentice. Nineteen were killed outright or burned to death. Churchill Harvey-Elder, assistant night editor, the last man to jump, died six hours later from burns, plus a broken leg. Sixteen of the dead men were mar-

THE LOS ANGELES *TIMES* BUILDING
AFTER THE EXPLOSION

ried; they left a like number of orphans. Seventeen persons were injured, including one woman.

Many residents of Los Angeles, awakened by the roar and shock, believed at first that the town had been struck by a major earthquake, and rushed panic-stricken from their homes. Then they saw the heavens lighted up. The telephone office was swamped with calls. Men and women rushed to the scene, business men, merchants, manufacturers, laboring men, wives and families of *Times* employees. The latter, held back by police lines, screamed and fainted. In less than an hour several thousand persons were milling in the neighborhood, many in night-clothes, others half-dressed. The whole town was up.

The *Times* executives rounded up their forces, went to an auxiliary plant several blocks away, the existence of which most people were unaware of, and got out their paper. In the morning it appeared as usual, carrying the story and making the direct charge that the *Times* had been bombed by the unions. The eight-column streamer read: " UNIONIST BOMBS WRECK THE TIMES." The front page carried: " A Plain Statement. By the Managing Editor of the *Times*." It read:

" The *Times* building was destroyed this morning by the enemies of industrial freedom by dynamite bombs and fire.

" Numerous threats to do this dastardly deed had been received.

" The *Times* itself cannot be destroyed. It will be issued every day and will fight its battles to the end.

" The elements that conspired to perpetrate this horror must not be permitted to pursue their awful campaign of intimidation and terror. Never will the *Times* cease its warfare against them.

" General Otis, the principal owner of the *Times*, is on his way home from Mexico and will arrive here this afternoon.

" The *Times* has a complete auxiliary plant from which this issue was printed on its own presses.

" The management is under great obligations to the *Herald* for hearty assistance and to the *Examiner* for friendly offers.

" The *Times* will soon be itself again. All business will be conducted at the Times Branch Office, 531 South Spring Street.

" A further statement cannot be made at this hour in the presence of frightful death and destruction.

" Harry Chandler, assistant general manager of the *Times*, happened to be on the street when the explosion occurred and immediately took command of the situation.

" They can kill our men and can wreck our buildings, but by the God above they cannot kill the *Times*.

HARRY E. ANDREWS.
Managing Editor of the *Times*."

It was a good statement, effective and, under the circumstances, rather restrained. Then Otis returned.

" O you anarchic scum," he wrote, " you cowardly murderers, you leeches upon honest labor, you midnight assassins, you whose hands are dripping with the innocent blood of your victims, you against whom the wails of poor widows and the cries of fatherless children are ascending to the Great White Throne, go, mingle with the crowd on the street corners, look upon the crumbled and blackened walls, look at the ruins wherein are buried the calcined remains of those whom you murdered. . . ."

II

What had caused the *Times* explosion?

" Dynamite! " shrieked the *Times*.

" Gas! " yelled the unions.

" Who knows? " others asked.

The day of the explosion the Los Angeles *Examiner* said: " There were a number of theories by those familiar with the geography of the *Times* building to account for the explosion. In addition to the declaration that the building had been dynamited, there was the theory that the explosion came from an ignition of the stock of ink, oils and other highly inflammable and explosive materials used in the printing and kindred processes. They were kept in the alley separating the tall *Times* building from the main structure on the corner. This was known as Ink Alley. There was also the report that the explosion had been caused by gas, which several in the building smelled during the evening."

C. C. Travers, foreman of the *Examiner* composing room, was half a block from the *Times* Building at the time of the explosion. He said: " Immediately I got busy and started to telephone the news to the *Examiner*, but before I could use the phone some of the boys from the *Times*, I think they came from the press room, beat me to the phone. I asked one of them, ' What do you think caused it? ' He replied quickly: ' There's going to be hell to pay for this. The gas has been terrible all night. Everybody noticed it.' "

The day after the explosion it was " reported " that

unexploded bombs had been found at the homes of Otis and Zeehandelaar. Strangely enough, no one had thought to look for them until twenty-four hours later. Los Angeles was in a panic. Every capitalist, every merchant in the city, was fearful that a bomb was hidden somewhere in his place of business or beneath his house. Tourists rushed to get out of the town. Angelenos found business elsewhere; wealthy men sent their families to Pasadena and Santa Barbara.

Five days later they were still taking bodies and bones out of the wreckage of the *Times* Building. The positions of some of the charred bodies showed that men had rushed to elevator shafts and other exits, found them blocked with machinery and fallen timbers, and slowly burned to death. The *Times* ran pen-and-ink drawings depicting the shrouded remains of bodies being carried from the ruins to the dead-wagons. One such drawing, on the front page of October 5, carried the following underlines: " Placing One of the Seven Bodies Recovered Tuesday in Dead Wagon for Removal to Morgue to Await Inquest. Thus Far the Remains of Fifteen Victims of the Unionist Assassins have been Taken from the Debris."

Huge rewards totaling nearly three hundred thousand dollars were offered for the apprehension of the " criminals." William J. Burns, the detective, was in Los Angeles the day of the explosion. He was on his way, he said, to attend the convention of the American Bankers' Association. He was immediately hired by Mayor Alexander.

Investigations were made by the police, the grand jury, a Mayor's committee, the City Council, and the Labor Council. All but one determined that the building had been dynamited and the gas set afire by the explosion. Job Harriman, the unions' attorney, was in charge of the investigation ordered by the Labor Council. His finding was that the *Times* had not been dynamited at all, but had been destroyed by fire caused by a gas explosion.

Harriman said he had positive proof that men had been carried out of the *Times* Building overcome by gas fumes; that the explosion was the result of a faulty gas system, " criminal negligence " on the part of the *Times*, and that Otis would probably be tried for manslaughter. The *Citizen* shouted: " Dynamite! That's the kind of stuff that occupies the place in Otis' head where brains are supposed to be! If sufficient dynamite had exploded to blow up that building, every window for three blocks would have been broken and not a soul in the basement would have come out alive. Any person may go and see that the floor of the basement directly beneath where Alexander's committee said the dynamite was placed shows no effect of the downward action of dynamite. Windows directly across the street were unbroken, and the windows of the building itself were not destroyed until the heat demolished them. The *Times* building was an unsafe, unsanitary, gas-polluted, fire-trap."

The explosion, of course, was front-page news throughout the United States.

To the open-shop employers Otis became a great hero. He went on a national lecture tour. The National Association of Manufacturers, in convention in New York, wired him sympathies, urging him to keep up the splendid fight for " industrial freedom," condemning " the doctrine of rule and ruin which employs dynamite as the instrument." Expressions of sympathy and offers of help poured in on the *Times* from many cities. *American Industries,* an organ of the N. A. of M., immediately implicated Samuel Gompers and other officers of the A. F. of L., by printing, verbatim, the secret resolution which had been passed at the Norfolk convention of the A. F. of L. in 1907 providing for " *a war fund* for use in attacking the Los Angeles *Times.*"

" Gompers," says Mr. Adamic, " refused to answer the accusation; the mere suggestion of such a thing was absurd! "

Throughout the United States the Socialists raised a tremendous howl. In the *Appeal to Reason* (October 15, 1910) Debs printed a long article, which he elaborated in every issue. " I want to express my deliberate opinion," he said, " that the *Times* and its crowd of union-haters are the instigators, if not the actual perpetrators, of that crime and the murder of twenty human beings." All kinds of rumors and insinuations were going round. " Wasn't it strange that all the big officials and chief editors had been out of the building when the explosion occurred? " " Why was Otis out of town at this time? " " How did Harry Chandler just happen to be on the street? " The *Times* itself said: " Some of the more hardy of the *Times'* enemies industriously spread the report that the *Times* had blown up its own building and killed its own men for the dual purpose of getting the insurance and fastening the crime on organized labor."

On Christmas night, almost three months after the *Times* explosion, a bomb wrecked part of the Llewellyn Iron Works, where men were still on strike. This threw Los Angeles into another panic. The following day the *Times* said: " As a result of the dynamite outrages a

Vigilance Committee may be formed by the representative business men of Los Angeles. The matter was discussed with gravity yesterday morning at a joint meeting of some of the most representative civic organizations, but definite action was postponed until a future date. . . . It was the sentiment of the assemblage that the situation demands immediate attention, and that it is of a character that might not necessitate gloves. The Chamber of Commerce and the Merchants and Manufacturers Association held this meeting . . . all appeared united in the belief that the time has arrived for the creation of a vigilance committee."

III

On April 12, 1911, seven months after the *Times* explosion, agents of Burns arrested two men at the Oxford Hotel in Detroit. They were rushed to Chicago, where they were incarcerated, not in jail, but in the home of a Chicago police sergeant. There the detectives went to work on one of the men, Ortie McManigal, and after a few days, on a promise of immunity, he made a statement saying that he had bombed the Llewellyn Iron Works; that his companion, J. B. McNamara, had dynamited the Los Angeles *Times* Building; that they had done other "jobs" together; and that they had been directed and supplied with funds by J. B. McNamara's brother, J. J. McNamara, of Indianapolis, secretary of the Structural Iron Workers Union.

Burns wired his agents in Los Angeles requesting that extradition papers be rushed immediately for the three suspects. After the two men had been held illegally and incommunicado in the Chicago cop's house for more than a week, the extradition papers arrived. They were signed by the Governor of Illinois, and the two men were rushed to Joliet in a closed car and placed aboard a limited train to Los Angeles. Burns then went to Indianapolis, where fraudulent extradition papers for J. J. McNamara were signed by the Governor, prior to McNamara's arrest. Armed with these papers, Burns and local officers invaded the union headquarters late Saturday afternoon, arrested McNamara, denied him a lawyer, rushed him to a magistrate, who, without any authority, recognized the extradition papers, and he, too, was handcuffed and rushed to Los Angeles. Fraud, illegality, and crime marked the arrest of the three men. In a word, they were kidnapped.

On April 23, when the three men were safely on their way to Los Angeles, the *Times,* which was " in " on the catch, broke the story. It was a nation-wide sensation. The news startled the country. The *Times* headlines read: " DYNAMITERS OF THE TIMES BUILDING CAUGHT — CRIME TRACED DIRECTLY TO HIGH UNION OFFICIALS — RED-HANDED UNION CHIEFS IMPLICATED IN CONSPIRACY."

The same day the *Times* said editorially: " These villains are the Camorrists of the United States and in running them down Detective Burns has unearthed the most tremendous criminal conspiracy in the history of America."

The reaction was not such as might have been expected. For the Pettibone, Moyer, Big Bill Haywood trial had not been forgotten. In 1907 during the Capital-Labor war in Idaho, those men had been arrested in Colorado on a Saturday afternoon when the courts were closed, by agents of the McPartland Private Detective Agency, kidnapped, rushed to Idaho, and placed on trial for the murder of former Governor Frank Steunenberg, who had been killed, as he entered his home, by a dynamite bomb attached to the front gate. The chief witness against them was one Harry Orchard, who confessed to the murder and swore that he had been paid by the trio to kill Steunenberg. The three men were prosecuted by William E. Borah and defended by Clarence Darrow. They were acquitted, and the evidence brought out at the trial was a damning indictment of capitalistic brutality, crime, and crookedness. The circumstances surrounding the arrest of the McNamaras were virtually parallel.

All over the country a terrific cry went up against the kidnapping of these men, led by union men and radicals, but seconded by many conservatives. Debs telegraphed to the *Appeal to Reason:* " Sound the alarm to the working class! There is to be a repetition of the Moyer-Haywood-Pettibone outrage upon the labor movement. The secret arrest of John McNamara, by a corporation detective agency, has all the ear-marks of another conspiracy to fasten the crime of murder on the labor union officials to discredit and destroy organized labor in the United States. . . . Arouse, ye hosts of labor, and swear that the villainous plot shall not be consummated! Be not deceived by the capitalist press! "

O. A. Tveitmoe, of San Francisco, as secretary of the California Building Trades Council, offered a seven-thousand-dollar reward " for the apprehension of the person or persons really responsible for the destruction of the *Times* Building and the killing of twenty men."

Samuel Gompers appealed to working men and women throughout the country to subscribe to a defense fund. " We know," declared Gompers, " that these men have been arrested on charges that are absolutely false. I have investigated the whole case. Burns has lied! "

The McNamara brothers and McManigal were placed in the Los Angeles County jail on April 27. J. B. McNamara was charged with dynamiting the *Times* Building (murder), and J. J. McNamara of complicity in the dynamiting of the Llewellyn Iron Works. McManigal was closely guarded and given every attention. The prosecution feared that he was going insane, in which case his confession would be discredited as the ravings of a lunatic. J. J. McNamara was well known in national labor circles. " He was," says Mr. Adamic, " a stalwart, well dressed, smiling, clean-shaven man. His brother, Jim, slightly older, was slight, with a thin face, enlivened by a bitter, uncertain smile, and a fanatical look in his shifty eyes."

Job Harriman, as attorney for the Los Angeles Labor Council, was temporarily placed in charge of the defense. " We have witnesses," he declared, " who will be called to the stand and will prove that they left the *Times* Building early in the evening [before the explosion] utterly unable to stand the odor of gas that flooded it." Burns said: " We shall have no trouble convicting these men. We have a complete case against them."

Less than a month after the McNamaras were jailed, Harriman was nominated for Mayor of Los Angeles by the Socialist-Labor party. The open shop and the McNamara " frame-up " were the main issues. From his cell in the county jail J. J. McNamara supported Harriman, saying: " There is but one way for the working class to get justice. Elect its own representatives to office." While in his cell, McNamara himself was re-elected secretary of the Iron Workers Union. Both brothers were flooded with telegrams, expressing faith in their innocence.

The *Citizen* said: " That Otis is guilty of one of the greatest crimes of this or any other century is amply proven. The character assassin and passion incendiary is the most damnable kind of an anarchist. . . . Burns stands charged with fraud, falsehood, inciting to perjury, and kidnapping. Organized Labor . . . does not believe that anyone destroyed the *Times* Building unless it was the greedy owner, Harrison Gray Otis."

On June 11, after a new series of strikes and streetfights, the *Times* said: " Against any public acts of disorder, against boycotting and picketing, and rioting and mob assaults upon non-union workmen, the police are able to efficiently guard the people of Los Angeles. Back of the police is the sheriff with power to swear in an armed *posse comitatus* to preserve the public peace and arrest offenders. There is no reputable citizen of Los Angeles who would decline membership in such a posse, and in an hour, if necessary, a brigade could be organized and armed with pick handles that would drive the lawless union laborite, closed-shop, murderous vermin into the sea."

The next day, by a coincidence, the *Outlook* magazine appeared on the news-stands of Los Angeles with an editorial by Theodore Roosevelt, in which the former President said of Otis: " He is a consistent enemy of every movement for social and economic betterment; a consistent enemy of men in California who have dared resolutely to stand against corruption and in favor of honesty. The attitude of General Otis in his paper affords a curious instance of the anarchy of soul which comes to a man who in conscienceless fashion deifies property at the expense of human rights, no less surely than it comes to a man who in the name of human rights, wars upon all men of property, good and bad. It may be quite true that the paper (The *Times*) has again and again shown itself to be as much an enemy of good citizenship, honest, decent government, and every effective effort to secure fair play for the working men and women, as any anarchist could show itself. . . ."

Otis replied to Roosevelt, calling him a " Virtuous Vaulter " and referring to the *Outlook* editorial as " hydrophobia frothings "; he spoke of the " manly refusal of General Otis to endorse the views and accept the dictation of that sore-pated labor despot and demagogue, Samuel Gompers, at whose foul feet Colonel Theodore Roosevelt, the man of once boasted independence, seems willing to grovel in these days of his political despair. . . . The many-colored coat of Joseph was uniform and sombre compared with the colorings of the Roosevelt political robe. Of all the Janus-faced, chameleon hued, upright and downright fabricators . . . here certainly is the limit."

IV

Clarence Darrow was engaged by the American Federation of Labor to defend the McNamaras. He went to Los Angeles, surrounded himself with local associates, and rented a whole floor of an office building. Early in July the McNamara brothers appeared in court and pleaded not guilty. Fredericks, the prosecuting attorney, asked for a trial at once. Darrow requested that it be postponed until December. It was finally set for October 11. Each side got busy, checking up on prospective jurors and otherwise preparing to build up one side and tear down the other. Both defense and prosecution employed spies and " stool-pigeons." On July 27 the A. F. of L. issued an official appeal to the working class of America to stand by the McNamaras, " innocent victims of capitalist greed." Money poured into the defense fund.

In the early part of August, Big Bill Haywood toured southern California, speaking to huge crowds, pointing out the similarity of the McNamara case to the Idaho frame-up against himself, urging defense of the McNamaras and election of Harriman.

By the middle of August it became apparent that Harriman would probably be elected. His campaign and the McNamara case went side by side. His leading opponent was Mayor Alexander, the *Times'* candidate, seeking re-election on the ticket of the so-called Good Government League, or " Goo-Goos." Besides the laborites and Socialists, hundreds of Los Angeles citizens believed that Otis and other capitalists had hired Burns to " frame " the McNamaras. Many supported Harriman for that reason alone; others because they hated Otis and believed that he belonged in a padded cell.

" In September," relates Mr. Adamic, " Gompers came to Los Angeles. He visited the McNamaras in jail, was photographed with them, conferred with Clarence Darrow, and spoke before a vast audience, endorsing Job Harriman, ' candidate of the people,' for Mayor of the city of Los Angeles. He also issued a statement to the working people of the United States, assuring them that ' the boys ' were innocent, urging them to stand by the case and hasten with their contributions to the defense fund."

Money poured in. Practically every town and city in

the country had a McNamara Defense League, collecting quarters and dollars from the laboring people. Labor Day 1911 was dedicated in the United States to the McNamara brothers. Huge demonstrations demanding their freedom were held in New York, Chicago, Philadelphia, St. Louis, Cleveland, Indianapolis, Portland, Seattle, Memphis, Atlanta, San Francisco, San Diego, and elsewhere. A tremendous demonstration was held in Los Angeles. Twenty thousand persons paraded through the town, many on horseback, carrying banners reading: " Register Your Protest Against the McNamara Frame-Up! " " Down with Otis! " " Harriman for Mayor! " " Carry Los Angeles for Socialism! " From his cell J. J. McNamara issued a " Labor Day Message to the Toilers of America."

The *Times* said: " Socialism is not anarchy, but it is a half-way house on the road to anarchy. It is not itself an abandonment of law and order and the establishment of a rule of blood and rapine, but it is the prelude to such a rule . . . in the present condition of civilized society it would only prove the inevitable precursor of a condition of lawlessness, of robbery, of riot and of murder. . . . ' Carry Los Angeles for Socialism? ' Carry it for business stagnation. Carry it for closed-shop labor unionism. Carry it for abandoned industries. Carry it for an exodus of capital. Carry it for smokeless chimneys, unused factories and silent marts. Carry it for bankruptcy. Carry it for ruined homes, and carry it for chaos of civil government. Carry it for hell! "

As the trial neared, the *Appeal to Reason* had a circulation of forty thousand in Los Angeles. It announced that " forty thousand Los Angeles voters will get the paper every week from now until after the election."

In a front-page box it said: " One of the star witnesses for the defense at Los Angeles will be Dr. J. A. Holmes, director of the United States Bureau of Mines."

The *Times* replied: " That the venal experts who will be secured to swear that gas and not dynamite was the cause of the explosion will be well paid for their perjuries, is altogether probable."

On October 10, the day before the trial opened, Gompers addressed a crowd of fifteen thousand people at the Labor Lyceum in Philadelphia. The address was followed by a street parade of seventeen thousand, with men and women carrying banners reading: " Down with Otis! " " Down with Detective Burns, the Kidnapper! " and other sentiments of a like nature.

A few days after Gompers spoke, when the trial was just getting under way, it was reported that an effort had been made to blow up the Southern Pacific Railroad bridge near Santa Barbara just before a train bearing President Taft was due to cross it! It was said that thirty-nine sticks of dynamite, with fuses attached, had been found in the bridge structure by a watchman. Few, perhaps, actually believed this report. There were entirely too many " unexploded bombs " being found. Many expressed the opinion that non-union forces had " planted " the dynamite and then dramatically " discovered " it, just as the trial was starting, in an effort to influence public opinion.

J. B. McNamara went on trial first. When his trial opened, the press boxes were packed with reporters, special writers, and feature correspondents from various parts of the country. The National Manufacturers' Association and the National Erectors' Association announced " support of the *Times* " and sent funds, the

latter thirteen thousand dollars, to " assist in the prosecution." The American Bankers' Association, convening at New Orleans, passed resolutions defending Burns.
The American Federation of Labor, convening at Atlanta at the same time, passed resolutions denouncing
the bankers.

A Black "Bargain-Day" for Labor

*T*hings were going on behind the scenes. Both sides were worried, afraid.

The McNamaras were guilty. Darrow said later that the prosecution had " an open and shut hanging case " against J. B. McNamara. Since 1905 there had been more than a hundred dynamitings on open-shop construction jobs throughout the United States, and Burns had been employed by the National Erectors' Association to run down the dynamiters. Weeks before the *Times* explosion his agents had been trailing J. B. McNamara and Ortie McManigal. Burns had a " line " on them when the *Times* was dynamited; in fact, on that day, when he arrived in Los Angeles, he told Mayor Alexander their names. But the case against their employers, the higher-ups, was not conclusive. Accordingly, Burns's men trailed J. B. McNamara for seven months after the *Times* explosion, gradually tightening the net. " We were determined," he wrote later, " to find from whom

they were getting money and orders for their work —
and it would have been fatal to let them suspect that
they were being watched." The evidence was complete,
he said, when the men were arrested in Detroit.

There were twenty-one separate indictments against
each of the two brothers, charging them with dynamitings in various parts of the country. Darrow sent investigators to each of the cities where dynamitings had occurred, to gather evidence as to what happened in those
cities in relation to the *Times* Building explosion. What
his investigators found evidently satisfied him, for he
says in *The Story of My Life* that he had determined
long before the trial that the case against his clients was
hopeless.

More, the prosecution claimed that dictographs (at
that time a new, almost unknown device) had been
placed in J. J. McNamara's cell and in Darrow's offices,
and that conversations recorded between J. J. McNamara and a priest, and the defense lawyers, had clinched
the case.

But this was not the worst of the defense's worries;
at least, not of the A. F. of L. officials who had retained
Darrow. They had more to worry about than J. B.
McNamara; to wit, themselves. This trial (and they
knew it) was being skillfully prepared by the prosecution, not only to establish the guilt of the McNamaras,
but also to tear down the whole union smoke-screen and
thereby to involve at least fifty other men, some of
them high in A. F. of L. ranks, in a national dynamite
conspiracy. Organized Labor itself — not merely the
McNamaras — was on the spot.

The *Times*, the prosecution, and the politicians and
capitalists who controlled Los Angeles were also wor-

ried. Public opinion, the mob, was with the defendants. Otis and his allies could hang the McNamaras, no doubt; but there was more to it than that. They knew Clarence Darrow, and they feared him. He was planning to put them on the stand and strip them down to their underwear, so to speak. They did not relish the prospect. Burns was about to be indicted by the Indianapolis grand jury for kidnapping. Moreover, regardless of a conviction, there would be thousands of people in Los Angeles, and millions throughout the country, who would believe that the McNamaras had been " framed " and murdered. The McNamaras would remain martyrs to a " cause."

Worst of all, perhaps, Los Angeles was going Socialistic, unless the McNamaras' guilt was established before election day. A wave of Socialism, more feared by capitalists than a plague, was sweeping over Los Angeles, as it was over the entire country. " In the spring of 1910," records Mr. Adamic, " the Socialist Party experienced its first success at the polls, which was followed by more victories in the fall and in 1911. Milwaukee and Schenectady elected Socialist mayors. St. Louis nearly went Socialist. The States of New York, Massachusetts, Pennsylvania, Minnesota, and Rhode Island had Socialists in the legislatures. Victor Berger went to Congress. By the autumn of 1911 over 500 Socialists were elected to office. In May 1911 the *Atlantic Monthly* published as its leading article of the month a piece entitled ' Prepare for Socialism.' " Charles Yale Harrison has noted that " C. P. Connolly, writing in *Collier's*, described this period as follows: ' Socialist enthusiasm was like the swell of a great sea. Its adherents seemed to come from everywhere, from crevices and crannies, from the tops of trees and from under the ground.' Meeting halls that normally held two or three thousand were packed to the doors and overflow meetings were held in the streets outside." Berkeley, San Diego, and other California towns, influenced by the McNamara trial, were about to elect Socialist mayors.

" Protect Los Angeles Homes! " cried the *Times* hysterically. " Don't let Socialist Harriman and his hungry crowd of office seekers fool you, home-owning, working, and other voters of Los Angeles! Socialism in the saddle will mean less civic and private credit, less building, less industry, and thereby less work and less wages . . . less money with which to comfort your family, and far less protection for your home than you now so happily enjoy! "

Los Angeles at this time had a population of 329,000, and the Men of Vision could already see the first million. But not under Socialism. The National Headquarters of the Socialist Party sent Alexander Irvine, a highly competent politician, to manage Harriman's campaign. In the primary election on October 30, Harriman was the leading man with 15,000 votes. Alexander was second with 13,000. The third candidate, receiving 6,000 votes, was eliminated in the primary. The run-off election was to be held on December 5.

" Can Los Angeles sell $17,000,000 of its bonds in the next year if Harriman is elected mayor? " asked the *Times*, frantically. " In that question is presented the real issue of the campaign that is to be decided December 5. If Los Angeles fails to sell bonds in that sum it cannot carry on the great undertakings on the success of which its continued growth and future prosperity alike depend. *Failure in those undertakings means*

municipal disaster! " The Los Angeles *Express* cried:
" Harriman must not win! " But how to prevent it?

Darrow was dragging the trial, so that nothing detrimental to his clients, or to the Socialist-Labor cause, would come out of it before election day. The awful specter of Socialism which was hanging over the heads of the capitalists was his chief weapon in his desire to get a settlement out of court, and he was making the most of it. In the first two weeks of the trial only one juryman was accepted. The days dragged on. By November 15 only six jurors had been chosen; more than five hundred talesmen had been examined to get them. If Harriman was elected, as was almost certain, it was openly stated that when he and his gang came into power, Otis would be indicted for " criminal libel " and for " manslaughter." That would further confuse the situation " already in a frightful mess." Darrow employed engineers to build a model of the *Times* Building, which he was preparing to blow up in court, to prove something.

II

On both sides, no doubt, there were other factors, still hidden from the light of day, which operated to stop this trial. It is impossible for anyone to make a study of the case without emerging from it with that conviction. At any rate, they struck a bargain — judge and all.

The McNamaras were to change their plea from not guilty to guilty. J. B. was to receive a life sentence, and J. J. ten years in San Quentin Prison. The brothers were to admit their guilt in open court before election day, which would unquestionably result in the defeat of Job Harriman and the Socialist-Labor ticket. On the other hand, there was to be no public confession, and no one else was to be implicated. The prosecution was to drop the pursuit of all other suspects, and the prosecuting attorney was to recommend the McNamaras to the mercy of the court.

This remarkable bargain was made with the utmost secrecy. Neither the public nor the newspapers had any inkling of it; even Job Harriman, who was one of the defense attorneys, was not told of it.

The " settlement " was arranged largely by Lincoln Steffens, the well-known liberal (at that time famous throughout the country as the king of the " muck-rakers "), who acted as a sort of unofficial go-between. Mr. Steffens was a pleasant, noble little man, with a Vandyke beard and a cane; jaunty, cock-sure, naïve, and excessively vain. He could also see farther than his nose; he believed in the essential goodness of man; he was full of humane instincts. As Mr. Harrison says, with penetrating satire: " Steffens preached Christianity; it worked, he thought, with sinners. Earlier in his career he had ' made ' Wall Street men contribute to Brand Whitlock's campaign for Mayor of Toledo. He had ' compelled ' Wall Street bankers to contribute money for radical purposes based on purely Christian appeals, ' especially for mercy.' ' Mercy is scientific,' Steffens wrote, thus establishing a new religio-ethical science."

Steffens was in London when the McNamara trial started. He returned to New York and arranged to analyze the case for a syndicate of twenty newspapers. He arrived in Los Angeles in mid November, while the jury was still being selected, and started to write a series of articles on the theory that the McNamaras were guilty, " and that Capital and the world should be told

SOME OF THE BIZA
REFRESH
WHICH DELIGHT THE EY
VISITORS

RESTAURANTS AND
STANDS

TICKLE THE PALATE OF
ANGELES

why "; a series of sociological articles depicting the "wrongs of Capital against Labor," as a background to the trial itself.

Steffens jauntily informed Judge Bordwell, the trial judge, that he had come to Los Angeles " to try the case "; he visited the McNamaras in their cells. He was close to Darrow; they were personal friends. His idea in his series of articles was to influence public opinion, to hint that the McNamaras were guilty; but to show that they were guilty " because of Capital." Seeking mercy " scientifically," and with uncommon sense, he said to Judge Bordwell: " It is a social manifestation of a condition, not a mere legal offense, this crime. If these men did it, they did it as the appointed agents of Labor, and they and their organizations of ordinary working men must have suffered something worth our knowing about to get worked up to a state of mind where they deliberately, as a policy, could carry on for years dynamiting, arson, murder. What were those real or fancied wrongs, what were the conditions that produced this — this act of war? That's what has to be gone into."

Steffens was well known in Los Angeles, popular, liked by nearly everybody. After the San Francisco graft trials, when the Los Angeles Capital-Labor war was reaching a climax, he had addressed a group of prominent citizens at the Jonathan Club, indicated to them by theoretical illustration what was wrong with Los Angeles, and advised them, abstractly, how to run the Angel City. According to his own account, he had flabbergasted the business men and left them speechless with the force of his symbolic logic. As a matter of fact, his audience had put him down as a dreamer, a " good man," a harmless idealist.

Steffens's theory was that Capital and Labor were both guilty — which of course they were — and that each should admit its mistakes, kiss, and make up. Accordingly, he held a series of secret conferences with the leading Los Angeles business men and capitalists (about twenty), and (so he relates in his *Autobiography*) it was agreed that in addition to the court settlement there was to be a further compromise. He is somewhat vague, but it appears that it was agreed that the McNamara case, and the whole Los Angeles Capital-Labor war, was to be settled on the basis of the Golden Rule, with the Judge making a merciful speech from the bench, the McNamaras probably to be pardoned later on as " political prisoners," and — immediately after the trial — a friendly, round-table, get-together conference between Capital and Labor, to bring Los Angeles permanent " industrial peace." Steffens says that all the dominant Los Angeles business men, including Otis and Harry Chandler, agreed that this was a noble idea; told him, indeed, that they were heartily in favor of *letting the McNamaras off scot-free*, and that it was too bad that the hard-hearted prosecuting attorney would not permit it. It seems, however, in the light of subsequent events, that that was merely what they told Mr. Steffens. And it also seems, from reading his *Autobiography*, that Mr. Steffens, all his life, had the happy faculty of believing what anybody told him.

III

In court, of course, the case was proceeding as usual; the jurors were still being chosen. Sentiment in Los Angeles and throughout the country was overwhelm-

ingly in favor of the McNamaras. In New York, Chicago, Philadelphia, Pittsburgh, Cleveland — in nearly
all large American cities, plans were under way for huge
demonstrations to be held the first week in December,
the purpose of which was to protest against the " dastardly frame-up," as Debs called it; to " *force* the capitalist class to release J. J. and J. B. McNamara." Money
was still pouring into the defense fund.

On December 1 the McNamara brothers were
brought into court. As J. B. alone was on trial, and J. J.
had not been in the courtroom before, reporters sensed
that something unusual was about to happen. But none
was prepared for what did happen. Suddenly, without
any preliminaries, LeCompte Davis, one of the defense
attorneys, rose and announced that the defendants desired to change their pleas from not guilty to guilty.

" A psychical explosion," says Mr. Harrison, " took
place in the courtroom. Reporters leaped to their feet
and ran to telephones to notify their offices. In the courtroom, in the hallways, in the street outside, everyone
was electrified, bewildered."

" A reporter," says Mr. Adamic, " rushing to his
office, paused on a corner to tell the news to a laborite
he recognized; the latter, outraged, called him a liar and
knocked him down with his fist. The effect of the confession upon Los Angeles was terrific. People would not
believe the headlines in the afternoon papers, thinking it
all some kind of political trick. Harriman denied all
knowledge of the affair. There was an enraged mob of
Socialists and radicals in front of his campaign headquarters; he and Alexander Irvine, his campaign manager,
became alarmed, jumped into an automobile, and drove
off."

That night the gutters of Los Angeles were strewn with the buttons inscribed " McNamaras Not Guilty! " and " Vote for Harriman! "

" Not a few radicals," to quote Mr. Adamic further, " and labor sympathizers in Los Angeles, as well as elsewhere in the United States, on hearing of the confession, went insane; at least three persons committed suicide because of the McNamara debacle.

" In the United States as a whole the reaction was but slightly less intense than in Los Angeles. For months millions and millions had believed the McNamaras innocent; Darrow, Gompers, Debs and others had been assuring them to that effect — now this terrible fiasco! "

Theodore Roosevelt wired William J. Burns: " All good Americans feel that they owe you a great debt of gratitude for your signal service to American citizenship."

The next morning press services and newspapers throughout the United States carried confused stories that the case had been settled somehow according to the Golden Rule.

The following day Steffens called upon Judge Bordwell, to discuss what the Judge would say when he sentenced the McNamaras; to see that the Judge's address from the bench would be full of mercy and reason. According to Steffens, " Judge Bordwell asked me how I would say what he had to say, and I advised him to speak as one man to another, as one criminal to another, with imagination, so that the prisoners might go off to the penitentiary feeling that they and the judge were human beings. Something like this I said, and I remember his answer: ' I think I can do that.' Anyway I went back to the jail the next day when the priest and the attorneys were there, and I declared my belief that the judge would be ' all right.' "

The day was Sunday. That day preachers in the City of the Angels, and all over the United States, preached sermons on the McNamara case. These sermons, wired to Los Angeles and carefully culled, appeared in the Los Angeles papers Monday morning, election day. A typical one preached in Los Angeles said: " We were standing on the edge of a yawning cliff. The volcano of prejudice and class strife was ready to belch out a lava of turmoil and stagnation. But now the hand of God has visibly taken hold of the ship of State, and the voice of God echoes in the ears of the world in the one word ' Guilty! ' This clears the air like an electric storm. Many thousands who honestly believed the Mc-Namaras innocent now will prove their honesty by voting for the cause of Good Government."

A few hours later Judge Bordwell summoned the McNamaras into court and sentenced them; J. B. to life imprisonment, J. J. to fifteen years, in San Quentin Prison. There was no recommendation for mercy by the prosecuting attorney. In passing sentence the Judge denounced the criminals in strong terms. The defense attorneys were astounded; Steffens was bewildered; Darrow was so overcome that he had to be helped out of the courtroom. A howling mob of former Mc-Namara sympathizers met them with curses and shouts of " Traitors! "

On the same day that the McNamaras were sentenced, Job Harriman was overwhelmingly defeated in the election for Mayor of Los Angeles.

" The God that is still in Israel," said the *Times*, " filled the guilty souls of the dynamiters with a torment that they could not bear! . . . Viewed fundamentally, the stupendous climax of the case was in essential particulars the most consequential event that has occurred in this country since the close of the Civil War. . . . The class bitterness which has been engendered by the demagogic and inflammatory appeals and misrepresentations of Debs, Gompers, the ' Appeal to *Treason*,' Job Harriman, and such leaders was frightful to contemplate. Murder and arson were openly urged by some of these shouters. ' Deliver the carcasses of the plutocrats to the furies! ' wrote Debs. The tide of feeling rose to a fearful height. Many sober observers detected signs of impending revolution, and trembled for the safety of their families and their country.

" But the crisis has passed. The firebugs are quenched. It will be impossible for inciters of crime and violence to longer deceive honest men. Their influence is gone. Their bedevilment is at an end. The country will settle down. Years of peace are assured because Liberty and Law will triumph and prevail.

" If the McNamaras had been found guilty by juries and had been sentenced to be hanged, God only knows what the effect on the country would have been. No matter how complete the evidence — no matter how fair the trial — tens of thousands of men would have asserted that the accused were martyrs. Tens of thousands of throats would have shouted that the condemned had been railroaded to the gallows. Probably there would have been riots and bloodshed. Monuments would have been erected to the McNamaras, and memorial exercises would have been held in their honor, so intense has this craftily cultivated class hatred become. Now, no monuments, no memorials, no misapprehensions. It is all an open book. The *Times* Building *was* dynamited by agents of the vicious elements of union labor, as the owners believed from the very beginning. With their own lips, in open court, have those dynamiters confessed. Not only is the *Times* vindicated, but the cause of Industrial Freedom and Law Enforcement is assured."

There was no round-table, get-together "Capital-Labor conference," and no abandonment of the pursuit of other suspects. On the contrary, some of the leaders of the dynamite ring — those who had been protected by the "bargain" — were subsequently rounded up by Federal authorities. Fifty-four men, some of them high in union ranks, were indicted in Indianapolis, and thirty-two were tried and sentenced to penitentiaries. Mr. Steffens claims that he was double-crossed by the Los Angeles business men (as no doubt he was), but insists that Otis and Chandler, from first to last, were *privately* in favor of a settlement based on mercy.

J. J. McNamara served not quite ten years in San Quentin, being released May 10, 1921. J. B. McNamara is still in the penitentiary, the oldest inmate in point of years of servitude in San Quentin. His job is to wait upon the condemned men in "Death Row."

IV

Just how was the *Times* Building dynamited? Did J. B. McNamara ever confess to the crime? The answer to the latter question is yes despite the evasions of most labor writers and the actual denials of others. Mr. Harrison, for example, in his biography of Clarence Darrow, says: "However, the first dispatches stated that a confession had been obtained; and to this day so-called well-informed writers speak of the ' confession.' " Well, the fact is that on December 4, 1911, three days after he had pleaded guilty in open court, and the day before he was sentenced, J. B. McNamara in his cell, in the presence of Darrow and Fredericks, wrote out and signed a confession. A facsimile of it was published in the Los Angeles *Times* on October 1, 1929. It reads (I give the exact spelling and punctuation):

" I, J. B. McNamara, defendant in the case of the people against McNamara and others, having heretofore plead guilty to the crime of murder, desire to make this statement of facts concerning the same. And this is the truth, on the night of September 30, 1910, at 5:45 P.M. I placed in ink alley a portion of the *Times* Building a suitcase containing sixteen sticks of 80 per cent dynamite, set to explode at one o'clock the next morning. It was my intention to injure the building and scare the owners. I did not intend to take the life of anyone. I sincerely regret that these unfortunate men lost their lives, if the giving of my life would bring them back I would freely give it. In fact in pleading guilty to murder in the first degree I have placed my life in the hands of the state. J. B. McNamara." Thus J. B. McNamara did confess to the crime with which he was charged; to wit, dynamiting the *Times* Building and killing the men who lost their lives in the explosion and subsequent fire.

The *Times* said: " Shortly after nightfall on the last day of September, 1910, several persons saw a slender, stooping, rat-like man turn the corner of the *Times* Building at First and Broadway, carrying a heavy suitcase. He walked along the side of the building for about twenty steps and, after a hurried glance around, turned into a short blind passage, opening from the street into the building itself. This entrance was called Ink Alley because it was here that the big containers of printers ink for the *Times* presses were unloaded and temporarily stored. Just below it was the huge iron gas main that supplied fuel to the building.

" The rat-like stranger carried his burden to a point halfway to the end of this alley and gingerly set it down against the wall in the shadow of the ink barrels. He stooped over it for a minute as though listening, straightened up, apparently satisfied, and hurried out of the Alley leaving the suitcase behind."

But let us look closely at McNamara's confession, and also at the *Times'* account of how the deed was done. Here was a city in the throes of mob violence, with bombs being reported found, and the *Times* daily expecting to be blown up. According to McNamara, and the *Times*, the suit-case full of dynamite stayed in Ink Alley for seven hours and twenty-two minutes without being discovered. Is it not strange that some of the " several persons " who saw the suspicious " rat-like stranger " did not investigate the matter, or report it? If " several persons " saw what the *Times* said they saw, they would have had to *follow* McNamara. Where were the police? Where was the night-watchman? How did this suspicious " rat-like stranger " get into Ink Alley without being stopped?

The answer is, I think, that he did not. McNamara made a confession, to be sure, but there seems to be good reason now to doubt both his confession and the *Times'* account of how the crime was committed. For in an interview with David Lawrence in the *Saturday*

Evening Post of April 25, 1931 Harry Chandler was quoted as saying: " There was only one bomb set in the *Times* office, and that was, as McNamara, after he had confessed the crime, explained, tied to the gas main up under the ground floor just under, and a few feet away from, where my desk was located. . . . Our theory and the theory of the detectives as to the location of the bombs was quite different from the actual situation, in the light of the explanations the McNamaras later made."

That the Los Angeles *Times* Building was dynamited, and that J. B. McNamara was implicated in the dynamiting, there seems to be no doubt. But there is grave doubt that J. B. McNamara actually placed the dynamite; there is good reason to believe, on the other hand, that the dynamite was actually placed by one or two accomplices and that it was an " inside " job. " Only six men," as the *Times* said on October 1, 1929, " know all the facts, and they have guarded the secret well."

At any rate, the conviction of the McNamaras, and the subsequent convictions in Indianapolis, ruined the Socialist movement in America, killed the militancy of the American labor movement, and dealt the American Federation of Labor a blow from which it has never recovered. It was a great victory for Capitalism.

The Fruits of "Victory"

In 1917 — six years after his great triumph over organized Labor — Otis died, at the age of eighty. Members of his family received hundreds of messages of condolence, and friends and admirers erected a monument to the memory of the old soldier in Westlake Park. Few Americans have ever seen or heard of this monument to Otis, but certainly many have either seen or heard of his real and living monument, the *Times.* " Otis lived," said the magazine *Time,* " to make the *Times* the most rabid Labor-baiting, Red-hating paper in the United States; a potent builder of Southern California resources; dominant in influence if not in circulation (dominant in circulation, too, as long as Otis lived); and, for all of its claims of independence, a hide-bound Republican organ." Otis also lived to become one of the best-known characters in the United States; and he remains to this day the chief figure in the whole history of southern California.

He was born on a farm near Marietta, Ohio, and was named after his uncle, Senator Harrison Gray Otis of Massachusetts. The boy attended a country school until he was fourteen, when he left home to work in a printer's shop at Sarahsville. Three years later he returned home, entered an academy at Lowell, and later took a commercial course at Columbus, both in Ohio. At the age of twenty he married Miss Eliza Wetherby, a young lady of the neighborhood.

Otis had been married two years when the Civil War broke out. He promptly enlisted as a private on the Union side, took part in fifteen battles, was wounded several times, and came out a Captain. The man was a natural warrior. Apparently he was meant to be a soldier, for no such success as he had known on the battlefields followed him with his return to civil life. He served for a time as clerk of the Ohio House of Representatives, and then for years as a compositor in the Government Printing Office, and later as a foreman there. For a while he was editor of the *Grand Army Journal*.

Finally he was appointed Treasury Agent of Seal Islands — those bleak spots, St. Paul and St. George — in the Bering Sea. There he was a sort of game-warden, a " copper on the seal poachers." After three years he returned to the United States and asked for a better government place, meantime taking a job as editor of the Santa Barbara *Press*, a little weekly in a country town of two thousand. This was Otis's first taste of newspaper work. He tried to be appointed Collector of the Port at San Diego, but failed to land. He was finally offered the consulship in two God-forsaken places, Apia and Tientsin, which he declined, and thereupon he became a permanent ornament of the Fourth Estate.

In 1882, when he was forty-four, Otis and his good wife journeyed down to Los Angeles and bought a one-fourth interest in the *Times*, a bankrupt sheet in a sleepy, struggling town of eleven thousand. Four years later he acquired control of the paper; with the arrival of the boom, wealth descended upon him.

"Otis," wrote Louis Sherwin, one of his editorial writers, "never got very far beyond the Third Reader." He loved a fight. As I have previously said, he was a large, aggressive man, with a walrus mustache, a goatee, and a warlike demeanor. He resembled Buffalo Bill, General Custer, and Henry Watterson. The military bee buzzed incessantly in his bonnet. He was a holy terror in his newspaper plant; his natural voice was that of a game-warden roaring at seal poachers. He was politically ambitious all of his life; though he never ran for an office he asked for many. When McKinley, his former army commander, was elected President, he asked to be appointed an Assistant Secretary of War, but Secretary Alger would not have him.

When the four Los Angeles newspapers first locked horns with the local typographers, the union men believed that Otis would make a personal effort to settle the squabble amicably. For he had been a union printer himself for years before he became a newspaper owner, had paid his dues and taken his orders. But Otis did nothing of the kind. In fact, his was the only paper that did not compromise. He accepted the gauge of battle, fighting the unions with their own weapons, and for years he licked them, almost single-handedly. He had the rare virtue of courage and he stood out as an unusually courageous man among his wealthy associates because most of them, as Otis himself said, were such craven cowards.

Ironically enough, the year he died, the unions were stronger in his beloved Los Angeles than they had been since 1890, and stronger than they have ever been since. In the first year of America's participation in the World War, Los Angeles was almost entirely " closed shop." The employers were greatly disturbed by rumors of a Mexican-German invasion of southern California and were, no doubt, also moved by a spirit of patriotism and profitism. They preferred, temporarily, to recognize the unions and meet their demands for a share of the huge war-profits, rather than argue. It was a bitter blow for Otis.

Thus the Capital-Labor struggle in Los Angeles, which he did so much to keep alive and in which he was the central figure, did not end with his victory, nor has it ended since, though the " open-shoppers " have continued to hold the upper hand and have gradually pushed the unions into a sullen, underground position, mainly by linking them with Reds and radicals and by passing laws hamstringing their actions. Nevertheless — or perhaps for those reasons — since 1912 Los Angeles has probably witnessed more industrial unrest than any other city in America. It has been shaken every year by disorders and class conflicts. The town's Capital-Labor record for the last twenty years is a sordid, unrelieved record of unceasing warfare; I omit it here because it is a monotonous repetition of strikes, lock-outs, violence, and bloodshed. Most of it is set forth in detail in an illustrated, thirty-thousand-word, twenty-eight-page supplement of the Los Angeles *Times*, issued Oc-

tober 1, 1929, under the title: *The Forty Years War.*
There is unconscious humor in this account, as well as
hatred; high humor, for example, in the following eulogy
of the professional strike-breakers and " scabs " who
were imported from Chicago, Kansas City, and St.
Louis to fight the unions:

" These men came to Los Angeles much as the first
settlers of New England came from the old country to
escape religious intolerance and to gain personal freedom to worship as they saw fit. Like their hardy, selected forbears, these liberty-loving Los Angeles immi-
grants were pioneers who laid the foundation for the
future growth of their adopted land."

I suppress a smile. These noble industrial pioneers,
in fact, remain such passionate liberty-lovers, so firmly
dedicated to the high cause of " industrial freedom,"
that they will go anywhere to uphold it — provided
they are transported, well paid, well fed, and well protected. Since 1912 the Merchants and Manufacturers
Association has trained hundreds of strike-breakers and
on several occasions has sent them to distant cities to aid
in breaking strikes.

" It has been War," concludes the *Times,* " war in
which many lives have been lost, millions of dollars of
property destroyed, other millions lost through suspen-
sion of production. The cost to the city has been great,
yet its profit infinitely greater. The fruits of freedom
will increasingly benefit the city — so long as that freedom is maintained. But, as in the past, the price of liberty will be unceasing vigilance."

And again: " For the war is neither over nor won. The
forces which for four decades have sought by strategy
and violence to enchain the industries of Los Angeles are

far from being beaten or even discouraged by their long series of reverses. While their major attacks have met defeat on all fronts, they have made formidable progress in the 'organization' of many key industries — holes in the dike, which, in the absence of constant vigilance, can easily spread till the whole protective barrier is swept away."

II

Unquestionably, the fruit of the "Forty Years' War" in Los Angeles — sweet to the open-shop employers, bitter to the unions — is the dominance of the employers there today. They do not take orders from Labor. Labor takes orders from them. There are also some other general fruits. Two of the first were the famous Los Angeles anti-picketing ordinance, and then the injunction which converted the police into an armed force for the employers, virtually into strike-breakers. Another fruit was the celebrated Criminal Syndicalism Act. In 1923, during the great harbor strike, twenty-seven men were convicted and sentenced to terms in San Quentin Prison under this statute; men whose main crime, it appeared, was in listening to the capitalist-baiter Upton Sinclair while he sardonically read the Bill of Rights from private property. Mr. Sinclair himself was arrested and thrown into jail for a day, much to his delight.

In his authoritative book *Our Lawless Police* (1931) Mr. Ernest Jerome Hopkins, whose nation-wide research formed the groundwork for the Wickersham Commission's *Federal Report on the Lawless Enforcement of the Law*, has this to say:

"On the surface it seemed supremely inconsistent

that Los Angeles police should still use the old-fashioned methods in dealing with crime, and should express a theory of law enforcement more openly opposed to the Constitution than any I had yet encountered.

" There had been a series of abnormal pressures. . . . The first outside pressure was exerted by a dominant financial group, fanatically anti-labor, which utilized the police as an adjunct to its open-shop industrial policies. Very early, the Los Angeles police ceased to distinguish between the *economic dissenter* (italics mine M.M.) and the criminal. This line of activity, kept alive by hysterical propaganda, had passed through successive phases: assistance in strike-breaking, espionage upon labor-union organizers, suppression of free speech during the war, the 'Bolshevik' scare, attacks upon Socialist meetings, and a continuous series of unlawful beatings and assaults upon Communists. This 'Red Squad' activity was undiminished in 1931. Radicalism, of course, throve under the lash. . . .

" The criminal problem, beneath it all, has always been sufficiently difficult. A city with an area of 250 (440) square miles is very difficult to patrol and guard. Among the tourists attracted by the advertising or by the climatic advantages, there appeared two unwanted classes: the migratory unemployed, always open to the baneful suspicion of being a 'Red,' and the professional criminal. . . .

" So false arrest, brutality with arrest, unlawful detention, incommunicado, and the third degree, with the relative incompetence at skillful or lawful detective work which these imply, tended to last as basic police conditions, underneath the glittering surface of innovations.

" The Bar Association's Committee on Constitutional Rights unearthed two hundred complaints of police brutality in eighteen months' time, and found fifty of them well grounded.

" It was in the wordy controversy with the Bar Association that police orators had openly defied the Constitution . . . police spokesmen accused the Bar Association committee of 'encouraging the criminal,' to which one attorney responded: 'I am opposed to criminals, whether they are in uniform or not.' Police officials with whom I talked acknowledged that the department had incurred needless odium and that the public advocacy of brutality had been a mistake."

The fact is that the Los Angeles police and those who control them have gradually linked together all the social groups on the opposite side of the economic fence from themselves — that is, liberals, Socialists, communists, union laborers, and the unemployed. They seem to be unable to differentiate between a Red and a man out of work. Idle hands, an unshaven face, and tattered clothes appear to constitute proof *per se* that the man beneath is a revolutionist. Elsewhere in the capitalistic world it seems to be the general belief that the traditional trades-union man constitutes the strongest bulwark against the communist; that it is sound policy to keep the *status quo* of underdogs divided among themselves. Los Angeles does not subscribe to this doctrine. In Los Angeles they have all been thrown together. No matter what his political belief (he may be a Mellon Republican), a union man in Los Angeles automatically becomes a " Red " in spite of himself.

In that splendid book *Only Yesterday*, discussing

the anti-Red hysteria which swept America directly after the war, Frederick Lewis Allen has this to say:

" Innumerable patriotic societies had sprung up, each with its executive secretary, and executive secretaries must live, and therefore must conjure new and ever greater menaces. Innumerable other gentlemen now discovered that they could defeat whatever they wanted to defeat by tarring it conspicuously with the Bolshevist brush. Big navy men, believers in compulsory military service, drys, anti-cigarette campaigners, anti-evolution Fundamentalists, defenders of the moral order, book censors, Jew-haters, Negro-haters, landlords, manufacturers, utility executives, upholders of every sort of cause, good, bad, and indifferent, all wrapped themselves in Old Glory and the mantle of the Founding Fathers and allied their opponents with Lenin. The open shop, for example, became the ' American Plan.' "

The " American Plan " was born in Los Angeles. Also one of the most active of all the patriotic organizations, the Better America Federation, came into being and still functions there, wielding a powerful influence. " Miss Hermine Schwed," says Mr. Allen, " speaking for the Better America Federation, a band of California patriots, disapproved of *Main Street* because it ' created a distaste for the conventional good life of the American,' and called John Dewey and James Harvey Robinson, ' most dangerous to young people.' "

The Better America Federation is composed of unintelligent rich men (some of them of dubious reputation) who have set themselves up, not as Americans, but as *Better Americans.* Thus if one lives in Los Angeles and happens to belong to the Better America Federation, he is, it appears, a " better " American than his neighbor, John Smith, who is only an Elk, or maybe a chiropractor. And if he does not belong to it, he is just a garden variety of an American, and not so good a citizen as his " Better American " neighbor. Alas, in 1927, during the Julian oil scandals, a half-dozen " Better Americans," including the president of the organization, were indicted for usury.

The Better America Federation is kept alive by a small, clever group of salaried parasites who capitalize hysteria and fear in the name of patriotism. Theirs is a racket, and their racketeering job is to keep the manufacturers, bankers, and merchants who support them in fear of a Red uprising. The Better America Federation gets out a magazine which is a masterpiece of blood, fear, and alarm. I do not know the technique of the able editor, but it seems to be to clip and reprint every " Red " scare story which he can find in the world's press, plus " special dispatches " from other super-patriotic organizations. The result — copies of which are on file at the New York Public Library — is a fearful thing. Reading it, one gathers the impression that Soviet Russia has been behind every unpleasant thing which has recently happened in America, and also that a proletarian revolution is ready to start in the United States tomorrow, beginning at Los Angeles. No wonder the members of the B. A. F. can see a Bolshevik lurking behind every palm tree.

What has happened in Los Angeles is simply that the underdogs, over a period of years, have been driven further and further under cover instead of being permitted to operate in the open. The Babbitts of Los Angeles, led by the *Times*, appear to believe that they can keep the have-nots under better control by this simple expedient. Perhaps they can, but if so, it will be the first time in history. For radicalism, as Mr. Hopkins says, thrives under the lash. At any rate, in 1933 it seems to be generally agreed that there is more class bitterness per square inch in this otherwise cordial, friendly city than anywhere else in America.

PART FOUR

Abbot Kinney's Dream

*A*t the close of the nineteenth century, among the milling herd of Middle Western farmers who were moving in on southern California, there arrived a Rich Man of Artistic Impulses. His name was Abbot Kinney, and he had built up a great fortune, first as a commission merchant, and later as the manufacturer of Sweet Caporal cigarettes. Now, Mr. Kinney was no mere pre-Lewis Babbitt of the Gay Nineties. He was a botanical expert, a former Indian commissioner, a globe-trotter, a student of art and culture. Having amassed a prosaic fortune, he was looking round for some way to make an æsthetic contribution to the human race.

Chance took Mr. Kinney to an uninhabited stretch of the beach, twenty-five miles from Los Angeles, and there, standing upon the barren sand-dunes, gazing out over the blue Pacific, he thought — for some unknown reason — of Italy, and especially of the ancient and lovely city of Venice. He saw the square of St. Mark with its Basilica scintillating with gold, the solemn lines of the Procuratie, the Ducal Palace. He recalled the lagoon at sunset, guarded by the bell-tower, and the dome of the Church of Santa Maria della Salute, with colors splashing. With intense emotion he remembered the Grand Canal with its marble palaces, the gondolas slipping silently through the water past the churches, those museums of the fine arts, with their majestic façades.

A great inspiration descended upon Abbot Kinney. Standing in the mellow sunshine, on the barren sand-dunes, he determined to create there a replica of Venice! He dreamed of a southern California cultural center set along canals similar to those of the Gem of the Adriatic. He saw world-famous opera stars, painters, poets, lecturers, and other artistic folk contributing to the glory of his Italian-American dream-city. He visualized a great educational center for *all* the people, a second Chautauqua.

With this great cigarette-manufacturer, to think was to act. Accordingly, Mr. Kinney bought up a hundred and sixty acres of sand-dunes and marshes fronting on the Pacific Ocean and started at once to build " Venice in America." He employed world-famous architects and engineers; nothing of a technical nature was overlooked. They built an elaborate system of canals, each four feet deep and forty feet wide, modeled after the water-ways of old Venice. The canals were filled with ocean water, forced in by high tide and retained by locks, the main canal connecting with the ocean at a spot which was appropriately named Playa del Rey. Along these watery streets they constructed pure Italian stuccoed bungalows and a few public buildings of Renaissance architecture, including a Music Hall and a Civic Forum.

Boats could be made in southern California, but that idea did not appeal to Mr. Kinney. He imported from old Venice a fleet of graceful gondolas, and to man the water-taxis he brought over from the same place twenty-four real, live gondoliers. These Italians were transported across the waters and then across the American continent; and pretty soon they found themselves seven thousand miles from home, putting their gondolas through their paces in the water boulevards of New Venice. Mr. Kinney's plan, according to the reporter Joseph L. Mears, was to provide " entertainment for the cultured, good music for the masses, wholesome playgrounds for children, and artistic home-sites for writers, musicians, sculptors, painters, and retired capitalists, along the romantic, winding canals."

" Venice in America " was opened in 1905, and the watery home-sites were offered for a song. Crowds went to see and to admire; it was like going to a circus. The Italian gondoliers sculled their gondolas round through the sand-dunes in sunshine and moonlight, singing snatches from operas.

It was all very elegant and æsthetic, but, alas, the project was doomed to failure from the start. Benjamin Fay Mills, the great evangelist, put on a Chautauqua course for the cultured, but the crowds were small. Madame Johnstone Bishop sang for the masses, but they remained cold. Helen Hunt Jackson, who had been associated with Kinney in Indian welfare work, lent her presence to the promotion. The celebrated author of *Ramona* gave a series of lectures, but most of those who came to hear her were patriotic Mexicans and half-breeds rounded up from the Plaza of Los Angeles. Finally, in desperation Kinney engaged Sarah Bernhardt, and there, surrounded by hot sands, salt water, and Kansas farmers, the Divine Sarah did her stuff in *Camille* and other masterpieces. But even Sarah failed to arouse lovers of the drama.

Mr. Kinney was bitterly disappointed, but, with all his artistic temperament, he was a business man. For a little while he bemoaned the failure of his artistic dream — but not for long. The people of southern California did not want art? Very well; he would give them what they would enjoy, understand, and appreciate. So in 1906 he converted Venice into a tenth-rate Coney Island, importing all the amusements, freaks, and sideshows bodily from the Portland Fair. This struck the right note. Folks built pink bungalows and wooden shacks along the canals; farm boys late from South Dakota and western Texas paddled sightseers round in skiffs to the hot-dog stands, roller coasters, and other amusements.

The Italian gondoliers were not happy. No doubt they thought of their glorious traditions, and of the many virtues of their ancestors. No doubt they pined for the regal beauty of old Venice, with its shades and colors, for San Simone il Piccolo; for the fairy-like sequence of the palaces of all ages; for the greenish water, with its polychrome reflections, bathing the Giudecca Isle, caressing the granite steps of San Giorgio Maggiore, winding its way in song and color through the damp canals until it reaches the Lido. No, the gondoliers were not happy. Their songs died out. Gradually they disappeared. One of them became so desolate and so desperate that he got into his gondola and propelled him-

STREET SCENE IN VENICE

THE GONDOLAS WERE IMPORTED FROM ITALY

self through the main canal out into the Pacific Ocean, determined to scull his way back to Italy. He was blown ashore at Ocean Park, a few miles down the beach, a town which was later to become famous as the scene of Aimee Semple McPherson's disappearance, and shortly thereafter he entered the real-estate business.

Venice prospered as a unique beach amusement city for years, with hundreds of pleasure-seekers rowing in the canals in bathing-suits, darting round in out-board motor-boats and canoes, riding the roller coasters, shooting-the-shoots, and dancing in the penny dance-halls. But, alas, seaweed drifted into the canals, and hidden springs broke into them; fungus growth began to take root and thrive faster than it could be cleaned out. Eventually the canals gave forth an aroma more pungent than the Chicago stockyards, the perfume of dying kelp and dead fish.

In 1925 Venice became thirsty for fresh water. Los Angeles not only gave it a drink, but reached out twenty-five miles and took it under the motherly wing, thereby acquiring ten thousand new residents and a flock of roller coasters, dance-halls, Ferris wheels, flying jinneys, freak shows, carnival concessions, canals, and smells. The Angel City immediately began to fill in the canals, turning them into modern streets.

The native Venetians objected strenuously, for despite the dead-fish aroma they had grown to love their canals. Moreover, the parental Venetians announced that automobile traffic in Los Angeles was a public menace, and that they preferred to take chances on having their children drowned in the water-ways (as many were) to having them run over by automobiles. On one occasion three hundred outraged Venetians went out with picks and shovels and started removing rocks, dirt, and tin cans as fast as the Los Angeles Street Department could dump truck-loads into the canals.

But Progress triumphed, as Progress will, when a small oil-field was struck at Playa del Rey. Black oil shot into the air, spattering the stucco Italian architecture and converting the beautiful smelly canals into ditches filled with greasy slime. The Venetians capitulated. Spurred on by the Chamber of Commerce, Los Angeles filled in the canals; water gave way to asphalt; the bridges were torn down; gasoline service stations replaced the boat-landings.

The transformation of the New Venice was announced in advertisements in the Los Angeles press on June 28, 1929, in part as follows:

" Heralding the official start of another million dollar civic improvement, the filling of the famed canals of Venice, and their transformation into much needed roadways, all Los Angeles is preparing to celebrate this onward step of progress at the beach city when an elaborate program sponsored by civic organizations will be presented. . . .

" The Venice branch of the Los Angeles Chamber of Commerce has prepared a proclamation of ' Joy and Happiness' to fittingly initiate this day of days for Venice and Los Angeles.

" Five years ago a constructive movement was started in Venice looking toward the demands of progress, which plainly indicated the need of abandoning the ornamental canals so that streets might give better access to the heart of the city. Today the fulfillment of this objective is being celebrated. . . . The actual work of filling the old waterways, which served such a useful purpose in drawing people to Venice in the early days of her unique existence, is now in progress. The canals are a thing of the past and in celebrating their elimination, all the representative organizations and community-building forces in Venice join together in demonstrating the fact that this is a day of days long looked for and eagerly greeted in the spirit of congratulation and felicitation.

" To all Los Angeles territory, from which millions of people are entertained every year by the hospitality that Venice is so justly proud of, we send this proclamation of joy and happiness, marking the sacrifice of ornamental beauty and of traditional characteristics upon the altar of progress so that you, the people, may find here better facilities for your accommodation and to encourage the normal development that is so well justified by the trend of Los Angeles to the sea."

Los Angeles, in acquiring Venice, acquired a perpetual problem, for a large block of good Los Angeles people demand that the pagan beach amusements be closed on Sunday. Nevertheless, the Devil seems to have won out, for the toys of Satan are running wide open on the Sabbath as I write, while Los Angeles gets the Sunday tax. The reason for this desecration is perhaps because the pleasure resort of Santa Monica, up the beach a few miles, is an independent community, has no objection to Sunday dancing or roller coasting, and would get all the trade and taxes if Venice were closed on Sunday.

Just as there remains at Santa Monica a relic of Collis P. Huntington's dream harbor — a jetty and rails half buried in the sand — so there remains at Venice a relic of Kinney's æsthetic nightmare. Part of the once main water boulevard has never been filled in and remains today in its pristine glory on the outskirts of the town. Along its banks are rows of faded frame bungalows, mostly the homes of oil-field laborers. The concrete sides of the canal have fallen in. On the scummy waters, covered with a film of greasy black oil, small boys with mongrel dogs play pirate on improvised rafts. Nailed to a telephone pole near the fallen " Ponte di Rialto " there is a crude wooden sign, a pine board awkwardly lettered, which some romanticist no doubt made and put up tenderly with his own hands. Bravely and sadly it reads: " The Grand Canal."

Venice today is the favorite resort of the sailors when the fleet is in San Pedro. Some of the Venetian architecture is still there, visible in spots behind the " Two Suits for the Price of One " billboards.

Pasadena — Millionaires' Retreat

Pasadena is ten miles from Los Angeles. It is the scientific center of the West — the home of the highly publicized California Institute of Technology — one of the prettiest towns in America and probably the richest. Millions listen to the descriptions of its Tournament of Roses and East-West football game every New Year's Day. This community is the *crême de la crême* of California; a beautiful residential city to look at, a delightful place to live in. It makes the elegant suburbs of Boston, New York, and Chicago look positively sad. The place is not merely a community, it is a symbol. It symbolizes American plutocracy at its ripest.

The town was founded, oddly enough, by a group of frozen Hoosiers from Indianapolis, in 1873. Neither love of gold nor lure of high adventure sent those weak pioneers west. What sent them, according to the documents of the original "Indiana Colony," was a harsh winter, hard times, and a great, overwhelming desire

" to get where life was easy." The Hoosiers have long since given way to the Crœsuses, but the same desire, conscious or otherwise, accounts for nine tenths of the present population. Where life is easy! That is the sociological significance of this lovely millionaires' retreat.

Twenty years ago, on one street, a reporter counted the adjoining palaces of fifty-two millionaires and wrote a feature story entitled, " Orange Grove Avenue: A Millionaire for Every Week." Since then the total number has probably quadrupled. Playing golf and drinking Scotch (the town goes dry in all prohibition polls), the millionaires serve unknowingly, and hence happily, as guinea-pigs for the ecologists of the Carnegie Institution. What the scientific findings are, I don't know. A lyrical Swedish priest from gloomiest Wisconsin recently stated, somewhat bitterly, that Pasadena was a municipal flower-garden populated by lilies of the field. He said he saw in the inhabitants and in the environment unmistakable signs of national decadence.

Up and down the Pacific coast Pasadena is known as " the Millionaire Town." The local Chamber of Commerce objects to this designation, and accordingly the word " millionaire " is taboo in the local press. The sobriquet, the commerce boys claim, has kept hundreds of middling well-to-do people from settling there. The characterization awes them and scares them off to such places as Whittier, Monrovia, and Glendale. The Pasadena business men welcome millionaires, to be sure. But they would like to see a larger group of dependable, steady, middle-class buyers filling in the crevasses. For, contrary to what might be supposed, an extremely rich winter-resort is rather a poor place for the majority of merchants. The wealthy customers do not respond to " local-pride " appeals. They are practical men and women, discouraging realists. They buy in Los Angeles and, worse, order consistently from New York, London, Paris, and Berlin. Moreover, the millionaires are absent about half the year. In winter, when the census is taken, the population of Pasadena is approximately 100,-000; in summer it dwindles to about 35,000.

This population falls logically into three main classes: plutocrats, domestic servants, and tradesmen. They are garnished with perhaps two thousand retired folk of modest means; people who live in pretty bungalows, drive their own medium-priced cars, and have incomes of, say, five thousand dollars a year. There is also a generous sprinkling of chiropractors, osteopaths, fortune-tellers, swamis, and purveyors of " electronic vibrations." Last year when a Hindu snake-charmer lost his snakes in Los Angeles, he folded himself in his flowing robes and hied himself to the most inaccessible part of Pasadena's Arroyo Seco. Within a few days reports were going round the town about a mysterious East Indian prophet and seer, and shortly thereafter limousines were threading the tortuous bed of the canyon, loaded with vivacious ladies anxious to know if the seer could glimpse any husbands going on long journeys, or any tall dark men appearing on the horizon. Quacks are plentiful in Pasadena, and they are very popular, especially with the wealthy, middle-aged matrons on whose diamond-studded hands time, alas, hangs heavy. The Pasadena Community Playhouse and the Pasadena Art Institute, especially the former, are life-savers for these ladies. The young matrons and débutantes go in mainly for Junior League high-jinks, homes for Mexican orphans, and genteel whoopee.

There is a saying in Los Angeles that rich people who move to southern California do not go to Pasadena to live unless they have had money for at least two decades. That may have been true at one time, but it has not been true for ten years, for during the prosperity era a flock of new millionaires built homes in the Oak Knoll district and, more particularly, in the near-by suburbs of Altadena and Flintridge. But it is true that most of the *nouveaux riches*, and especially the traditional types, prefer Beverly Hills, Malibu Beach, and Hollywood. They see nothing in Pasadena and are somewhat ill at ease there; the town is too conservative, too reserved, and too rich. Moreover, these good people ordinarily do not desire a home in a quiet setting where gold does not glitter. What appeals to their taste is a Chinese-Kansas castle in Beverly Hills, an Arabian-Iowa mansion at Malibu, or a grand apartment-house on Hollywood Boulevard. In short, they desire to flash, and money does not flash in Pasadena. In the whole history of the town no movie star has ever lived there.

The conservative Pasadena millionaires frown severely upon gold-green villas, pink-striped automobiles, and candidates for the social register. They ask very little for their money. They request good liquor, and the town's millionaire bootlegger supplies it. They insist upon being let alone, and their commercial attachés see to that. They ask that industries be kept out of the town, and the Chamber of Commerce co-operates. They ask for fifty-one weeks of perfect golfing weather every year, and Nature complies. They demand the most efficient police force in the United States, and they have it.

THE ARROYO SECO BRIDGE
TO LOVELY PASADENA

The gentlemen of great wealth are very proud of the Pasadena Police Department. Some time ago when a burglar, who must have been insane, tried to rob a Pasadena castle the millionaires gave the police officer who killed him a medal, a public benefit, and a huge cash prize. They also retain what seems to be several army corps of watchmen and private detectives. These lurk behind stone walls, doze in patios, and ride bicycles through the streets at all hours of the night. Locked and barricaded in their castles against the Russians (reported to be approaching the city limits every morning by the Los Angeles *Times*), the millionaires snooze safely, police whistles on their beds.

II

The Chamber of Commerce, as I have said, objects to Pasadena's being called " the millionaire town." The plutocrats, on the other hand, object to its being called anything else. Aside from their own domestic servants and commercial attachés, these retired men of great wealth do not want any working people in the town. The working classes, they point out with unimpeachable logic, can go to San Pedro, or, better still, to hell. They know by experience that whenever working people congregate near them, social unrest inevitably follows. Naturally, a retired underwear-manufacturer has seen enough of such monkey business in his active years of sweating women and children. Now, as peace reigns and his arteries harden and the Angel of Death begins to flash a coy eye at him, he does not want to hear any more about that.

These vigilant old men — these amiable old rogues —

are surely not babes in the woods when it comes to strategy. They join the Pasadena Chamber of Commerce for the unique purpose of keeping commerce out of the town. It is a charming idea. And, however selfish their motives, however personal their interest, however incongruous their position, it seems to me that they perform a real service. For the active Babbitts of Pasadena, like business men everywhere, are natural vandals. Tomorrow, if it were possible, they would convert Busch Sunken Gardens into a site for a glue-manufacturing plant, and chop down every unprogressive, obstructing tree in order to display their exquisite advertising signs. They have endeavored to improve and Americanize the town for years, and only a moss-backed, city-planning commission, composed of retired millionaires, has prevented it.

Thus it is dog eat dog. Many are the fights in the Chamber of Commerce between the practising, red-blooded go-getters who yell: " We must have more pay-rolls! " and the retired, nature-loving millionaires who shout back apoplectically: " When the smoke-stacks come, we go! " As a result, there is much surreptitious activity on the part of the business men to get " desirable industry " quietly; many secret, solemn conferences and much plain and fancy double-crossing all round. It is interesting to note that some of the most violent beauty-lovers are retired manufacturers from such centers of culture and loveliness as Brockton, Massachusetts, East St. Louis, Scranton, Pennsylvania, and Bluefields, West Virginia. The spectacle is a sort of *reductio ad absurdum* of something; I confess that I do not know exactly what.

The town glides along from day to day, tranquil, sun-shiny, warm, friendly, complacent, and rich. The Los

Angeles patriots go into hysterics at the mere mention of the word " radical," but the Pasadena plutocrats are more tolerant of this strange species. Pasadena is probably the only town in the country where Mr. Upton Sinclair could live for years without creating a ripple on the surface. Mr. Sinclair, alas, was never taken seriously. He was simply dismissed with a vague, cordial wave of the hand, as one might say to a lunatic: " Sure, sure, that's right, Napoleon." Mr. Roger Baldwin, of the American Civil Liberties Union, was permitted to speak in Pasadena in spite of the American Legion and the Better America Federation. He arrived in a Hispano-Suiza piloted by the Socialistic croix-de-guerre owner, Crane Gartz, which, in itself, was enough to insure a hearing. Pasadena police have ousted Los Angeles " open-shop " bands bodily from the town's annual Tournament of Roses parades. This small metropolis, indeed, is a paradox. The richest city in America, it is also one of the friendliest to organized Labor, a friendliness which goes back to the days of the McNamara case. The files of the Los Angeles *Citizen* disclose that during those hectic days the labor organ received most of its advertising from Pasadena merchants.

Mainly responsible for this state of affairs is Charles H. Prisk, editor and owner of the Pasadena *Star-News*. In an article in the *American Mercury* a few years ago on the California literati, George W. West referred to this journal as " an oasis in the desert." After years of easy but persistent pressure Mr. Prisk has gradually created a spirit of live-and-let-live in the community. The *Star-News* has long been the envy and wonder of newspaper publishers on the Pacific coast. Its policy of giving all sides in a controversy an " even break " is often termed spineless by persons whose idea of courage is to suppress the opposition.

Mr. Prisk is a modest, genial, dignified, mild-mannered man, a former president of the town's Rotary Club. Thirty years ago, just out of Stanford, a cantankerous young man from the wilds of Grass Valley, he went to Pasadena and started a paper. A short time after he arrived, the political boss of the town went to his office and tried to dictate to the young editor. The conference ended in a knock-down, drag-out fight between the two. They rolled over the floor. The battle finally ended in the traditional manner, after noses were bloodied, glasses broken, and furniture wrecked, when " Kid " Prisk threw his opponent bodily through the front door, glass and all. Many times since then the man has had occasion to show his courage, his generosity, and his intelligence. He had one fight with Labor and won, but since he was not vindictive, he was willing to shake hands after the fight. Today not only is his paper, in an open-shop paradise, run mechanically by union labor; the heads of the mechanical departments are officials of national and international unions. Mr. Prisk is the despair of all the Los Angeles Red-baiters and Labor-haters; he is full of humor and common decency, and hence among most of the capitalists of southern California he stands out like a redwood in a growth of stunted pine.

III

The millionaires of Pasadena have exhibited heat and passion only once. That was when the King of Belgium visited the town shortly after the war. That was a great day. An official half-holiday was declared. Covers were laid for a thousand luncheon guests at the Maryland Hotel — the King was coming for lunch. A triumphal rose-covered arch, paid for with the nickels and dimes of school-children, was erected on the main street. Thousands of people lined the sidewalks. For once the plutocrats came out of their shells *en masse*, resplendent and hot in morning clothes, to welcome the King. But the King was late.

And, lo and behold, when he did arrive, the royal automobile shot through the town — on a side street at fifty miles an hour — to a siding where the royal train was parked, and a moment later the King was gone. He passed up Pasadena like a pay-car passing a tramp. A few cops and railroad switch-men got a fleeting glimpse of His Majesty; that was all. It was explained that the movie folk in Hollywood had kept him two hours past his schedule, and consequently he was forced to deprive himself of the pleasure of Pasadena's hospitality. He also passed up the monster afternoon reception which Mrs. Anita Baldwin had been planning for three weeks. Mrs. Baldwin had not only spent fifty thousand dollars; she had also invited every prominent person in California to meet the King.

Alas and alack-a-day. Before the sun went down behind the purple mountains, the hot, pathetic herd of outraged millionaires announced publicly that the movie magnates in Hollywood were a gang of unspeakable yahoos, and that, furthermore, they put no faith whatever in the ridiculous and utterly absurd stories of German atrocities in Belgium!

The Rape of Owens Valley

*F*rom an airplane Los Angeles today resembles half a hundred Middle-Western-Egyptian-Italian-English-Spanish communities, repainted and sprinkled about. Its population is about 1,400,000. It is, and has been for ten years, the largest city in America in area, and people often wonder why. The answer is Water.

Water is scarce in southern California — so scarce that since 1913 Los Angeles has obtained its main supply from a source two hundred and fifty miles away. Since then, whenever a new town has bloomed ten, fifteen, or twenty miles away and reached the point where the water-supply from its artesian wells and underground streams has become inadequate, Los Angeles has given it a drink and taken it under the motherly wing. That is the way in which ungrateful Hollywood and a score of other towns were saved from dying of thirst, and that is the way in which Long Beach, Beverly Hills, and Pasadena would probably have been annexed by now but for their threat to defeat the building of the new aqueduct from the Colorado River when the Hoover Dam impounds its waters.

As a result of these repeated annexations the sunshine metropolis now winds in and around southern California from the mountains to the sea, squirms through " bottle necks," attaches itself to its Wilmington and San Pedro by means of a " shoe-string " district a half-mile wide and fifteen miles long, drapes itself over deserts, mountains, and sand-dunes, and altogether sprawls grotesquely over *442 square miles* — a " municipal " area three times the size of Chicago — including leagues of farms and virgin soil. The result, *legally*, is " Los Angeles." It must be obvious, however, that all this vast area is no more one " city," properly so called, than, say, Merced, California, would be one " city," the largest on earth, if it should suddenly annex Yosemite National Park.

How Los Angeles got this way — how it got the water which it uses as a club — is a story of business beside which Teapot Dome pales into insignificance. It constitutes one of the most dramatic epics ever enacted in America.

II

Two hundred and fifty miles northeast of Los Angeles, in Inyo County, near the Nevada line, there is a long, slender, arid region, about ten miles wide and one hundred miles long, known as Owens Valley. This is Mary Austin's original " Land of Little Rain." In its natural state the valley supports little life except cactus, sagebrush and chaparral, tarantulas, horned toads and rattlesnakes. But this desert valley has one freakish, inexhaustible, priceless treasure, bestowed upon it when it was created by the geological convulsion which threw that chain of mountain peaks (the highest in America) into the air on one side of it, and the Inyo and White Mountains on the other. Right down through the center of this arid valley runs Owens River, a life-giving, permanent stream, fed by the melted snows of the High Sierras — including the melted snows of Mount Whitney, towering twelve thousand feet above it — a permanent supply of pure, fresh water. This strange river terminates at the southern end of the valley in a saline lake which has no outlet. And this lake, though its water is unfit for irrigation, tempers the curse of the desert heat (like the Salt Lake of Utah) and serves as a cooling agent. Eleven months a year, except right along the banks of Owens River, the valley *in its natural state* would be as dry as the Mojave Desert.

But Owens Valley, until recently, has not been in its natural state for seventy years. Everyone who has traveled through the Southwest — indeed, everyone who has seen the orange groves of southern California — has seen what water can do to desert land. Hospitable to nothing in its natural state, the desert land, when irrigated, seems to be richer than any other soil. Thus seventy years ago homesteaders selected this region, because of its permanent river, as one of the potentially richest sections in California. It would take water and work and time to make something out of this God-forsaken country; but these struggling, pioneer men and women were not afraid to work. In time they would make something out of this burning desert, a little for themselves, more for their children. These people, take note, were not mere farmers setting out to rob the soil and lead an easy life. They were pioneers, faced with the prospect of creating something out of nothing.

The first settlers went, with no illusions, into this un-inhabited, scorching valley in covered wagons in 1861, taking with them their children and all their earthly belongings; seed, live stock, and crude tools. They settled along the river and near the outflowing canyon streams, dug irrigation ditches with hand tools, women wielding picks and shovels along with the men. Gradu-ally they turned little streams of water on the parched land, an acre or so at a time. They carried out boulders, plowed up the hot earth, planted little orchards, vege-table gardens, and patches of wheat — and watched them die, for this desert did not respond to water at once. It drank thirstily and cried for more. It was a slow process. For years these isolated pioneers battled earth, heat, dis-ease, famine, floods, and Piute and Mojave Indians. It would be difficult to imagine men and women having a worse time. There was something heroic about them, as there is something heroic about people everywhere who grapple with Nature, against terrific odds, in an effort to tame and civilize it.

Slowly the desert bloomed — two narrow, cultivated strips on each side of the river — two strips gradually widening as the water was led out from the stream, acre by acre. Orchards began to bear; wheat, corn, and clover grew in the fields; cattle grazed in pasture-land. Farther and farther from the river homesteaders took up land. Finally, there were flood-diversion canals running down from the hills, and irrigation ditches running out five miles from the river, with homesteaders living near them, and all working to build up the country, to keep the canals open and clean, the water moving.

Gradually a part of this desert was transformed into a rich agricultural valley. Along the river a series of little towns sprang up and prospered — Bishop, Independence, Laws, Manzanar, Lone Pine, and others. Unproductive acres blossomed into prosperous ranches, desert shacks into fine farm-houses, flanked by barns, silos, shade trees, and flowers. Roads and schoolhouses were built. A railroad came up from Los Angeles. There were eight thousand people in Owens Valley. Their agricultural exhibits were among the finest at the State fairs. Specifically, they were the best in California and captured first prizes year after year, in hard grain, in apples, in corn, and in honey.

III

Two hundred and thirty miles south of Owens Valley, *twenty miles northwest of Los Angeles*, there was another arid valley of about a hundred and fifty thousand acres, San Fernando Valley, where the land got little water, and which, in its natural state, was virtually desert land.

Some time between 1899 and 1903, when Los Angeles was growing hand over fist — and the orange-growers were beginning to drain the Los Angeles River and the artesian wells — a select group of public-spirited Los Angeles business men, bankers, and real-estate operators hit upon a great idea. Just who conceived it I do not know, but he was a genius. It was a fantastic scheme, but they were Men of Vision. They decided to buy up the worthless San Fernando Valley land, acquire control of the Owens River, and then frighten the taxpayers of Los Angeles into paying for a huge aqueduct to bring the water down two hundred and fifty miles over mountain and desert — to give Los Angeles an added water-supply and, incidentally, to use a great portion of the water to irrigate the San Fernando Valley and thus convert that desert region into a fertile farming section, just outside the city. It was a bold, tremendous enterprise, a piece of business in the grand manner. For several years the little group conspired secretly, and eventually they worked out and perfected their scheme.

In 1903 the United States Reclamation Service became suddenly interested in Owens Valley. J. B. Lippincott, chief engineer of the U. S. Reclamation Service in California, appeared on the scene and began to explain to the ranchers that a benevolent Government was working out a plan to place about two hundred thousand additional acres of their desert valley land under irrigation, for the purpose of further promoting settlement, prosperity, and development. The people of Owens Valley were overjoyed.

Meanwhile down in Los Angeles a small real-estate syndicate began buying up San Fernando Valley land at five, ten, twenty, fifty dollars an acre.

The U. S. Reclamation engineers working under Lippincott went into Owens Valley, " made extensive investigations, tested the soil, measured the area of farming lands, determined the duty of water in the soil and climate, surveyed sites of proposed storage dams," and otherwise went ahead with the Federal project. Lippincott told the farmers and mutual water companies that they should co-ordinate their forces with the Government in order to advance the Government's plans; that is, they should pool their interests, and turn over their rights and claims to the Government, so that Uncle Sam could get the whole thing in hand at once and go ahead. By doing this, he said, when the project was completed, they would be able to get the water-improved lands, most of which they already owned, for the actual cost of the development, estimated at twenty-three dollars an acre. If for any reason the Government should not go through with the project, their priority rights would of course be returned to them, the Government would restore all reservoir and power filings to their former status, and furthermore the Reclamation Service would turn over to the valley people all charts, maps, surveys, stream measurements, etc., so that in any case the farmers stood to gain by the transaction. The trusting citizens thereupon surrendered their claims and locations to the Federal Government, and every co-operation was given the National Reclamation Service by the people of Inyo County. These ranchers were naïve, unsophisticated people; that is, they had faith in the Federal Government.

In 1899–1900 Fred Eaton was Mayor of Los Angeles. In 1904 Mr. Eaton, representing himself as Lippincott's agent, went into Owens Valley and began taking options on land which was riparian to the Owens River. He was in possession of the United States Reclamation Service maps and surveys (the property of the Federal Government), and the ranchers believed that he was obtaining the lands for the Government. In obtaining these options Eaton followed what is known as the " checkerboard " or " spot-zone " system; that is, he followed the irrigation canals from the river, obtaining options, if possible, on every other ranch on each side.

The following year Eaton returned to the valley,

acquiring more land, and bringing with him William Mulholland, chief of the Los Angeles Water Department, and a group of Los Angeles bankers. The presence of these bankers aroused the suspicions of the Owens Valley ranchers for the first time; the presence of the bankers, plus vague rumors which now began to reach the valley, that somebody down in Los Angeles, two hundred and fifty miles southward, was after their water. At the same time Lippincott began to hint that the reclamation project might be abandoned.

On June 27, 1905 S. W. Austin, Land Registrar at Independence, wrote a letter to the United States Land Office at Washington, from which I quote a few excerpts: "In the spring of 1905 Mr. Eaton returned to the Valley, representing himself as Mr. Lippincott's agent in examining right-of-way applications for power purposes which had been filed by the government. He had then in his possession maps which had been prepared by the Reclamation Service. In April 1905 Mr. Eaton began to secure options on land and water rights in Owens Valley to the value of about a million dollars and shortly thereafter he brought a number of well known Los Angeles capitalists and bankers into the valley to look over these properties. . . . The well known friendship between him and Mr. Lippincott and the fact that Mr. Eaton had represented the Supervising Engineer for the Government (Lippincott), made it easier for these rights to be secured, for the people were all generously inclined toward the government project, and believed Mr. Eaton to be the agent of the Reclamation Service. Mr. Eaton's own statement was that he had bought these lands for a cattle ranch. . . . About this time letters were received at the United States Land

THE RAPE OF OWENS VALLEY

Office from prospective homesteaders stating that it was understood in Southern California that these rights were being purchased for the purpose of carrying the water to the city of Los Angeles which was known to be in need of a new supply. . . .

" An abandonment of the project by the Government at this time will make it appear that the expensive surveys and measurements of the past two years have all been made in the interest of a band of speculators, and it will result in inflicting a severe loss upon all settlers and owners of property in Owens Valley."

By this time Eaton had obtained options on considerable riparian land along the river and elsewhere. He thereupon exercised his options and bought the land. Lippincott then announced definitely that the reclamation project had been abandoned by the Government. He resigned from the United States Reclamation Service and took a job with the Los Angeles Water Department, as assistant to Mulholland, turning over to the city all maps, charts, field surveys, stream measurements, etc. This data told the story of what could be done and what had been planned for Owens Valley, *and gave also the ownership, value, and status of every piece of land in the valley*. At the same time this information was denied to the people of Owens Valley. It was subsequently proved, and very shortly, that Lippincott had been receiving a salary from the city of Los Angeles while still a government officer and while he was ostensibly promoting the mythical Federal reclamation project in the valley.

On July 29, 1905 Arthur P. Davis, assistant chief engineer of the U. S. Reclamation Service, wrote a letter to F. H. Newell, chief engineer of the service, in which he said: "I think we cannot clear the skirts of the Reclamation Service too quickly nor completely."

Not a word of all this had appeared in the Los Angeles papers. For three years the people of Los Angeles were kept in ignorance while the scheme was being hatched. The city of Los Angeles was to get an aqueduct, but the city — even the City Council — was unaware of it. Only the little group of leading citizens and the newspapers (let in on the deal for fear that they might expose it) knew what was going on. For three years the newspapers suppressed the news. By July 1905, however, the time was ripe for printing it. Eaton now owned much of the land riparian to Owens River and was ready to deed it to the city. The syndicate now owned virtually all of near-by San Fernando Valley. Money was needed to pay Eaton, to gain control of the full flow of Owens River, and to bring the water down to Los Angeles. The papers agreed to break the story simultaneously, part in the morning and part in the afternoon papers. Louis Sherwin, writing in the *American Mercury*, said: "One morning [July 29, 1905] the *Times* came out with the scoop of the century plastered all over its first three pages. The city had for years been quietly preparing to build an enormous aqueduct from the Owens River Valley. In order that the poor, downtrodden farmers in that region should not get wind of the project and hold the wicked city up for blackmail, all the Los Angeles papers had agreed to suppress the news until the necessary land had been acquired. The *Times* broke the agreement, double-crossed everybody, and beat the town by a day. Lordy, how the others yelped. And nobody saw the humor in the situation."

Obviously Mr. Sherwin, a former editorial writer on

the *Times,* saw the " humor " in the situation. His account, however, is slightly misleading. " The *city* had for years been quietly preparing to build an enormous aqueduct from the Owens River Valley." The city had been doing no such thing. The people of Los Angeles knew nothing of what was going on. Even the members of the City Council, as William R. Stewart pointed out in the *World's Work* for November 1907, had not the slightest inkling of what was going on until the little group that controlled them was ready for these puppets to go through their paces. As for " the poor, downtrodden farmers " of Owens Valley getting wind of the project and holding " the wicked city up for blackmail," the real reason the whole matter was kept secret was that the conspirators did not want the *people of Los Angeles to get wind of the San Fernando scheme;* nor did they want to waste any more time than was absolutely necessary to get the water.

As a matter of fact, the " poor, downtrodden farmers " of Owens Valley did not have the slightest objection to the city of Los Angeles acquiring an additional water-supply from the High Sierras by impounding the melted snows, storing the flood-waters, and augmenting the flow of Owens River. There was not the slightest need for secrecy, not the slightest need for conspiracy. Enough water comes down from the High Sierras each year, ninety-nine per cent of it wasted, to supply the needs of half the people in the State of California. There was not the slightest reason why the people of Owens Valley, the Federal Government, and the Angel City should not have co-operated on the entire project. All that was necessary to give Owens Valley twice as much water as it was getting, and Los Angeles twice as much as it has ever received from its aqueduct, was to build a storage reservoir above Owens Valley.

But the San Fernando land-grabbers and the politicians of the Water Department, whom they controlled, had no time to waste upon such a public project. The city (that is, the small group who ran it) simply announced that it was going to stick an aqueduct into the Owens River and divert *all* that life-giving water to Los Angeles, two hundred and fifty miles away, and furthermore that it was out to buy, and proposed to acquire, some seventy thousand additional acres still owned by the ranchers in order to gain full control of the river.

On August 4, 1905 Mr. Austin, getting no satisfaction from the United States Land Office, wrote directly to President Roosevelt. His letter reads, in part, as follows:

" I am Registrar of the United States Land Office at this place. In behalf of the people of this district, and of the Government which I have served for nearly eight years, I wish to protest against the proposed abandonment of the Owens River Project by the Reclamation Service. . . .

" Mr. Lippincott while drawing a large salary from the Government was employed by the City of Los Angeles to assist in securing this water for the City. He agreed to turn down this project at a critical moment when the Los Angeles men had secured other rights here which they wanted. . . . As these matters came before this office, I am stating what I know to be true. The connection between Mr. Lippincott and Mr. Eaton deceived the people of this valley, and they supposed that these rights were being indirectly secured for the Government. They could not believe that a plan to rob the valley of its water and turn down the Government's irrigation project was being carried out with the consent of the Supervising Engineer. The people of Owens Valley trusted to the Reclamation Service, and by so doing all who own property here, and all who have located under the provisions of the Reclamation Act, (under the implied promise of the Government to build the reservoir, if feasible) will lose a great deal if this project is abandoned. . . .

" In justice, therefore, to the people here, in the interest of fairness and of the honor of the Reclamation Service, I appeal to you not to abandon the Owens River Project, but if feasible, carry it out in accordance with the spirit of the Act of June 17th, 1902."

Protest after protest rained upon Roosevelt, the Secretary of the Interior, and United States Senators, but without avail. The way had been greased. On the contrary, a bill was prepared granting to Los Angeles a free right of way for an aqueduct on government lands through Inyo, Kern, and Los Angeles counties.

At the same time Los Angeles, through the press, through pamphlets, and otherwise, began to impress upon its citizens, most of whom were newcomers, the need for an immediate supply of water. Unless they voted bonds for building an aqueduct and getting water from Owens River, they were told that the country would soon dry up. Water was run into the sewers — " for purposes of necessary sanitation, to flush the system " — decreasing the supply in the reservoirs. The people were forbidden to water their lawns and gardens. This drought, artificial or real, lasted throughout the dry summer months; lawns in the city turned brown and flowers died.

On election day the people of Los Angeles voted the aqueduct bonds — twenty-two and a half million dollars' worth — to build an aqueduct from Owens River to Los Angeles and to defray other expenses of the project to bring Los Angeles a domestic water-supply.

With this money in hand the city " acquired " all the land that Eaton had acquired in Owens Valley, and Mulholland started to build the longest aqueduct in the world. Los Angeles, to be sure, did not yet own all the water-rights land in Owens Valley; and there was no assurance that it could acquire it. Ranchers still owned much of it. Moreover, all of Owens Valley was homestead land, and homesteaders were still moving into the valley and acquiring their share of the water rights. However, as it soon appeared, there was a way to take care of *that*.

In 1906 the Honorable Gifford Pinchot (now Governor of Pennsylvania), at that time chief of the United States Forest Service under Roosevelt, issued an order transforming a great portion of the desert land of Owens Valley into a *Federal forest district!* — thereby withdrawing approximately two hundred thousand acres of land from its homestead status. I quote herewith from a volume entitled *The Story of Inyo*, by W. A. Chalfant:

" Additional settlement of vacant lands at that period was not desired by the aqueduct promoters, for such development might reduce the water supply available for the scheme. Los Angeles' bureau, which proved its efficiency in many ways during the period, headed off such possibilities by the simple expedient of having the Forest Service, then under ultra-conservationist Gifford Pinchot, withdraw all vacant land in the Owens Valley watershed on the preposterous pretense of its being

' forest.' This included square leagues covered with grass and sagebrush, where the only trees within any reasonable distance were those that had been planted by settlers. It was further directed that all applications for land permitted under forest regulations be referred to the city of Los Angeles for approval."

From a series of articles by Frederick R. Faulkner, which appeared in the Sacramento *Union* from March 28 to April 2, 1927, I quote the following:

"In its procedure of usurping the Owens Valley water supply, Los Angeles found an ally in the Federal Government. . . . In 1906 Gifford Pinchot, chief forester under President Roosevelt, issued an order creating a federal forest district in Owens Valley.

" This was one of the most picturesque decrees any government ever issued. There was not a tree in the entire area except the slender, graceful poplars, locusts and cottonwoods the settlers had planted.

" Pinchot's order stopped development, for it closed the government's desert lands against homesteading."

From a written statement presented to the Owens Valley Investigating Committee of the California State Senate on April 1, 1931 by Andrae B. Nordskog of Los Angeles I quote the following:

" Two hundred thousand acres of desert land were withdrawn under the United States Forestry Act in favor of Los Angeles when in fact not an acre of said lands was forestry land; and done in this manner because Forest land in Inyo County was not subject to entry by homesteaders, whereas desert land was open for entry, and the land could and would have been developed by progressive farmers had they been given the opportunity which they should have had under our Federal laws.

I possess an astounding admission in writing from the former Chief Forester as to the real motive in this unusual withdrawal of Government lands."

I am aware of the fact that the reprinting of these charges here, without repudiation, casts grave reflection upon a public man. It happens, however, that in my researches on this subject I have found nothing to repudiate or even vitiate them. Moreover, in 1911 President Taft rescinded Mr. Pinchot's order and returned the Owens Valley land to its homestead status. Accordingly I wrote to Governor Pinchot (pointing out what I have just said) and asking him to give me the facts which would repudiate these charges, or at least refer me to them. To make myself perfectly clear, I concluded my letter to Governor Pinchot as follows: " In brief, what I would like to know is: Was this properly desert land, or forest land? If it was not forest land, were you deceived, and if so, by whom? If it was forest land why was your order rescinded by President Taft? If the letter referred to by Mr. Nordskog was from you, could I see a copy of it? " Mr. Pinchot's reply is as follows:

COMMONWEALTH OF PENNSYLVANIA
GOVERNOR'S OFFICE
Harrisburg
January 12, 1932

The Governor

Mr. Morrow Mayo,
4 Milligan Place,
New York, New York.

Dear Mr. Mayo:
Many thanks for yours of December 31st, which I have just found in working through the enormous mail which is reaching me these days.

I remember, of course, very well indeed the whole case of the Los Angeles-Owens Valley water controversy, and it is perfectly true that I did what in me lay to prevent the people of Los Angeles from being held up by a handful of people — and a very small handful of people — living along the line of the proposed canal.

I appreciate immensely your interest, and I wish it were possible for me to stop in the rush of the present unemployment situation to refresh my mind by a reference to the sources, and write you in detail with reference to the controversy. I will, however, write to a friend of mine and see if he can help you out. The essential fact is that I used the power that lay in me for the greatest good of the greatest number, and that the results have abundantly justified my action. I would do the same thing again.

Sincerely yours,
(Signed) GIFFORD PINCHOT

To date I have not heard from Governor Pinchot's " friend."

At any rate, Pinchot's order immediately stopped all further settlement in Owens Valley and closed these government desert lands against homesteading. The land was closed for six years, during which time Los Angeles prepared, and filed in advance, applications for its use. In 1911 when President Taft rescinded Pinchot's order and returned the land to a homestead status, the claims of Los Angeles were accepted, and the city thereupon obtained possession of all this land.

Meanwhile the Los Angeles Aqueduct Bill was being rushed through Congress. In the presence of Secretary of the Interior Hitchcock, Chief Forester Pinchot, and

Director Walcott of the Geological Survey, President Roosevelt dictated a letter to the Secretary of the Interior approving the bill. Roosevelt included a writ of prohibition against using the water for agricultural purposes. However, he was assured (so he said) by Senator Flint of California (Los Angeles) that Los Angeles had no such intention; that the water was to be used for domestic purposes only. The Senator added that the writ of prohibition would kill the passage of the bond issue, because many people wanted to use a little of the water on their gardens outside the city proper, and, denied that use, they would vote against the bonds.

Whatever the facts, Roosevelt struck out the writ of prohibition and in its stead inserted the following clause:

"Under the circumstances I decide, in accordance with the recommendations of the Director of the Geological Survey and the Chief of the Forestry Service, that the bill be approved, with the prohibition against the use of the water by the municipality for irrigation struck out."

Accordingly, the Aqueduct Bill was passed by Congress and signed by Roosevelt. He had hardly signed it before the syndicate which owned San Fernando Valley began to advertise that the aqueduct would go through San Fernando Valley, and that early investors in the thousands of acres of dusty stubble fields there would make lots of money with the use of Owens River water on that land.

In the meantime, Los Angeles started devastating the ranches which it had acquired in Owens Valley, by withholding water from them; and also it began to force the other ranchers to sell out. This was accomplished by a deliberate process of ruination. The city not only permitted no water on its own land, but also placed hundreds of pumps on the edges of it, drawing the water from its own land and also from that near by. Owning much of the land along the irrigation ditches, it refused to do any work on them or pay any of the expense towards keeping them clean; in fact, it did everything possible to clog them up and stop the flow of water. The City of the Angels built dikes in front of these irrigation ditches, altered the course of the river, and even dynamited private storage reservoirs. Thus it forced the ranchers to sell their land to the city at condemnation prices and get out. Long before the city had acquired legal control of the flow of the river, it stuck the nose of the aqueduct into the stream and began taking the water by force, with armed men patrolling the aqueduct and the river day and night.

The great pipe-line was a " patriotic " project, built entirely with American labor. Not a foreign workman was permitted to contaminate it. It was built 233 miles, but not to Los Angeles. It was built to the San Fernando Valley, and there it stopped, and there a great part of the flow of the water was distributed. Members of the real-estate syndicate subdivided their land and sold it at from five hundred to a thousand dollars an acre, clearing profits estimated at one hundred million dollars on their elegant San Fernando subdivision. But, you will say, both the bond issue and the Aqueduct Bill called for the building of the aqueduct to Los Angeles. Well, the land speculators took care of that by the simple expedient of annexing 100,800 acres of agricultural San Fernando land to the city, thus *taking Los Angeles to the aqueduct*. San Fernando Valley is today

A VIEW OF THE LOS ANGELES AQUEDUCT, DYNAMITED NINE TIMES

a part of the City of the Angels, and that is another reason why this municipal monstrosity covers so much territory. In 1930, eighty-eight thousand acre feet of Owens River water, taken through the Los Angeles aqueduct, was used for irrigation in San Fernando Valley. It was enough water to provide each and every one of the 1,300,000 people in Los Angeles fifty gallons a day for one year.

The apologists for the destruction of Owens Valley emphasize that it was for the " greatest good for the greatest number." This seems to be the position of Mr. Pinchot, plus the implication that the ends justified the means. This is good democratic doctrine, often used by majorities in crushing minorities, but, whatever its dubious merits, it does not apply in this case. The manner in which Los Angeles took the water from the Owens River did not accomplish the greatest good for the greatest number. The greatest good for the greatest number would have been a project which would have provided water both for Owens Valley and for Los Angeles. There was, and is, plenty of water for both. There was not the slightest necessity for secrecy, fraud, and ruination. New York, San Francisco, and other cities have built aqueducts and brought water from a distance without ruining agricultural communities.

The whole project could have been accomplished to the advantage of everybody concerned (except perhaps the San Fernando land-grabbers) simply by building a storage reservoir in Long Valley, a natural reservoir above Owens Valley. Long Valley is one of the finest reservoir sites in America — a level stretch of meadow land, twenty square miles in extent. It is twenty-five miles above the highest diversion point in Owens

Valley, at an altitude of about 6,500 feet, where the water is uncontaminated by human habitation.

As Mr. Faulkner wrote in the Sacramento *Union:* "On April 17, 1920, at a hearing before the Public Lands Committee of the United States Senate, W. B. Matthews, counsel for the city of Los Angeles, testified in response to a question by the late Congressman Raker regarding Long Valley: 'It is the largest and finest reservoir in the country.' In December 1906 a board of distinguished consulting engineers, John R. Freeman, Frederick B. Sterns, and James D. Schuyler, recommended the use of this storage reservoir in Long Valley. They found a foundation capable of supporting a dam of any construction. A dam 165 feet high and only 525 feet long at the top would store approximately 350,000 acre feet of water in Long Valley.

"If this storage facility had been developed, it would have provided an equated water flow of over nine hundred second cubic feet at the diversion point above the valley. Proper conservation of the water coming down from the various streams in the valley would have produced a total volume sufficient to have kept under cultivation the eighty thousand acres of first-class farming land in the valley, and still have given Los Angeles twice as much water every day in the year as has ever been in the aqueduct on any day since the aqueduct entered service. These are the facts of record from government engineers and the city's own engineers. The engineering project which Los Angeles planned and executed, indeed, is the most remarkable in engineering history. It is the only project of comparable size in the world which did not provide for the storage of water near the source. Not a gallon of water storage has been provided by Los Angeles at Long Valley or at any other of the adaptable sites above the former diversion points of Owens Valley irrigation."

In short, the nose of the aqueduct was simply stuck into the Owens River, diverting the water, while pumps were installed in the ground to suck into the aqueduct water from all the surrounding farming land. In other words, the water was simply stolen from one valley, already under cultivation, and distributed upon another, uncultivated valley 233 miles away.

IV

It takes some time to destroy an agricultural section. It took Los Angeles fourteen years to ruin Owens Valley. The aqueduct was completed in 1913. In the early spring of 1927 there appeared a full-page advertisement in most of the large California papers beginning: " *We, the farming communities of Owens Valley, being about to die, salute you!* " The ranchers were giving up the ghost.

As I write, the New York *Times* of August 26, 1932 lies before me, containing one of Will Rogers's syndicated dispatches. I quote the first paragraph: " Bishop, Cal., Aug. 25 — Ten years ago this was a wonderful valley with one-quarter of a million acres of fruit and alfalfa. But, Los Angeles had to have more water for the Chamber of Commerce to drink more toasts to its growth, more water to dilute its orange juice and more water for its geraniums to delight the tourists, while the giant cottonwoods here died. So, now, this is a valley of desolation."

Owens Valley is rapidly returning to sagebrush and

desert waste; to the coyotes and jack-rabbits. All around are the ruins of homes and ranches. The Los Angeles Water Department is using tractors to pull up the fruit trees. Inyo County has had no exhibit at the State Fair since 1927. It has had nothing to exhibit. About ninety per cent of the former cultivated area has been acquired by the City of the Angels, and the water withdrawn from it.

As one motors along what was once the McNalley irrigation canal, one of the first sights is the former Trowbridge ranch, the house empty, the barns falling down, trees dying. Los Angeles turned the water out of the ditch in 1923; today sagebrush is growing in the patio of the house. And so along the road, to the river. In this stretch of five miles there were eighty-five farmhouses, with a total acreage of 13,712 acres. On all sides were young orchards, prosperous alfalfa ranches and gardens, dairy and beef cattle. Today there are two privately owned farms, 112 acres in all. Los Angeles owns the balance; along this one irrigation canal it has " retired " 13,600 acres of fine farm land. It is a lovely picture of wrecked homes, broken-down silos, and empty stock corrals.

The desolate trail leads on to the once prosperous town of Laws. The alfalfa association's warehouse is empty, silent, the windows broken. The main street of this ghost town is lined with empty homes, empty restaurants, and vacant stores. Manzanar was once famous for its apples. The orchardists won first prizes at the State Fair at Sacramento and at the Watsonville apple show. They had a large packing plant. Los Angeles bought up every orchard and ranch that its agents could trick and browbeat the owners into selling. It immediately diverted the water from the ditches into the aqueduct and dug wells and installed pumps to exhaust the underground supply. The Angel City has acquired 99 of the 116 farms along the irrigation canal here and pulled up the apple trees by the roots.

Two miles east of Lone Pine, in the southern end of the valley, is the Mount Whitney station of the narrow-gauge railway running between Keeler and Mina. Some time ago the railroad sold the depot; there was no longer anything to stop for at Mount Whitney station. This was where the William Penn colony existed. The colony owned thirty thousand acres of land around its irrigation ditches. More than forty houses had been built when Eaton entered the valley. It was a thriving community of farms, alfalfa-fields, orchards, truck gardens, stock pastures; the place where most of the honey was produced. Today there is not a trace of the William Penn colony. Chaparral and alkali compose the whole landscape. From Independence to Big Pine the Angel City has purchased 12,000 acres, 123 farms, and consigned it all to desert.

Diversion of the Owens River naturally is drying up the saline Owens Lake below the aqueduct intake. Desert winds scatter the alkali; clouds of soda dust sweep over the valley. Owens Lake has been a great cooling agent. When it is dried up, the heat of midsummer will make the valley more difficult to live in — for the centipedes and horned toads who will be there then.

A few years ago the State of California decided to build a highway up from Los Angeles through Owens Valley to reach the scenery of the High Sierras. Los Angeles fought the building of this road in every possible manner, but nevertheless the road was built, a paved highway leading through Owens Valley to Lake Tahoe and on to Yosemite National Park. I surely do not need to say that ordinarily the Los Angeles boosters would have whooped this project up to the skies. Why was it opposed? The Angel City did not want the world to see its destruction of Owens Valley. It was cutting down the shade trees along the county road; poplars, locusts, and cottonwoods from twenty to sixty years old. " Tree-lover " Pinchot should have seen that " conservation."

But the State highway was built, right up through the valley, and as the tourist drives along it today, his eyes feast upon a picture of desolation — dying orchards, empty schoolhouses, and abandoned farms. It looks like a country devastated by war. Los Angeles cannot permit this sight to remain for tourists and travelers to see. Consequently, the city is removing all traces of civilization; putting the firebrand to dead orchards, deserted farmhouses, schools, and other buildings. The houses are burned, the trees are pulled out by the roots and burned, and the ashes are scattered. In a few more years — as already in many places — the sagebrush and tumbleweed will conceal the scars from the eyes of tourists. The Angel City is covering her trail.

There has been a great deal of violence in the valley. The aqueduct was dynamited nine times. In 1927 the spillway in the Alabama Hills was opened by three hundred enraged ranchers, who kept it open for four days to get some water on their land. Los Angeles, however, first introduced lawlessness and dynamite in Owens Valley. Agents of the city, officials and employees of the Public Service Commission, dynamited storage dams at Lake Mary, on Fishlake Creek, and Hot Springs Creek, to get water for the aqueduct. Working in the dead of night, they threw dikes around irrigation-canal intakes.

In rushing the water down to San Fernando Valley and controlling it at its terminus, instead of at its source, Mulholland built a series of dams all around Los Angeles, the largest at San Francisquito Canyon, near Saugus. This dam was condemned by engineers in high standing as a death-trap. Two years after its construction, on the night of March 12, 1928, it fell apart, and waters rushed down through the valleys taking a toll of six hundred lives and millions of dollars' worth of property. Another dam was started in San Gabriel Canyon. The fork sites there had been condemned since 1906. It was started, but finally abandoned, after five million dollars had been spent on it, when the foundation took a slide. Another dam was built above Hollywood. As late as 1928 pictures were printed showing cracks in it, and a protest was made by Hollywood citizens, but nothing apparently was done about it. If that dam ever fails, they will have a real movie in Hollywood.

Ninety per cent of the people of Los Angeles have no idea of the colossal swindle which was put over on them, nor do they have the slightest inkling of what has gone on in Owens Valley. Few of them have ever seen Owens Valley. Throughout the years occasional pieces appeared in the Los Angeles papers, simply saying that the city's water-supply was being contested by "a small group of disgruntled ranchers."

In conclusion, it may be said that Los Angeles gets its water by reason of one of the costliest, crookedest, most unscrupulous deals ever perpetrated, plus one of the greatest pieces of engineering folly ever heard of. Owens Valley is there for anybody to see. The City of the Angels moved through this valley like a devastating plague. It was ruthless, stupid, cruel, and crooked. It deliberately ruined Owens Valley. It stole the waters of the Owens River. It drove the people of Owens Valley from their home, a home which they had built from the desert. It turned a rich, reclaimed, agricultural section of a thousand square miles back into primitive desert. For no sound reason, for no sane reason, it destroyed a helpless agricultural section and a dozen towns. It was an obscene enterprise from beginning to end.

Today there is a saying in California about this funeral ground, which may well remain as its epitaph:

" The Federal Government of the United States held Owens Valley while Los Angeles raped it."

Hollywood

*A*mong the Middle Westerners who went to Los Angeles during the boom were Mr. and Mrs. Horace H. Wilcox, a wealthy Christian couple from Topeka, Kansas. Mr. and Mrs. Wilcox (the former Miss Daeida Hartell) were active in the Methodist Church, pioneer temperance workers, leaders in the movement that "abolished" the liquor traffic in holy Kansas thirty years before the blessings of Prohibition were extended to the rest of the backward Union. These good people did not go to southern California primarily to speculate; they went to settle down and incidentally to add to the moral tone of a new country. First, they acquired a small home with a fig and apricot orchard on it, and later, when the boom collapsed, they bought a full section of land beneath the foot-hills. They subdivided this land, laid out a town site, offered free lots to all churches, and set out to build an ideal community near a grove of sycamore trees where Father Serra had once said the Mass of the Holy Wood of the Cross.

There is some question as to the original name of the community. Some say that Mr. and Mrs. Wilcox first called their ideal community Holywood. Others say that it was called Hollywood because of the holly trees in the hills. The Los Angeles *Examiner* says that Mrs. Wilcox called it Hollywood because she had once met a woman on a train whose country home was called Hollywood. At any rate — " With such noblemen as founders," inquires the historian Laurance L. Hill, " is it any wonder that such good things have continued to come out of Hollywood? "

Holywood, or Hollywood, was indeed a good town, and a very select one, despite the fact that most of it was a sheep ranch. Even the town livery stable " was without the proverbial department of profane languages where ambitious youths could build up a vocabulary for men only." A Board of Trade booster booklet published in 1904, when the population of the whole immediate countryside was four thousand, spoke of the high-school baseball team as being made up of " boys of such refined rearing that never so much as a word of profanity had been overheard by teachers and bystanders." A wicked city trustee, who voted to license a pool-room, was defeated for re-election. When the Hotel Hollywood asked for a liquor license " as an accommodation to our winter tourists," the city fathers refused the petition.

Retired folk from the Middle West made up the population for the most part. They built houses, surrounding them with orange, lemon, and fig orchards; they lined the roads with pepper and palm trees. Life among these good people was described as " simple and sweet." In 1900 there were five hundred people in Hollywood. When the town was incorporated, in 1903, a law was passed forbidding anyone to drive more than two thousand sheep down Hollywood Boulevard at one time. No jail was needed in this new ideal community. The town marshal was paid the first year in honor and glory. He carried no arms and locked up the occasional errant brother or sister in a spare bedroom of his own home. Later he received ten dollars a month and was provided with a " little rose-covered bungalow as a lock-up."

II

At the close of the century, in New York City, a number of Fourteenth Street showmen and Coney Island impresarios started making the first moving pictures. These gentlemen, mainly proprietors of penny picture galleries, nickelodeons, and honky-tonk shows, sensed something new and good, and, accordingly, the motion-picture industry was started, built up, and is today still largely controlled by them. This new business had a peculiar appeal to their philosophy, the philosophy of the midway, which is described clearly and penetratingly in one of Wilbur Daniel Steele's short stories, *The Shame Dance*. " Just give me," says the main character, " something good that sells for a nickel, that's all. That *makes* me! "

Their new business caught on quickly, and it was not long before nearly every town in the country had a picture show where *The Great Train Robbery* and other thrillers were shown. But not Hollywood. These moving pictures, born in the Sodom of New York, were barred in Hollywood as being sinful. Almost every country town in America had a well-patronized motion-picture theater in operation, not only before a single motion-picture studio was built in Hollywood, but before motion pictures were even allowed to be shown in Hollywood. The residents of Hollywood missed the first masterpieces of Biograph, Vitagraph, and Essanay.

There was one drawback about the business in New York. In those days sunlight was required for the outdoor " shots," and there were many gloomy days in Brooklyn, where the first studios were built. In 1910, therefore, two young Hebrew pioneers pulled up stakes and took their business to southern California, where the sun shines about three hundred and fifty-five days a year. Looking round for a workshop, they rented an old barn in peaceful Hollywood (of all places), and there, among pastoral scenes and Hard-shell Baptists, the first crude motion-picture studio was established, quickly to be followed by half a dozen others. The population of the town was seven thousand. There was strong protest among the populace against this invasion of sin, but the real-estate dealers won out, as usual. The protests were hushed, and Hollywood entered upon a new life.

The first producers were short on art, short on cash, but long on business acumen. They had no money to employ well-known actors, nor was that necessary, or even possible; for well-known actors laughed at them. So they went through the stock companies and agencies and took on cheap " ham " actors out of work. They had no money to pay for good stories; nor were good stories needed; accordingly, they employed the worst of the pulp-wood hacks to throw their crazy narratives together. Thus the motion-picture industry, from the beginning, was almost exclusively in the hands of the lowest type of business men, the lowest type of actors, and the lowest type of writers; to wit, honky-tonk impresarios, hams and hacks.

A little later the producers even quit looking for professional ham actors; for even a professional " ham " had some " artistic " scruples and dignity, some dramatic training, which was an obstacle to the business. The producers began picking up anybody, everybody, to do the play-acting: amateurs, hash-house waitresses, clerks, home-talent performers, cowboys — *types*. It was not necessary then, nor was it ever necessary until the advent of the talkies, for a person to have any experience or any intelligence whatsoever to become a motion-picture star. That should be clearly understood.

Indeed, the dumber the " actor " — some of them were illiterate — the better material he or she was for " stardom " in the hands of the cloak-and-suit directors and the pulp-wood dramatists. Anybody could be a motion-picture actor who could do what he or she was told to do. There were no lines to learn or speak; nothing to remember; no audiences to face; no theatrical training of any kind was needed. All one had to do was what the " director " said to do, while a camera took pictures of it. If it wasn't done satisfactorily, it was done over until the æsthetic demands of the director were satisfied. The less one knew, the better. Any knowledge of acting, of the drama, of the theater, was a hindrance. This was demonstrated in the case of Lionel Barrymore, who was somehow seduced into the movies twenty years ago and played in many of the " middle-period " pictures. In the hands of the morons who directed him and with whom he acted, he was never a success and remained a failure as a motion-picture star until the movies caught up with him a few years ago.

Everybody knows why the movies made so much money from the start. If you take a photograph with your pocket camera, pay ten cents to have the negative developed, five cents each for fifty additional prints, and get one hundred legal voters to look at each print for one cent a look, you will make plenty of money. That is the economic foundation upon which the motion-picture industry rests, and it was, as I have said, one which appealed peculiarly to the gentlemen who started the business in New York and expanded it in Hollywood. They made a picture, and a hundred prints of it were made, sent out, and shown simultaneously for five, ten, or twenty-five cents in a hundred towns this week, a hundred more next week, and so on. Money poured in to the producers.

Of this returning flow, all who had contributed to the picture demanded an increasing share of the profits. First and foremost of these was the "star." Had not actors always been paid according to their drawing or box-office power? They had, and now when these hams appeared in a picture, they appeared in a hundred towns simultaneously. The returns from one town might be poor, but the total of all for a particular night, week after week, was more than Duse, Bernhardt, and Jefferson combined ever dreamed of. The flood of publicity served further to popularize the actors, and the returning "fan" mail added to their conceit and gave them a definite financial club to use on the producers. Thus within a very few years the moving-picture actors — the best of them stock-company hams, and the worst of them of types so low as to beggar description — were demanding and getting increasing " cuts " of the profits — a thousand dollars, five, ten, fifteen thousand dollars a week! Next came the " scenarists " — that is, the pulp-wood hacks. Their salaries jumped from thirty-five to a thousand dollars a week. As for the business men who ran the works and were soon rolling in wealth, they had only one thought: the more they made, the more they were willing to pay.

The growth of the motion-picture industry in Hollywood resulted in two things. First, this growing group of Thespians were not moving round, but were staying in one place. For the first time in the history of the whole theater the actor ceased to be a transient, a wanderer on the face of the earth, a trouper. For the first time he was able to take root, identify himself with the community, acquire and live in a permanent home. And this happened, bear in mind, to the most grotesque gang of play-acting mummers ever assembled in Christendom. Secondly, the fabulous sums coming in to them created in Hollywood an altogether new type of *nouveaux riches*, the most interesting and amazing of all. The movie actors were (and are) far more comical than newly rich oil millionaires, war profiteers, or ordinary folk suddenly left large sums of money. For, in addition to all the other contributing factors, the movie stars were " public characters," besought by fan mail, covered with the axle-grease of publicity; unreal dummies built up into something artificially real.

Outside of investing in fake oil stocks and perpetual-motion machines, and buying diamond fountain-pens, gold brassières, red-white-and-blue automobiles, and German police dogs, these morons — with very few exceptions — had, and have, no more idea of what to do with money than so many Osage Indians. They were (and are) angels from heaven for anybody and everybody who had something to sell, provided only that it was *costly, gaudy, and bizarre*, and provided the salesman had " front." Particularly, they were made to order for realtors, architects, clothiers, interior decorators, landscape gardeners, and domestic servants. There sprang up in Hollywood, therefore, and in the surrounding hills, ravines, canyons, and sand-dunes, the most amazing collection of " homes " ever seen on earth. Could Valencia Sunburst (*née* Minnie Jones, 226½ Dallas Avenue, ring O'Flaherty's number, or leave message at Schulte's delicatessen store), the great mysterious star of the silver screen and silent drama, be content with a mere Italian, or Russian, or German castle? The answer is: No.

She must have — and you will find her (or her male counterpart) in it today — a home concocted from the best of all styles and periods and climes. The movie stars built English manors with French drawing-rooms, Spanish patios, Pittsburgh dining-rooms, Italian gardens, German music-rooms, Greek sun-rooms, Swiss kitchens, and Kansas City libraries. They put Russian brasses in the Pittsburgh dining-rooms, Chippendale chairs in the Spanish patios, Czechoslovakian tapestries in the Greek sun-rooms, Chinese urns in the Swiss kitchens, mechanical pianos in the German music-rooms, Indian throw-rugs in the English butlers' pantries, " Los Angeles " settees in the French salons, Irish heather in the Italian gardens, and, what seemed even more unusual, books in the libraries. Throw in nine automobiles, a flock of English and Japanese servants, stucco sculpture, an onyx swimming-pool, some swans, some dogs, and a huge American flag waving from the top, and you have a typical motion-picture star's home in southern California.

The uneducated reader may wonder what a " Los Angeles " settee is. This style of furniture was officially described at the National Home Furnishing Style Show held two years ago in Los Angeles as follows: " To the long list of special periods such as Chippendale, Georgian, Hepplewhite, Federal American, Louis XV, and Louis XVI, is now added the new expression ' Los Angeles.' In ' Los Angeles ' furniture there is a trace of the old Spanish, a bit of the missions, a touch of the Orient, a shadow of the past, or of some period once recognized as separate and apart." " All of which," adds Mr. Rob Wagner, editor of *Rob Wagner's Script*, " adequately describes the kitchen stove."

Anne O'Hare McCormick, in a recent article in the *New York Times Magazine*, describes Hollywood " at its best." " At the top of a climbing road, hidden behind a white wall, Pickfair. . . . The house is just remodeled, white inside and out, the rooms white-paneled, carpeted in white or faded green, furnished with eighteenth-century treasures, with cabinets full of white jade, blond de chine and Waterford glass, with old brocades and new chintzes. . . . Douglas's Chinese dressing room, with its panels from a Ming temple. Mary's collection of Cinderella slippers . . ." If this is Hollywood at its best — and we have Miss McCormick's word for it — the reader may imagine Hollywood at its worst.

Recently Hollywood and Beverly Hills automobile-dealers, real-estate firms, florists, grocers, and other mer-

chants were offering " $5,000 reward for evidence show-
ing that we pay commissions to any butler, housekeeper
or other servant " of motion-picture stars. This led one
butler to depose in the *Script* as follows: " Of course
there is graft among the butlers here. The picture
people? I've worked for many. They are a fine lot,
most of them. Of course they don't know service,
but why should they? They hire me for that. Mr.
Goldwyn has the best service in Hollywood. He's had
good butlers for twenty years. In two years he gave me
thirty suits of clothes. Of course we ' graft ' as you call
it. Aren't we entitled to our commissions? Most of the
people we work for don't know glass from plate, leave
the table to answer the telephone, and get in and out of
their automobiles without waiting to have the door
opened. Most of them are just bums and we have to
teach them etiquette. They even ask us to word in-
vitations. All that is worth extra, but we don't get it,
so we take it out in commissions. Anyway, most of them
throw their money away, so why shouldn't we get a
slice? "

From a discussion here of all the Hollywood scandals,
orgies, dope parties, sexual obscenities, and murders
which have entertained the public in recent years I must
respectfully ask to be excused. This book is intended
for family reading. As night editor of the Associated
Press at Los Angeles I put many of them on the wire.
It will suffice merely to recall that in 1923, when " Woe
was deep in the Kingdom of the Screen," all of these
morons, like the professional baseball-players, had to
have a sort of guardian placed over them. The job was
offered to William Gibbs McAdoo, who threw up his
hands in holy horror. It was subsequently accepted by

Deacon Will Hays, since known in Hollywood as " the Deliverer."

Take the stars, press agents, directors, literary hacks, producers, and their families and servants, add to them thousands of technicians and other honest working people connected with the industry, plus hundreds of " unprofessional " *nouveaux riches*, plus the average run of merchants, bootleggers, bankers, realtors, school-teachers, and plumbers, plus seventeen thousand " extras," and you have Hollywood. Physically the town proper looks like any other part of Los Angeles; you do not know when you come to it, nor when you leave it, except for the signs and Hollywood Boulevard, the Main Street. This is a broad thoroughfare with street-car tracks in the middle, lined with bizarre, claptrap buildings in pinks, greens, and eye-blinding, sunstruck whites. The best-looking building in the town is the popular Krotona Institute of Theosophy.

" Hollywood at night," says Cornelius Vanderbilt, Jr., " is marvelous. Those new Neon lights with their soft optic-pleasantness. No Eastern city with so many; they are still in the mechanical Mazda stage. The brilliant Neons make of Hollywood Bull the lane of lanes."

The business men of Hollywood are full of ingenuity and dignity, as befits caterers to the film stars. A few years ago they decided that the word " merchant " was beneath their dignity, and the name of their organiza-tion, the Retail Merchants Association, too common. So they changed the name of their organization to the " Merchantors' Bureau," and became themselves " Merchantors." This title, however, is conferred only upon green-grocers, interior decorators, and automobile-salesmen who belong to the Chamber of Commerce.

The word " Merchantor," like the distinguished noun " realtor," is copyrighted, and, for all I know, I may be arrested, and my publisher sued, for using it here. However, as we say in Kiwanis: " *Absit Invidia. Ære perennius Merchantor est. E pluribus unum.*"

III

Ten years ago Mr. Sid Grauman, a veteran San Francisco showman, decided that it was meet and proper that Hollywood, the film capital of the world, should have the finest, the most artistic, movie theater in the world. He also perceived that no ordinary theater would fit into that bizarre atmosphere. So he built on Hollywood Boulevard the first " movie cathedral " in America, and he went as far as he could go, both in miles from Hollywood and into antiquity, for his leit-motif; no doubt on the theory that the less the movie stars and the other patrons knew about the subject, the more freely he could express himself. The result was a perfect addition to Hollywood, an architectural crazy-house; to wit, Grauman's Egyptian Theatre.

" Nestled beneath the empurpled hills of the cinema capital of the world, Grauman's Egyptian Theatre, as an internationally famed palace dedicated to Thespis, conjures visions of ancient Egypt in all its triumphant glory. This temple of art is a replica of a palace of ancient Thebes, profusely embellished with Egyptian hieroglyphics, drawn from the monuments to the Theban kings, and presenting the symbolic stories of the gods and goddesses of the Nile. At night it glistens in the aura of brilliant lights. The façade of the theatre presents huge Egyptian columns surmounted by a massive strut of stone. Along the top of the walls, all day long, silently promenades a Libyan sheik in the garb of the desert. Entering the great foyer the visitor is greeted by beautiful girls as usherettes, dressed after the manner of handmaidens of Cleopatra. The auditorium is surmounted by a great dome from which hangs an enormous chandelier of Egyptian design, all wrought in colors of gold with golden iridescent rays emanating from an ingenious system of concealed lights, giving the effect of a colossal sunburst."

Thus runs, in part, the official description of the "Egyptian." This amazing theater was a great success from the start — so great a success that Mr. Grauman soon built a second monument to the art of Hollywood and the ages; this time, Grauman's "Chinese" Theatre.

"The usherettes, the majority of whom are Chinese girls, are given a rigid schooling for their tasks. They are garbed in gorgeous oriental costumes and are trained to the minute in courtesy to guests.

"The use of the Chinese style as a source of inspiration has followed along a totally unexpected and spectacular line.

"The giant elliptical forecourt is an unique Grauman conception. High on one of its towering walls is the horn of the largest victrola in the world, which entertains visitors before performances and during intermissions with South Seas melodies.

"The finishing touches are now being put upon a replica of a Polynesian village in the forecourt arranged by Grauman to entertain patrons and sightseers. It will be complete in every detail and natives of the South Pacific islands will be seen about their daily tasks."

While the concrete in the forecourt of the "Chinese"

was still wet, Mr. Grauman had a number of the most *distingué* stars come down and put their feet in it. When it hardened, the footprints of the immortals were preserved for posterity, not in the sands of time, but in the concrete. Another *Oriental* feature of the " Chinese," along with the Polynesian village, is the huge " Royal Carriage of Napoleon," that well-known Chinaman.

Realizing that the stars would come to his theater to be seen by " their public," and that the public would pay huge prices to see the stars " in person," Mr. Grauman invented the " premier " — the initial showing of one of the " super-special " films. The tickets for a premier sell for five dollars each; they are bought by the public to see the stars, and by the stars to be seen by " their public." Mr. Wagner describes the premier in the *Script:*

" On the night of a Grauman pre-meer, Hollywood goes carnival. Atop skyscrapers huge squirt lights scrape the heavens with monstrous brushes of light, whose stacatic strokes wig-wag the exciting news that Phyllis Haver is to vamp around in her newest and stingiest undies, or that Daryl Zanuk is about to drown everybody on the Warner lot. Nor is the illumination confined to the heavens. Hollywood Boulevard is a blaze of light supplied by terrifying power wagons roaring their amperish tocsins, and the vari-colored flood- and bank lights that illumine the palace where the epic film is to be shown. Press and police cars rush hither and thither sirening a warning to the surging throngs to hurry if they wish to see the ' stars ' arriving in their golden chariots.

" Like all good medicine men, Sid stages a better

A "PREMEER"

AT GRAUMAN'S CHINESE THEATRE

ballyhoo than the show inside the main tent. With this in view he builds his theatres with huge plazas in front to accommodate non-paying rubbernecks that the biggest auditorium in the world could not contain. By three or four o'clock in the afternoon the excited yokelry begin to arrive, packing camp stools and box lunches against a five hour wait. Just to breathe the same air that royalty uses is thrill enough, but to be close enough to touch the hem of Joan Crawford's garment or to pick up Gary Cooper's unfinished cigarette simply turns their tired legs to tallow.

" At 8:30 the first royal carriage arrives; the queen, assisted to the pavement by two footmen in powder and plush, emerges and faces a battery of lights that would Klieg the eyes of a Salamander. Her Highness sweeps the multitude with her imperial and mascaraed eyes. ' Just a moment, Miss Garbo, while we take your picture! ' The loud-speaker gag serves two purposes — to identify the queen and to hold her long enough to give the crowd an eyefull. Instantly a great battery of cameras begins to click and the queen, feigning modesty, submits to a few seconds more of her daily grind. Only one — if any — of the cameras is loaded and it is cranked only on the most important celebrites. Stars of the second magnitude face filmless magazines.

" Following the phoney tableau, comes the grand trek to the palace entrance. The queen advances, followed by her solemn entourage. ' Look, there's Irene Rich! Isn't she dear? ' ' And, Oh, Min, here comes Patsy Ruth Miller! Jest look at them sables! I'll bet they cost ten thousand dollars! ' ' Good God, Gert, it's Lew Cody! —and he smiled at me! ' ' Stand back, please, lady's fainted.' "

And Anne O'Hare McCormick, writing in the *New York Times Magazine*, adds the following touch:

" The élite of the movies crossed a high bridge erected across the street in front of a theatre. This ' bridge of stars' was a temporary gangway ablaze with clusters of huge incandescent flowers and raked by Klieg lights like a battery of suns. The stars were announced by megaphones; in ermines, sables and similar equivalents of the imperial purple, like royalty on a balcony, they bowed to the plaudits of the populace.

" The throng was so dense that the pedestrian could not fight his way within a block of the place. The parade took place under an awning a block long, lighted like an operating table, between solid walls of gaping people. In the theatre the spot-light was thrown upon the audience, always the feature of these entertainments. Here, indeed, were the real figures of the screen, in full gala.

" They were a little stiff with awareness of that fact, a little blank with make-up and self-consciousness."

IV

All the wild wild excitement of the Hollywood studios, all the " artistic problems " of Hollywood, amount to nothing. All the directors and all the " stars " (however highly paid) are mere puppets; marionettes, and technicians who work them. There is not one of them who could not be replaced in ten minutes. Recently a director — to spite one of the highest paid female stars, who had rebelled against his authority; to show her that what she did was no more than any pretty moron could do — went out in Los Angeles and selected a hash-house waitress to play the stellar role in the love-story which had been selected for the star. I saw part of this picture made; the direction was something like this: " Your sweetheart has just left you, see? You love him. It makes you sad, see? You cry." Then a small orchestra played *Hearts and Flowers,* or something simi-lar, and the little hash-house waitress, urged on by the director, began feeling sorry for herself. Tears welled up in her eyes; she was emoting. Then the scene was shot. The picture was a success, the publicity faucet was turned on, and now the former little hash-house waitress is a famous star herself.

And why not? It makes no difference to the business men who control the industry which little Dottie Dimples is used, nor how, so long as the product sells. Holly-wood is merely the factory, the assembly plant where the film is canned for export. New York is the controlling point. In a recent discussion of the making of a picture called *Body and Soul* the magazine *Fortune* de-scribed the real, inside workings of the motion-picture industry:

" Meanwhile the Fox Film Corporation is to be found in several places at once throughout the Union. In the person of William Fox, it is striding across a cool November golf course on Long Island, in gray sweater and comfortable shoes. Once the absolute monarch of the corporation, Mr. Fox has been removed from every-thing except the board of directors and a $500,000 ' salary.' . . . Harley L. Clarke, new Fox president . . . is seated in the office of Fox's new banker, Albert H. Wiggin, in the Chase National Bank, Manhattan. They are discussing a proposition advocated by A. M. Bowles, division manager of Fox West Coast Theatres, for the purchase of a chain of seven Pacific coast theatres from Paramount Publix for $20,000,000; these to be added to the 1,250 theatres already under Mr. Clarke's wing. Since ' Body and Soul ' is merely one of fifty-three equivalent features produced by Fox in 1930, Financier Clarke is not particularly conscious of the gigantic preparations of Mr. Santell (the director) and his staff for the filming of it. Mr. Clarke is much more conscious of the fact that the fifty-three features, together with shorts and comics, together with the Fox theatres throughout the world, should earn a 1930 net of some $10,000,000 (after interest charges of more than $4,600,-000), in order to pay the important $1.00 quarterly dividend. . . .

" By way of contrast, there is Winfield Sheehan, vice president and general manager of Fox. . . . Mr. Sheehan came to the cinema by way of the newspapers and the secretaryship of the New York Police Department. . . . Mr. Sheehan is installed in his suite in the Savoy-Plaza, Manhattan, which includes an office and several telephones. While he is just as conscious as Mr. Clarke that the $55,000,000 of short-term notes must be refinanced next April (this will finally be done by the sale of Loew stock and by issuing $30,000,000 of five-year debentures) and while he too knows that the Fox 1930 net ought to equal $10,000,000, he is at the same time aware that ' Body and Soul,' specifically, should earn about $125,000 of this sum. . . . At the Savoy-Plaza today he is preparing to make a seven-league leap back to Hollywood where, in the ample sitting room of a mansion which he has assembled from all parts of the world, he will have the ' rushes ' of ' Body and Soul ' thrown onto his private screen, evening by evening, as the studio turns them out. And if he does not like them he will talk disagreeably the next morning through the side of his mouth."

A few months ago Mr. Ben Hecht, the distinguished author, broke a fifty-thousand-dollar contract in Hollywood and departed, leaving behind him this benediction:

Come flicker forth, you squawking hams,
You pasteboard heart and candied woes
You little gibbering diagrams
Of silly plot and infant prose.
Your hour is brief, make your salaams.
Grinning outside your pasteboard rows,
Lean and muttering fervent damns
Our gallant Thespis thumbs his nose.

Your gags and wows and slapstick whams,
And all your pansy Romeos,
And all your billboard oriflammes,
And all your Zukors, Myers and Loews
Will cash in for a load of clams.
Outside your door in threadbare hose
A-dreaming of his dithyrambs
Our gallant Thespis thumbs his nose.

Late weaned on penny arcade shams,
Oh, idiot child tricked out with Bows,
Whose adenoidal yapping crams
These Paramountish patios,
The ashcan waits your mechanams;
Art never yet turned up its toes —
There shivering on his outcast gams
Our gallant Thespis thumbs his nose.

Grind out your sterile panorams
Oh, Camera, God of Smirk and Pose,
Buy up the Friars and the Lambs.
All your Janes in underclothes
And all your bankers' high flim flams
Can't change the cabbage to a rose.
One look at you and Thespis scrams
Into the night to thumb his nose.

PART FIVE

Aimee Semple McPherson

*I*n addition to its pre-eminence in the fields of material progress, morality, and patriotism, it is universally recognized that Los Angeles leads the world in the advancement and practice of all the healing sciences, except perhaps medicine and surgery. Eastern medical science having failed either to rejuvenate the members of that multitude of the aged which each year escapes from harsh winter, or to perform magic for the accompanying army of the sick, many of these people gravitate naturally to the practitioners of divine healing, fortune-telling, and miracle-making, all of which are legalized professions in Los Angeles. The City of the Angels has more osteopaths than any city in the world, and in proportion to its own estimate of population three times as many chiropractors as any other municipality on earth.

The city is internationally famous for its metaphysical versatility, and each year erstwhile Christians in alarming numbers desert the orthodox evangelical churches for temples more bizarre. It is largely, perhaps, a climatic phenomenon. After the frozen folk of Vermont and Wisconsin have been exposed to the melting atmosphere of southern California for ninety days, a subtle change comes over them. Thereafter they demand something more exotic, if not more erotic, than the frigid stuff to which they have been accustomed. This accounts for all the theological love-cults and spiritual schools of sex aberration. Briefly, it may be set down that any geomancer, soothsayer, holy jumper, herb-doctor, whirling dervish, snake-charmer, medicaster, table turner, or Evil Eye — practising any form of black magic, demonology, joint-jerking, witchcraft, thaumaturgy, spirit-rapping, back-rubbing, physical torture, or dietical novelty — any such will find assured success and prosperity in Los Angeles despite fierce competition. All kinds of quacks, therefore, have poured into Los Angeles and southern California for the last twenty years.

The greatest of these, one of the most remarkable women on earth, was, and is, the Reverend Aimee Semple McPherson.

II

The world's leading evangelist was born in Canada, in answer to a prayer by her mother, Mrs. Minnie (" Ma ") Kennedy, who asked God for a baby girl, that she might be a preacher. Mrs. Kennedy had wanted to be a preacher herself, but an early marriage, motherhood, and other things had prevented it. Later, however, Mrs. Kennedy did become a preacher, for she was ordained by her daughter; and still later, when Mrs.

Kennedy married for the third time, her husband, Mr. G. (" Whataman ") Hudson, became a preacher, too, for Mrs. Kennedy ordained him; and the two ministers of the Gospel lived happily for a week until it was discovered that " Whataman " had another wife.

At any rate, God replied with a shaft of light that He would grant Mrs. Kennedy's prayer, and He did. In her autobiography Mrs. McPherson compares her birth to the coming of Samuel to Hannah. At an early age Aimee was converted at a Salvation Army meeting, but later she grew worldly and pleasure-loving, studied for the stage, and even became a school-teacher. She was reconverted, however, by a young Holy Roller pastor, the Reverend Robert Semple, who preached in " tongues " (that is, unintelligible words). She was so thoroughly converted, in fact, that she fell in love with and married the young disciple. The two young Holy Roller evangelists then went to China as Pentecostal missionaries; and it was not long before thousands of Orientals were being divinely healed, while countless other Chinamen were rolling and talking in tongues. Alas, a heathen mosquito, which knew nothing about divine healing, bit Dr. Semple, and he died of malaria. Mrs. McPherson returned to America, where she married a clerk named McPherson, continuing to preach and practice " tongues manifestations," until her husband " got the tongues " too. However, all did not go well; whereupon God told Aimee to desert her husband. She did so, her husband sued her for divorce, and it was granted him on the grounds of desertion.

Like many a leader of the people, therefore, Mrs. McPherson was educated in the School of Experience. Before she embarked upon her great career in Los

Angeles, she had been a wife twice, a widow once, a divorcee once, and was the mother of two children. She had knocked about the world, seen and known the seamy side of life, met and learned much about many kinds of people. She had been, among other things, a school-teacher in Canada, a missionary in China, a roaming rural evangelist, a barker for a side-show, and a few other things. When she made her great step, she was in the full bloom of womanhood, a mature, traveled woman of the world.

Mrs. McPherson is a strong, healthy, big-boned lady of medium height, about forty years old, and weighs, I judge, about a hundred and forty pounds. She has a proud walk, large wrists and ankles, a finely shaped head, wide hips, broad shoulders, a thick neck, and a mass of heavy dark-red hair — blond and bobbed at the moment. Her smile is wide, engaging, and friendly; her voice is the husky, vibrant contralto of the midway. Sister would be called a handsome woman. There is a certain electric quality about her. She is well fed, cheerful, shrewd, enthusiastic, voluptuous, and full of what the Christian Scientists call M.A.M. (" malicious animal magnetism "). Mrs. McPherson is an excellent sport. In private conversation one of her favorite colloquialisms is " That's Oke." She has a highly developed sense of humor, and more vitality and energy, perhaps, than any other woman alive.

From holy Kansas ten years ago Mrs. McPherson surveyed southern California. As a roaming Pentecostal missionary, which profession she had followed, more or less, for ten years, she had been in Los Angeles once, a half-dozen years before. There she had associated herself with the Holy Rollers holding forth at Victoria

MRS. AIMEE SEMPLE McPHERSON,
THE WORLD'S LEADING EVANGELIST

Hall (where the Holy Rollers still hold forth), and later she had held a tent meeting in Los Angeles which was so noisy and so full of "tongues manifestations" that the police had to be called out to protect the neighbors. She had made money even then, but the commands of God had sent her on. Now she was wiser and older; she had progressed to a conventional, hell-shouting, corn-belt revivalist; she had more vision, and Los Angeles was riper.

Gazing upon southern California, she saw a glorified carnival, with thousands of released Puritans, bewildered farmers, elderly folk, and mental and physical incurables, dallying along the gorgeous midway. Her thirty-two perfect strong white teeth flashed in a happy smile. She perceived that the spiritual needs of those people and her peculiar talents fitted together like ham and eggs. It was good. In the quaint phraseology of the cloth, Sister heard the Call — just as chiropractors, oil-stock promoters, and love-cult leaders were hearing it in all parts of the country — and never did a preacher hear a finer Call with a more unerring ear.

Aimee had no money when she arrived in Los Angeles. She had no friends there. She started her work on a street-corner. Within a few years she had thirty thousand devout and generous followers. They built her a $1,500,000 temple. It has a brass band bigger and louder than the late Sousa's, an organ worthy of any movie cathedral, a female choir bigger and more beautiful than the Metropolitan chorus, a costume wardrobe comparable to the late Ziegfeld's. Angelus Temple, indeed, boasts almost every appointment except a half-mile track and Swedish baths, including an auditorium with five thousand seats, a seventy-five-thousand-dollar broadcasting station, a great commissary, and the classrooms of a university from which five hundred young evangelists were graduated last year. The Temple payroll is seven thousand dollars a week. From the day its door opened, money has poured into it faster than the white-robed, walking cashiers have ever been able to make change.

It is possible, of course, that Sister did not analyze the situation in southern California. Yet it is probable that she did, for the real-estate beagles and patriotism quacks were doing it, and she was superior to all of them. Perhaps somebody told her it was the place for her. Maybe she just lit on it instinctively, as a gold-digger lights on a butter-and-egg man. At all events, she hit it.

There was, and is, nothing mysterious about her success; it was a kindergarten operation of supply and demand. The great majority of people that move to southern California each year are not Sinners. They have been Saved for years. Most of them have been going to church all their lives. Many of them are old, many are psychopathic, many are incurably sick. Eastern physicians prescribe southern California for such people. After six months in the new semi-tropic wonderland they demand new spiritual medicine and a new technique, the nature of both of which is strongly indicated. Fear is no longer effective. Threats of mundane calamities, floods, lightning-bolts, darkness, tornadoes, hail-storms, blizzards — immemorial medicine of theology — work forever in the Mississippi Valley, but they lose their potency in a land where such caprices of nature are unknown. The preachers are seriously handicapped. The only threat left to them is the earthquake; that is an ace, but, unfortunately, it is barred by the Chamber of Commerce. In bleakest Vermont a theological sadist might prosper for years by threatening old ladies eighty-seven years old with hell-fire and damnation; but he has a hard time keeping a sharp edge on their terror for more than six months in a sun-kissed, flower-garden land of eternal June. The Old Testament threats gradually fail to convince. Nature is too kind. In the orthodox evangelical churches where nothing better is offered, the pews become less crowded.

The 1925 church census of Los Angeles, compiled by the conventional churches themselves, told the sad story of decreasing attendance, and Aimee got most of the deserters. " Nine out of ten of her people," cried the Reverend R. P. (" Bob ") Shuler, pastor of the Trinity Methodist Church, " are converts from Protestant churches. Instead of her real estate being worth $300,000, it is worth nearer $1,000,000." And why? Well, these people, as always, were crying for religion. They needed it. They would pay for it. But they no longer cared to be told that a cyclone would hit the wheat back in Kansas if they didn't pile the offertory plate high, or that they were going to hell if they didn't stop necking. Forty years of that was almost enough. What they craved now was a few *assurances* —something brighter, happier, more beautiful. Mrs. McPherson supplied that from the start.

III

Sister substituted the " Gospel of Love " for the " Gospel of Fear." This doctrine, " Love," was as strange in southern California as it is elsewhere in

Christendom. No ambassador of Christ in that section had ever thought of it until Mrs. McPherson introduced it; the others had rejected it at once on principle. Sister substituted the cheerfulness of the play-room for the gloom of the morgue. She threw out the dirges and threats of hell, replacing them with jazz hymns and promises of Glory. The gospel she created was an ideal bedtime story. It had a pretty color and a sweet taste and was easy for the patients to take. She threatened nothing; she promised everything.

Plagiarizing from the Salvation Army, Aimee built Angelus Temple on that great question: " Are You Washed in the Blood of the Lamb? " But Sister went the Army one better. She not only propounded the poser; she answered it. She assured her customers that they were. Next, she invented the " Four-Square Gospel." This was a trade name, based on the supposition that heaven is surrounded by four walls. Mrs. McPherson described the Holy City *literally* — the jeweled walls, pearly gates, golden streets, milk and honey. She said she was not sure — she was not *sure*, mind you, but she had a pretty good idea that heaven would resemble a cross between Pasadena, California, and Washington, D. C. That will give you an idea of what may be expected at Angelus Temple.

The atmosphere bubbles over with love, joy, enthusiasm; the Temple is full of flowers, music, golden trumpets, red robes, angels, incense, nonsense, and sex appeal. The service may be described as supernatural whoopee.

The Temple service is balanced by the stronger medicine concocted and dispensed at the , " Gospel Lighthouse," Aimee's third creation. The " Lighthouses " have been so successful that Sister now has them scattered throughout the United States. Here she introduced a military note, with thrills and bold adventure. The " Lighthouse " was also built to a sure-fire theme-song: " Throw out the Life Line! " The ladies of the chorus are clad in dapper uniforms so much like those of American bluejackets that the Navy went to court in a vain effort to prevent Mrs. McPherson from be-littling the dignity of Our Boys. The typical " Light-house " service leads up to a " Rescue." The grand finale shows a dozen nightgowned virgins clinging to the Rock of Ages, while the wind howls, the thunder roars, the lightning flashes, and the waves beat about them. Sister — magnificent in an Admiral-General's uniform — directs the girl sailors as they throw out the life-line, while a corps of male Coast Guard workers for the Lord sweeps a prop sea with searchlights. The virgins are saved; the curtain descends as the band crashes, the audience stands and cheers, and the American Flag waves triumphantly over all. In New York this spectacle would cost $6.60 in a hellish theater, run by the Devil and Jake Shubert. Sister merely says: " Put your willing hand in your pocket, praise God, and bring out a five-dollar bill! "

Divine healing (though practiced by Dr. Semple) was not, at first, one of Sister's accomplishments. But it was too promising to leave to the lesser quacks; it came logically with time, observation, and prayer. Sister, I understand, has cured cases of spinal meningitis and club-feet. A mere doctor could never cure a veteran hypochondriac, for the simple reason that none would come within forty feet of him. But he goes to Angelus Temple, and when Sister fixes him with her large electric eyes, brushes his cheek with her frankincensed mane, and lays her moist, warm paws upon him, he leaps to his feet, shouts: " Glory to God! " and does a Charleston down the aisle. He is cured. He is cured as completely as if he had sat on a red-hot stove, and without the pain.

Some folks say that Mrs. McPherson does a lot of harm; others that she does a lot of good. Certainly she has never harmed anybody. That idea belongs to the nursery. On the contrary, she has pepped up thousands of elderly people until they see angels flying in a blue light over Hollywood. More, she has probably piped two thousand happy citizens into Ward Five, including one of her chief male disciples and the wife of another. A public service. Watching these good people joking with Napoleon, I always followed Pollyana. It happened for the best. There, gently rebuking Catherine of Russia, they are supremely happy; and, what is more, they are safe from the wolves. Let us be broad-minded, like the Rotarians. If they had not fallen under Sister's seductive spell, they surely would have been the victims of some other more painful quackery; probably Real Estate, or Oil Stock, or Patriotism. They might, indeed, have fallen under the sinister influence of the Better America Federation.

Sister advertised extensively in the papers. One advertisement taken at random from the Los Angeles *Herald* says: " The story of this evangelist is a marvelous one. Joan d'Arc, the loved maid of Orleans, has one no more wonderful." The accompanying picture shows Mrs. McPherson in armor, with a spear in her hand, mounted on a prancing white charger. She fed the poor and gave out clothing. She joined the Chamber of Commerce. Arrested for speeding, her picture appeared in the press the next day in the uniform of a motorcycle cop; overnight she had converted the police; they made her an honorary member of the Traffic Squad. She appeared in the costume of a dashing aviatrix. She made the Los Angeles firemen her " boys " and was credited with getting them a raise in pay. In return they made her an Honorary Chief; she had her picture taken in a fireman's helmet, snapped in the act of receiving a silver loving-cup. She boosted the politicians, posed with babies and tramps. Her flock were not holy snoopers nor vice crusaders, hence the underworld boosted her at every opportunity. She wrote innumerable tracts, and two books, both " inspired by the Lord." One was her *Autobiography*. The other is a *History of the Church from the day of Pentecost to* — the present? Ah, no — *to Christ's Return*. She preached twice a day and sometimes three times, broadcasting all sermons over her radio.

At first all this pleased Los Angeles. And then it began to infuriate the town when the clergy, the boosters, the civic-pride patriots, and the new æsthetes began to realize that Mrs. McPherson, by her success, was making a laughing-stock out of the Angel City in the eyes of the civilized world. She was a magnet, drawing to her the moronic, the bucolic, the sick, the aged — and a whole army of former back-east Christians who, growing mellowed in the warm sunshine of paradise, were turning against the hell-fire religion under which they had quaked all their lives. Angelus Temple was a mirror reflecting the mentality of a multitude of Los Angeles taxpayers and legal voters. How could they call Los Angeles the " New Athens," the " City of

Culture "? How could the city claim to have any dignity, with all this going on? Alas, their own propaganda, their bread cast upon the waters, was coming back, twofold, in their faces — " the Sunshine City of the Lord," they had called it, started by His own angels, the " New Eden," the " Paradise on Earth." The orthodox churches began to rave, all except the Catholic Church. The Protestant clergy thereupon claimed that the Holy Church was egging Aimee on; because, they said, she was " breaking up Protestantism."

Aimee, in short, was embarrassing the town. She became *persona non grata*, and the boosters went out to " get " her, just as they had always " got " everybody and everything else which had embarrassed the town. The campaign against her, from the start, was never an effort to expose mountebankery in terms of sense. There were too many mountebanks in Los Angeles for anything like that. They simply started an under-cover attempt to suppress Sister — and later an open civic crusade to punish her — for making a monkey out of southern California. The under-cover efforts to suppress her began in 1923, with sniping and sowing of discord at Angelus Temple. These under-cover efforts to put down Aimee went on for three years. The open crusade against her started in the summer of 1926, when Sister disappeared in the Pacific Ocean and reappeared thirty-two days later at Agua Prieta, Mexico, with her kidnapping story.

IV

On a Saturday in the spring of 1926 Aimee went to swim in a pea-green bathing-suit at Ocean Park, a beach resort between Santa Monica and Venice, the place where the Italian gondolier, hitherto mentioned, was washed ashore in his gondola. She went to swim, listen to the sad sea waves, and prepare her next day's sermon, taking Bibles and other scriptural books with her. For a while she and her secretary, a pious spinster, sat beneath a sunshade; then Aimee went to swim, while the secretary, Miss Emma Schaeffer, prepared a Sunday-school lesson for the kiddies. Two hours later the secretary calmly reported to the beach police that " a friend " of hers had been drowned. Who was it? Miss Schaeffer did not like to tell. The police insisted. Well, then, it was Sister McPherson! Miss Schaeffer had seen her swimming " way out "; then she had disappeared. An hour later the extras hit the street. Los Angeles went wild.

The following day the congregation of Angelus Temple moved *en masse* to the beach. It is doubtful if such devotion to a religious leader will ever be seen again in our day. The faithful sang hymns, prayed, built bonfires, wept, wailed, and moaned. They kept constant vigil night and day for thirty-two days, played the trumpets, beat the tomtoms, and danced on the wet sand in the moonlight. Fishermen dragged for the body, and deep-sea divers went down for it. Thousands patrolled the beach; airplanes searched, glass-bottom boats from Catalina Island were used. One diver died of exposure. One girl committed suicide, determined to follow Sister to a watery grave, and others were forcibly restrained from casting themselves into the sea. " Ma " posed with a deep-sea diver in his appalling submarine uniform and helmet, and she and Rolf, Aimee's son, posed scattering flowers on the waves.

Angelus Temple offered a twenty-five-thousand-dollar reward for the return of Sister, dead or alive. It stood a month; then it was withdrawn. Obviously, there was no use; Sister was gone. The next day twelve-hour memorial services were held at Angelus Temple. About twenty thousand persons attended. Strong men were required to carry the collection baskets. The collection in cash and subscriptions was forty thousand dollars. " Mother " Kennedy took the pulpit. The reason her daughter's body had not been found, she told them, was because God held it so precious that He had taken it direct to heaven, as He had taken Elijah and Enoch. Over and over she declared: " Aimee is with Jesus! " The Los Angeles *Daily News* pictured Aimee's body ascending from the waves.

The authorities were confused. While some of them officially pronounced Aimee drowned, the coroner refused to issue a death certificate.

The day after the great memorial service Mrs. McPherson staggered into Agua Prieta, Mexico. The facts, as related by her a few hours later at Douglas, Arizona, and a thousand times since, are well known. Sister had been kidnapped by Jake, Steve, and Mexicali Rose. While she was swimming, they came to the water's edge and called her. She was lured to a sedan on the pretext of healing a sick child. The two men pitched her into the car in her wet pea-green bathing-suit, smothered her cries with blankets, and chloroformed her. She woke up somewhere. Her captors held her there for several days. Then they moved to another place. Then they rode a long time. Finally they took her to a shack in the desert. Sister was watching every moment for a chance to escape, but thirty-one days passed before the opportunity came. Jake cut off a lock of her hair, and Steve burned her hand with a cigar.

The night of her escape, the two men had gone away, and Mexicali Rose got paralyzed on mescal. Aimee rolled from her couch, unable to stand from weakness, used an empty tomato-can to cut the thongs that bound her, jumped out of a window, lit in a cactus bed, and then trekked for seventeen hours, across the burning sands, eighteen miles into Agua Prieta. Falling repeatedly from exhaustion, she struggled into the Mexican village, where a kind Mexican family sheltered her, called an American " jitney " driver, and sent her over the international line to a hospital in Douglas. She was not sunburnt; the chapeau the kidnappers had given her was a big floppy hat. Her stockings were not damp; Sister had been too frightened to sweat.

It was the ideal newspaper story: sex, mystery, underworld characters, spooks, kidnappers, hot sands, salt water, cactus beds, public indignation, and religious fanaticism. There was great rejoicing at Angelus Temple. " Our own Sister in Jesus has been found in the Wilderness! Glory to God and Hallelujah! " In Oakland, California, a devout brother dropped dead from joy. The perfect newspaper story. The hunt was on; but not for kidnappers. The quarry was far more appealing — a woman, and not only a woman, but the best-known character on the Pacific coast. The police, however, bear in mind, were not after Aimee. They were after the kidnappers. The mystery therefore came, as few mysteries have ever come, directly and exclusively within the scope of the press. Public curiosity was boiling. The people of southern California, outside of Aimee's own flock, were crying to know every detail — and they wanted her punished. It was a direct challenge to the Fourth Estate.

Where had Aimee been? Whom had she been with? What had she done? The sky was the limit. The newspapers knew that nothing would be barred if they could expose the facts. All the papers and press services did their best; at Douglas, reporters handed out twenty-dollar bills like cigars. But always, directly ahead of them, and again directly behind them, was some emissary of the Lord with fifty-dollar bills.

Aimee enjoyed perhaps five hundred interviews and cross-examinations by reporters, not counting scores by detectives. Unable to pierce her mystery or break down her story, which they knew was fiction, the reporters grew desperate. News columns were turned into editorial columns; each succeeding article was more vicious and indignant. The reporters, I am sorry to say, bullied and browbeat Sister, but they could not make her lose her smile. Not once did she weaken under the threats. " That's my story," she said, " and I stick to it. If you don't believe it, disprove it." She flourished on publicity, which she loves as a calf loves milk. Yet there were some dark moments when she devoutly wished that all news-hounds were in hell.

v

The city, the great metropolitan city, was up in arms and ears. What to do! What to do! Deputy District Attorney Joseph Ryan and Herman Cline, Los Angeles chief of detectives, were ordered to Douglas to bring Aimee back. Aimee's faithful rushed with them, before them, and after them. Thousands went to the Southern Pacific station to see the runaway brought in. And what a return!

Thousands wept and cheered as she triumphantly returned to the Angel City. A pilot engine, loaded to the cow-catcher with armed guards, preceded her train, so that the kidnappers might not get her again. The Police Department detailed special guards to protect her on her arrival. The Fire Department turned out as a body. The City Council and the Sheriff's department welcomed her officially. Fifty thousand people rushed and crowded to get a glimpse of her. She was carried from the train in a chair of roses, and when her feet touched the pavements, the pavements were carpeted with flowers. Los Angeles police officers rushed to her side and became her personal body-guards. They escorted her back to her Temple with a demonstration never surpassed within the United States. Many presidents have visited Los Angeles, but no other man or woman was ever given such an ovation in the history of that city. She was met by Acting Mayor Boyle Workman. There were American flags, music, and flowers. She was photographed in front of the great multitude, standing with a posy in her hands, flanked by the acting Mayor and Superior Judge Carlos S. Hardy. For Aimee, you see, was a political power; her thirty-five thousand followers could swing any election.

Los Angeles was stunned. But then there was a reaction. What crime had she committed? She could not be charged with manslaughter. And a public hoax is not a felony. But catharsis, like love, will find a way, and the desire to do something to this bold woman became a civic mania. Those who shouted for her hide the loudest were the new æsthetes, the boosters, the " good people," the self-conscious civic patriots who were angry because Los Angeles was being ridiculed by the civilized world. They wanted to punish her; and their mouths were watering for salacious details. No, I am wrong; this group did not howl the loudest. The gang which howled the loudest for her hide was composed of the pious and devout brothers of the Los Angeles Church Federation! A half-dozen prominent preachers actually signed and published a demand that she answer certain questions of the most intimate nature. Well, it must have been a matter of business with them; anything to kill a competitor. They demanded a grand-jury investigation to determine where Aimee had been, whom she had been with, if anybody, and what she had been doing every hour of the day and night. For there were startling, awful rumors that the lady had actually been seen with a man!

Aimee was great. She went into action at once. " They will be sorry," she said, " when the next kidnapping victim is taken." For she had learned, while held captive, that another prominent woman among them was slated for the same fate by the same fiends, Jake, Steve, and Mexicali Rose! Who was it? " Mary Pickford; America's Sweetheart! " That held them for a while.

Daniel, Aimee shouted, was kidnapped; why not Aimee? St. Stephen was kidnapped; why not Aimee? Shadrach, Meshach, and Abednego were kidnapped; why not Aimee? Her shoes were not scratched by the desert journey, her clothes were not torn by the cactus? " Why," she said scornfully, " those three Hebrew children came out of a fiery furnace, even hotter than the Sonora sun, without their garments being singed! " Peter, she said, was kidnapped, and he returned with a tale stranger than her own. Even Jesus, she said, was more or less kidnapped, and the situation in Pilate's court must have been much like her own; with some trying to crucify her, and others washing their hands. " Ma " Kennedy was not so bad herself. " I am amazed," she said, " that the Los Angeles Church Federation should join hands with the bootleggers, dope peddlers, and white slavers, in an effort to ruin my daughter."

What chance did these small-town Babbitts, patriots, and quacks have against Aimee?

On the night of July 26 she held her " Devil's Convention " at Angelus Temple. The devils, armed with pitchforks, came out of a crevice filled with boiling fire and were duly presented to the audience as the ministers of Los Angeles, the Grand Jury, the investigating officers, the kidnappers, the Temple workers who had betrayed her, and politicians. Never had her followers given her such an ovation as when a flock of winged angels came out and chased all the devils back into hell. They went wild. " Thank you. God bless you! If you believe my story," she yelled, " shout ' Hallelujah! ' " They shouted — " Hallelujah! " " Now I am like David with Goliath's scalp to his belt! " One moment she declared herself heart-broken, the next she was laughing openly at her enemies and threatening them. " I saw the Lord," she yelled, " walking through the orchard with His ax in His hand! "

Unable to prove her a liar, her enemies finally got her arrested on a technical charge of " conspiracy to defeat justice," based on the claim that she was not trying to help the police find the kidnappers! She went to court in her Admiral-General's uniform, accompanied by a uniformed feminine body-guard of six — and they stole the show. When Mrs. McPherson beat that case in open court, they arrested her on another technical charge, "subornation of perjury," based on the claim that she was trying to prevent somebody from being a tattle-tale. In effect, this amounted simply to saying: "We still think you have been unchaste, and we insist on hearing the details." Under this barbaric assault even Aimee broke for a moment. "Am I," she cried, "a woman, to be deprived of the chivalrous protection with which Americans have always guarded any woman's name?"

The newspapers, of course, had not been moved by any real indignation. At first they had merely anticipated the cry of the mob. Later they were spurred on by the realization of their own failure. But they have never yet been able to tell the public where Sister was during those thirty-two days, how she got away from the beach, whom she was with, what she did, or how she reached Agua Prieta. All of this remains as much of a public mystery as ever. The papers, certainly, have printed tons of rumors, suppositions, insinuations, veiled references, fragmentary and questionable evidence — which failed to stand up in court — deductions, and so on, but that is all. They have never yet been able to print the actual story. The secret stuff is in the archives, to be sure, and I have seen it all. But facts in the archives are not worth much. Until they land on the front page they remain, for nearly all practical purposes save blackmail, as dead as a row of corpses in the morgue.

The Los Angeles *Record* said: " Let's forget it while we are still good neighbors and good friends. Let's leave the mystery of the whereabouts of Aimee Semple McPherson from May 18 to June 23 for time or Providence to reveal. At the worst, Mrs. McPherson is accused by rumor of a moral lapse, and of lying about it afterwards like a gentleman."

All through the battle against tremendous odds Sister fought willingly, with great good humor, and with a superior understanding of the mob mind. Her flock paid all the bills. The mob was an organ; she played on it ceaselessly, and her theme was always the same: " The Emissaries of Hell Persecuting Poor Sister in Jesus." Raising cash to stave off the bloodhounds, she called it the " Fight-the-Devil Fund." She returned every blow with a hearty kick in the pants. If there were times when she grew hysterical, scolded her advisers, and wept, the public was not allowed to witness them.

VI

If all the nonsensical articles and editorials written about Mrs. McPherson were placed end to end, they would reach from the pinnacle of idiocy into half the magazine offices in New York. There is nothing sinister about her. Voluptuous, yes, but not sinister. Sister is human. She has a hearty laugh. She has " It," and plenty of it. Aimee has neither the vinegar of a female wowser, nor the more peculiar acids of a political hell-cat. She is neither a radical-baiter, a scandalmonger, nor a social climber. Her disciples are not holy snoopers. They are not vice crusaders. Her flock spends its whole time getting Saved and rejoicing in the Lord; it is guilty of the great American heresy of minding its own business. Mrs. McPherson is not a political parson. She was one of the few evangelical leaders who did not join in the national crusade against Al Smith. The pull there was tremendous. Los Angeles, bear in mind, is Mrs. Mabel

Willebrandt's home town. Mr. Hoover was not only the favorite California prodigal son; he was also a native-son brother to every Iowa farmer in Los Angeles. In southern California they were howling for Al's gizzard. Sister herself was under attack. Here was a Heaven-sent opportunity for her to divert the indignation against herself into the greater wave of hatred and fear of Al Smith and to ride back to a popularity she had never yet attained on the crest of religious bigotry. There are not many Christians, I judge, and probably no other ambassador of God in the United States, who could have resisted that impulse. I do not say that a sentimental regard for common decency inspired Sister; nor do I say that it did not.

The California Legislature finally put Aimee on the rack in a final effort to make her confess adultery. Sister had confounded the Babbitts of southern California, their police, their newspapers, their courts, their clergy, and thousands of voluntary snoopers. This grand final trap was known as the impeachment trial of Superior Judge Carlos S. Hardy. The jurist, however, was only a ventriloquist's dummy. No one was interested in Hardy. He was just Exhibit A, displayed to prove that Mrs. McPherson exerted a sinister influence over Big Men, as well as over more obvious morons.

That was the final battle — the result of two years of consistent planning and scheming by her enemies. It was the last chance in California to ruin " that red-headed sorceress." In New England they only hanged witches, but we have progressed since then. Defeating the bloodhounds at Sacramento, with the aid of several San Francisco legislators who refused to join in the assault, Aimee has now beaten every interested agency, official and lay,

AIMEE LEAVES FOR THE HOLY LAND
NOTE FOLLOWERS KNEELING IN SUPPLICATION

in the State of California. That last battle was the end of a six-year war; the victory for her marked her complete triumph. She is now free to serve the Lord until the marines are called out. She has even married again.

VII

Mrs. McPherson meets a definite spiritual need in southern California, just as Dr. John Haynes Holmes, Rabbi Wise, and Cardinal Hayes meet it in New York, and just as Bishop Cannon meets it in *all* of his dioceses. She suffers considerably from being a transparent mountebank instead of an opaque one. She is a Fundamentalist; but she stresses Glory instead of hell. She is aware of the possibilities of that place, but she does not exploit it. Hear her: " Who cares about old hell, friends? Why, we all know what hell is. We've heard about it all our lives. A terrible place, where nobody wants to go. I think the less we hear about hell the better, don't you? Let's forget about hell. Lift up your hearts. What *we* are interested in, yes, Lord, is *heaven*, and how to get *there!* "

Does she tell them how to get there? Well, not exactly. She simply assures them, positively, beyond a shadow of a doubt, that they are going there. All old friends will be reunited. Everybody will be a young angel. She calls upon her congregation for confirmation, and they voice it lustily. The shouts of " Glory to God! " — " Hallelujah! " — " Amen! " are spiritual equivalents of " Atta Baby! " — " You Tell 'Em! " — " And How! " Aimee's Jesus is not the wraith of the modernist theologians. He is not Bruce Barton's slick Super-Salesman of Jerusalem. He bears no resemblance to the Anti-Saloon League's celestial Cop. Sister has a greater personal following, perhaps, than any preacher in America. She gives them exactly the type of theology they desire. Are they any more, or less, intelligent than the followers of Bishop Manning or the suave Dr. Fosdick? Do they follow a doctrine sounder, or less rational, fundamentally, than that put out by Dr. Cadman or the Pope? I surely would not say so. It is simply a matter of grading nonsense, with the customers of each doing the grading.

When Sister closes a sermon — she frequently preaches three hours at a stretch — her congregation is exalted and exhausted. She sends them back to their gardens and salmon-hued bungalows laughing and happy, the doubts, fears, and cares of this depressing world forgotten. When she paints the picture of That Beautiful Land on High, the chests of young morons heave; it is a wonderful light that comes into the eyes of the old men with the palsy and the old ladies with the ear-trumpets in the front row. Their faces are illumined, their eyes are stars. Unquestionably, Mrs. McPherson is sincere. She believes what she preaches when she preaches it, just as a politician of the better kind believes his campaign promises when he makes them, a lawyer believes his argument when he delivers it, an author believes his fiction when he composes it. Sincerity, like virtue, is an art. Is Mrs. McPherson a hypocrite? If she is not, living in the United States, she belongs in a museum. She is an opportunist, of course, but so was Lenin. Is she, lastly, a quack? Well, she is a preacher.

Strange Interlude — The Hickman Horror

On December 15, 1927 a " nice-looking, well-dressed " young man called at a Los Angeles junior high school and asked for twelve-year-old Marion Parker, daughter of Perry M. Parker, an official of the Los Angeles First National Trust and Savings Bank. He told the principal that the girl's father had been injured in an automobile accident, and that he had been sent for her. The child was called from the class-room; the young man escorted her into a sedan and drove away. An hour later her father, at his bank, received the following telegram from Pasadena:

DO POSITIVELY NOTHING TILL YOU RECEIVE SPECIAL
DELIVERY LETTER.   MARION PARKER   GEORGE FOX.

Mr. Parker, mystified and alarmed, called up the school and asked for his daughter. He was told by a surprised and quickly hysterical principal what had happened. Parker called his home and then the police.

A few hours later Parker received a second wire. It

had been sent from Alhambra, another suburban town, eight or ten miles from Pasadena, and read:

MARION SECURE. INTERFERENCE WITH MY PLANS DANGEROUS.   MARION PARKER   GEORGE FOX.

The following morning Parker received the special delivery letter:

Secure 75 $20 gold certificates, U. S. currency, $1500, at once. Keep this on your person, go about your business as usual. Leave police and detectives. Make no public notice, keep this affair strictly private. Make no search.

Fulfilling those terms and transfer of the currency will secure the return of the girl. Failure to comply with those requests will mean that no one will ever see the girl again, except the angels in heaven. The affair must end one way or another within 3 days — 72 hours. You will receive further notice, but the terms will be the same.

If you want aid against me, ask God, not man!

The following day, Friday, Parker received another letter:

Fox is my name. Very sly, you know. Set no traps. Your daughter's life hangs by a thread, and I have a razor handy.

Do you want the girl or the 75 $20 certificates, U. S. currency? You cannot have both. There is no other way out. Before the day is over, I will find out where you stand. I am playing a solo, so figure on meeting the terms of The Fox or else —

Fox

Enclosed with this letter was one from Marion Parker:

Dear Daddy and Mother:

I wish I could come home. I think I will die if I have to be like this much longer. Daddy, please do what this man tells you, or he will kill me if you don't.

Your loving daughter,

Marion Parker.

P.S. — Please daddy, I want to come home tonight.

That night, at eight o'clock, there came a telephone call to the Parker home. A male voice said: " Have you the money? Any police around? Will phone instructions in a few minutes."

The call was traced to a drug-store. Police rushed to the place, but the caller had vanished.

The second telephone call to Parker came at half past eight. This time the voice said: " Come to Tenth and Grammercy in your car alone. Dim your lights, bring no police if you want to see your daughter alive. Fox."

Police blockaded the section. Then Parker got in his car and drove to the appointed place. The " Fox " did not arrive.

On Saturday afternoon Parker received another letter. It contained one also from Marion.

Dear Daddy and Mother:

Please don't bring anyone with you today. I cried all last night. If you don't meet us this morning you will never see me again.

Love to all,

Marion Parker.

The other, headed " DEATH," read:

P. M. Parker:

Today is the last day. I mean Saturday, December 17, 1927. You are insane to ignore my terms, with death fast on its way. I cut the time to two days, and only once more will I phone you. I will be two billion times as cautious, as clever, as deadly from now on.

If by 8 o'clock you have not heard from me, then hold a quiet funeral at your cemetery on Sunday, December 18, without the body. Only God knows where the body of Marion Parker will rest in that event. Not much effort for me to take her life. She may pass out before 8 p.m. so I could not afford to call you and ask for the $1500 for a lifeless mass of flesh.

Final chance terms. Have $1500, 75 $20 gold certificates U. S. currency. Come alone in car, license number 594,955. Stay in the car.

If I call you, your girl will still be alive. When you go to the meeting you will have a chance to see her. Then without a second's hesitation you must hand over the money, any delay will cost her life.

Don't blunder. I have certainly done my part to warn and advise you.

Parker received another call at half past seven Saturday night. The same male voice said: " Meet me at eight o'clock at 435 South Manhattan Street, pay the ransom, and get your daughter."

At Parker's urgent request, police did not accompany him; nor did they surround the neighborhood as before. He drove to the appointed place, dimmed his lights, and parked. A few minutes later a sedan drew up beside him. A man with a white handkerchief tied over his face pointed a sawed-off shotgun at him and asked: " Where is the money? "

Beside the masked man Parker saw his daughter. He

handed out a package of money — seventy-five crisp new twenty-dollar bills.

The man said: " Don't follow me, and be careful. I'll drive up there and put her out and you can get her."

The man drove ahead a short distance, leaped out of his car and placed a form on the sidewalk, yelled: " There she is," and drove away. Parker hurried to the spot. He found only the torso of his daughter's body, horribly mutilated. The hair of the childish corpse had been carefully combed, the face powdered; the eyelids were held open with thread. The father screamed, and fainted.

II

Within a few minutes thousands of man-hunters were on the trail; radio stations broadcasted descriptions of the murderer; newspapers ran extras; terror-stricken parents shuddered and kept their children indoors.

The entire west coast, Mexico, and Canada were aroused. Never in the history of southern California had the populace been so inflamed.

Parker had recognized the kidnapper. His name was William Edward Hickman, a young man from Kansas City, who had formerly worked at the bank. He had been suspected all along, from descriptions given by the school principal, telegraph clerks, and others. The newspapers published full-face photographs of the " Fox." They revealed a handsome, husky, healthy-looking nineteen-year-old boy. The serial numbers of the seventy-five twenty-dollar bills were published and broadcast.

This grewsome crime threw Los Angeles into hysteria. Every man became a policeman. The papers screamed: " Every citizen has the right to arrest a criminal. If you see any person that looks like this man, hold him. Do not let him get away! "

As a result, a dozen young men were " arrested " by citizens; their lives were jeopardized, some were beaten up, others appealed to the police for protection. Every road, very street, every exit from Los Angeles was guarded. For three days practically every car going out of the city was stopped and searched.

The day after the torso was delivered, the other parts of the body were found in a suit-case containing blood-stained towels within a few feet of where the body was delivered. One of the towels bore the mark " Bellevue Arms Apartments." Police and detectives surrounded the building, but reported that nothing suspicious was found. That was on Sunday.

On December 22 Hickman was captured at Pendle-ton, Oregon. The emotional storm that for seven hectic days raged in Los Angeles, southern California, and even throughout the entire West was lashed to a feverish climax when wires from the north flashed news that " the Fox " had been caught.

" Hickman is caught! " It ran by word of mouth, by telephone, and then by newspapers, radio, and courier to the farthest corners of California.

Cries from the street, red flashes from the telephone switchboards, dashing of messengers here and there, swept the great city of Los Angeles and smaller subur-ban communities. When newspaper extras came out, men, women, and even children fought for them.

The *Times* said: " Last night the city rested, the first time in seven fearful days and nights. A measure of calmness had returned. But at that crowds waited late into the night around news-stands, newspaper offices and in places of congregation for further word and detail of the triumph of the community over crime. Something of the normalcy of business, community and individual life is expected to return with the coming of today. Children again are safe in the land! "

Captured in a breakneck race with police officers, spurred on by rewards totaling sixty thousand dollars, Hickman was arrested on the Columbia River Highway, near Pendleton, Oregon. He slipped through the net in Los Angeles, escaping a cordon of many thousand police officers, ran undetected through San Francisco in a stolen motor-car, and speeded northward through Portland and to Seattle. There he doubled back and was captured by Buck Lieuallen, Oregon State traffic officer, and Tom Gurdane, Chief of Police of Pendleton.

The prelude to the capture of " the Fox " came when Edward Aldrich, city editor of the *East Oregonian*, telephoned Gurdane: " Hickman in a green, stolen Hudson coach is headed east on the Old Oregon Trail from Portland. He last was seen at Arlington, Oregon, on the Columbia River, eighty-six miles west of Pendleton, where he cashed one of the twenty-dollar bills."

Gurdane and Lieuallen immediately took up the chase. They spied a green Hudson with Washington license plates. The driver wore dark glasses. They stopped him.

Hickman at first denied his identity. Lieuallen searched him and found a purse containing fourteen hundred dollars. Hickman looked at the bills and at the officers. An automatic was also found in the car.

" Well," he remarked then, " I guess it's all over."

It was; the handcuffs already were on his wrists. Aside from a hysterical outburst of laughter, Hickman remained calm.

"I'm the Lone Wolf," he said. "Do you think I will get as much publicity as Leopold and Loeb? "

He told of slipping through the cordon of police.

"I was stopped by four different Los Angeles police officers in making my get-away. Several other officers looked at me and acted as if they were going to hail me; then let me pass by."

III

It was not a sex crime. The child was strangled to death with a dish-towel in the apartment which Hickman had taken at the Bellevue Arms under an assumed name.

"I kidnapped her," said Hickman, "to defray my expenses through college. I killed her because the cops were closing in on me."

Hickman was a " good " boy; he never smoked or drank; he had been a good Sunday-school pupil. He received a voluminous mail while awaiting trial. Chief among the fans were women and girls throughout the United States who sent him love-notes. These epistles never reached Hickman. Each letter of this nature was answered by the county jailer, with a letter to the chief of police in the city from which it came, enclosing the love-note and requesting the officers to " advise the girl's parents." Some of the " girls," alas, were married women; others were widows.

Hickman was tried, found to be sane, and sentenced to die. Nothing exciting marked the trial except that

Judge Carlos P. Hardy, Aimee's friend, turned his courtroom into a theater, numbered the seats, and issued passes for the reserved seats. For this and other eccentricities he was expelled by the American Bar Association.

Hickman was hanged at San Quentin. A few days before he was hanged, he issued a statement:

" I know very well that I have been a most guilty sinner. Nevertheless, I have confessed my sins and I am now trying to do what is right. All glory be to Our Father in Heaven and on earth, good will toward men."

Thousands of southern California citizens made application to witness the hanging; unfortunately, only about four hundred could be accommodated.

He collapsed just as the black hood was dropped over his head. He was unconscious, I think, when the trap was sprung.

Said the Los Angeles *Times* the following day: " Now let's forget it."

Unfortunately, some Angelenos refused to forget it. Hickman's escape from the Los Angeles police, and various circumstances connected with his successful outwitting of the thousands of peace officers, resulted in severe criticism of the police and a storm of protests. For Hickman disclosed that when the cops searched the Bellevue Arms that Sunday, detectives came into his room and talked to him. At the time, he said, there was blood on the bath-room floor, the fifteen hundred dollars was lying on an ironing-board, two guns were hidden in the kitchen stove, and a sawed-off shotgun was lying between the window casing and the screen. For a long time many curious people wondered how the police could have been so dumb. Dumb?

The following interesting resolution was addressed to the City Council:

" Whereas, the Bellevue Arms Apartment is in this district, and one of the most respectable apartment houses in the city of Los Angeles and,

" Whereas, the Los Angeles police department called there Sunday morning, December 18, 1927, looking for the slayer of Marion Parker and,

" Whereas, they visited the apartment of William Edward Hickman with a towel from that apartment and with orders not to arrest him because the City Council, Board of County Supervisors, Los Angeles First National Trust & Savings Bank [employer of Parker] had not been in session [due to the fact that it was Sunday] and would no doubt offer big rewards Monday morning and,

" Whereas, it was agreed by the Los Angeles police department to let William Edward Hickman stay at this apartment until Tuesday until large rewards had been offered and,

" Whereas, William Edward Hickman stole a green Hudson Sunday, after the officers left him, and left town, and,

" Whereas, after the newspapers had printed that the police had been to the Bellevue Arms Apartments and let Hickman go Sunday morning, the police called again at the apartment and asked the manager to issue a statement denying that the police had been there and *let Hickman go* and,

" Whereas, the manager of the Bellevue Arms Apartments refused to make a false statement, the police department bothered the tenants, accusing them of being friends of Hickman, and the owner of this apartment lost thousands of dollars due to the way the police handled the affair,

" Therefore, be it resolved that the City Council demand the resignation of Chief of Police Davis.

Yours respectfully,
North Civic Center Improvement Ass'n.
by Mrs. Clara A. MacDermott, Sec'y."

This was not considered news. It was not printed by the newspapers and is here offered for the first time.

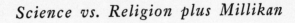

Science vs. Religion plus Millikan

No city followed the Scopes "monkey trial" at Dayton, Tennessee — better known as the " death-struggle between Genesis and the theory of organic evolution " — with more emotional fervor than Los Angeles. No people shouted louder than the Angelenos for William Jennings Bryan to scotch the Devil. For the Angel City was, and is, dominated overwhelmingly by Fundamentalist Methodists and Baptists, who believe not only the miracles of the Bible, but also those closer at hand, seen and unseen. In 1923, for example, so many angels were reported flying in a blue light over Hollywood that followers of a score of sects announced the immediate Second Coming. The Reformed Adventists and a sect of super-Methodists sold all their earthly property, prepared, I suppose, to take the cash to heaven with them when the Angel Gabriel stepped from the Angel Gabriel Mission and blew his horn. Nothing arrived, apparently, but a slight earthquake, causing no little chagrin, but that in itself was taken as evidence that the end had suddenly been postponed at the last minute.

On the one hand, the chief prosecutor of the young school-teacher, Scopes, was William Jennings Bryan. Since 1922 Mr. Bryan had spent his summers in Los Angeles; he maintained a home there, and the Los Angeles realtors were gradually luring him away from the Florida realtors. His son, William Jennings Bryan, Jr., another member of the prosecution counsel, was a Los Angeles attorney and a leading church light.

On the other hand, the chief counsel for Scopes was the despised Clarence Darrow, defender of the Mc-Namaras; one of his associates was Dudley Field Malone, a Catholic, who personified the sophisticated sin of the East; while the other associate was Arthur Garfield Hays, attorney for the American Civil Liberties Union, another slick New Yorker and also a well-known enemy of the labor injunction, the Criminal Syndicalism Act, and other obscenities.

Southern California followed the trial avidly, church congregations, womens' clubs, and civic organizations passing resolutions urging Bryan to " fight the good fight." The final cross-examination of Bryan by Darrow was pasted in huge bulletins on newspaper windows as fast as the questions and answers came over the wire. Huge crowds congregated in the streets, many wearing hat-bands reading " Jesus Saves," and expressing their sentiments in no uncertain terms as the questions of Darrow and the answers of the former Secretary of State of the United States unfolded in telegraph bulletins before their eyes:

DARROW: " And you believe that came about because Eve tempted Adam to eat the fruit? "

BRYAN: " Just as it says."

(Cheers from the crowd.)

DARROW: " And you believe that is the reason that God made the serpent to go on his belly after he tempted Eve? "

BRYAN: " I believe the Bible as it is, and I do not permit you to put your language in the place of the language of the Almighty. You read that Bible and ask me questions, and I will answer them. I will not answer your questions in your language."

(Loud applause from the assembled Angelenos.)

DARROW: " I will read it to you from the Bible: ' And the Lord said unto the serpent, because thou hast done this, thou art cursed above all cattle, and above every beast of the field: upon thy belly shalt thou go and dust shall thou eat all the days of thy life.' Do you think that is why the serpent is compelled to crawl upon its belly? "

BRYAN: " I believe that."

(Applause, and shouts of " Hallelujah " and " Glory to God.")

DARROW: " Have you any idea how the serpent walked before that time? "

BRYAN: " I have not."

(Silence.)

DARROW: " Did he walk on his tail? "

(Hisses and boos from the populace.)

BRYAN: " I don't know."

(Cries from the crowd: " That's telling him! " " That'll hold him! ")

Immediately after the trial, and Bryan's death, when William Jennings Bryan, Jr., came home to the Angelenos sharing the blaze of his "martyred" father's glory, an attack upon science was launched in Los Angeles. It was in three parts, each apparently separate from the other, but all dovetailing to make a perfect whole. The first was an effort to get the Bible placed in the class-rooms of every public school in California as a text-book. There was no chance to get such a measure past the State legislators — most of whom were from the northern and central, or more civilized, sections of the State — who had turned it down in 1923. Accordingly, proponents of the measure circulated petitions and got enough signers to introduce the "Bible Bill" as an initiative amendment to the State Constitution. The question was carried directly to the people. If the majority of them voted yes, the amendment would become the law of the land five days later. It would not be subject to the veto power of the Governor, nor to amendment or repeal by the Legislature. This was the question:

"The purchase with school funds and the use of the Holy Bible in the schools of this State shall not be deemed a violation of the constitution, and a copy of the Holy Bible shall be placed in every public school library and in every public school classroom, and may be studied in any school, or read by any teacher without comment as a part of the daily school exercises, but no pupil shall be required to read the Bible or hear it read contrary to the wishes of his parents or guardian."

The author of the proposed amendment was Mr.

Wiley J. Phillips, editor and publisher of the *California Voice*. This periodical describes itself as follows:

" Now in its fifty-sixth year. Oldest prohibition paper in the world, materially aided in the passing of the Eighteenth Amendment, led the forces that closed the ' Old Crib District ' of Los Angeles, originator and author of the amendment to put the Bible back into the public schools of California. Should be in every Protestant home in California."

The Bible Bill received the unqualified endorsement (by resolution) of the California State Church Federation, the Woman's Christian Temperance Union, the Federated Bible Classes of Southern California, all church brotherhoods and men's Bible classes throughout the State, the Masonic Lodge, the Junior Order of American Mechanics, the Anti-Saloon League, and many smaller organizations. It was also endorsed by many prominent ministers of the Gospel, including Elmer D. Helmes, D.D., Methodist; James Whitcomb Brougher, D.D., Baptist (now head of all the Northern Baptists in the United States); W. C. Buchanan, D.D., Christian; W. E. Edmonds, D.D., Presbyterian; R. P. (Bob) Shuler, D.D., Methodist (the leading rabble-rouser in Los Angeles); William Kirby, D.D., Friends; Bishop William Pierce, D.D., Methodist; C. H. Babcock, D.D., Nazarene; and Aimee Semple McPherson, A.B.C.D.E.F.G. Four Square, the world's leading evangelist. The Catholics, Lutherans, and Theosophists opposed the measure. The Jews, generally speaking, did likewise, although some of the Christianized rabbis favored the measure. The pussyfooting Congregational Church was on the fence; its members were advised to give the measure " careful consideration."

If the proposed amendment won at the polls, the Bible would be placed in 5,155 public-school libraries and in 33,394 public-school class-rooms. The amendment provided that the Bible " may be studied in any school " — in other words, it could be used as a text-book. In the strictest sense of the word, the amendment did not make study of the Bible compulsory, but left the matter optional with the local school-board in each town. Nor would the children be compelled to " read the Bible or hear it read " — if their parents or guardians objected. To be sure, the purpose of putting the Bible in the public schools was to have it read; it was not planned to have the book merely accumulate dust on the teachers' desks. But there would be no compulsion — that is, if you eliminated coercion, precept and example, and the natural tendency of obedience to the local *mores*. If the amendment won, the Fundamentalists announced that they would concentrate on any local school which did not provide for Bible study.

This was the first time in America that the Bible was ever placed directly on the ballot. To the sensitive mind there might seem to be something shocking in the spectacle of dragging the Bible through the muck of a California political campaign and general election. But the Fundamentalists did not see it that way. What they were doing was God's will. Nor did they hesitate to misrepresent the facts or to use any pious weapon in winning votes. Starting their crusade with the assertion that a discrimination was made against the Bible in the public schools which was not made against any other religious book (an obvious falsehood), they asked the individual voter if he would deny the teachings of Jesus Christ to little children — a sanctimonious lie by inference. As a matter of fact, neither the Bible, the Talmud, the Koran, nor any other religious book could be taught in the public schools of California, but all could be used for reference purposes in the library. The Fundamentalists, however, could not be bothered with facts; they were too busy threatening hell-fire and damnation for anyone who got in their way.

" This proposed amendment to the California State Constitution," wrote Mr. Phillips, its author, " will be a foundation, a beginning for an aggressive campaign for non-sectarian religious education of the rising generations. In certain States a program is already in operation which permits school children (if their parents or guardians do not object) to have a half-hour period or longer, on certain days of each week during school hours, to attend religious educational classes that are conducted by representative pastors of the community.

" No denomination or sectarian teaching is allowed in such classes, but children are taught the basic fundamental principles of Christianity; a foundation upon which a sound moral and spiritual structure of life may be built, making them grow into better Americans, with a better knowledge of right and wrong."

Accordingly, side by side with the Bible Bill went its stable-mate, the Miller Bill, which provided that children might be excused from school to attend week-day religious exercises during school hours. The measure protected schools from possible loss of appropriations because of absence of pupils attending church schools and stipulated that students must attend standardized religious schools approved by public-school authorities. These church schools were to be held in Protestant churches and conducted by local preachers. The Fundamentalists contended that separation of schools and religion contradicted the fundamental principal of the whole educational process, and that religious instruction could not and should not be left to the home and Sunday school.

Observing these two measures together, one was able to get the idea. If they became laws, the Bible would be studied in the public schools daily. Once a week the children would be excused to attend the church schools near by. Here the preachers would have a chance to find out what the teachers were telling the children about the Bible, and also to learn the pedagogical demeanor and attitude towards the Scriptures. Any heretics would be discovered and fired. Any children who did not take the Bible work would also be discovered, with subsequent concentration on individual parents and guardians. The groundwork for this holy snooping had been laid by personal-visitation evangelism, which already sent God's workers into individual homes in search of sinners. Thus one of these measures was a check-up on the other, and the two interlocked perfectly. They led to the final Fundamentalist scheme to outlaw teaching the theory of evolution in California. Here was the clear call of the Reverend Paul W. Rood, west-coast apostle of him whose soul went marching on:

" The Bryan Bible League was formed to honor the memory of William Jennings Bryan and to continue the fight he so nobly began in opposing the teaching of evolution in tax-supported schools, and in defending the historic position of evangelical Christianity. The purpose of God in so dramatically taking Bryan from the battlefield at this crisis can be no other than to rivet the attention of the nation on the tremendous issues involved. No man has had the ear of the country and the attention of the world as had William Jennings Bryan. God makes no mistakes. Through his death more people will be reached with his last message and noble fight for truth and righteousness than was done through his life. The psychological moment has arrived. The hour has struck. The call of God is clear. It is for us to take up the sword and continue to fight the battle of God and His Christ. The bugle call is sounded! "

III

Into this atmosphere — down into the busy street of irrational controversy — stepped a scientist peacemaker, Dr. Robert A. Millikan, A.B., A.M., Ph.D., Sc.D., LL.D., *et cetera*, *et cetera*, head of the California Institute of Technology.

Now, Dr. Millikan is a famous man, one of the world's leading experimental physicists. His original work in isolating and measuring the electron constitutes but one of many achievements, both lay and scientific. Anyone sufficiently interested will find under the name "Robert Andrews Millikan" one of the most formidable half-columns in *Who's Who*.

Dr. Millikan is not only a distinguished scientist, a winner of a Nobel prize in physics; he is also a competent business executive, a public-spirited citizen, and a constructive influence. He is popular with the Pasadena millionaires and has a way with them. A few years ago, at the home of the late Henry E. Huntington, he organized sixty millionaires (at a minimum of a thousand dollars per head per annum) into the California Institute Associates. He delivers appropriate addresses to American Legion boys, parenthood conferences, church congregations, and friends of radioland. No praise of the Los Angeles Chamber of Commerce is more unstinted than that to be found in one of his baccalaureate addresses. The newspaper advertisement he signed a few years ago urging the election of his favorite candidate to Congress carried much weight, but, unfortunately, not enough. Last year he wrote a letter to the *Outlook* reprimanding it for criticizing President Hoover.

All things considered, the ancient controversy between Science and Religion was made to order for Dr. Millikan — or, rather, he was made to order for it. He was a great leader of science. He was also (and still is, for that matter) a Christian gentleman; a devout Congregationalist, the son of a Congregationalist preacher. He was reared in that evangelical hotbed, the corn belt, and schooled to the A.B., A.M. point at the Christian college of Oberlin. In a word, Dr. Millikan was a scientist, but he was also a *Christian* scientist. The outlandish theories propounded by the eminent geologists, biologists, and anthropologists at Dayton were as painful to his faith as the effort to put down the theory of organic evolution by the police was to his intelligence.

Whether Dr. Millikan was moved by a desire to placate the fanatics and reassure the morons of southern California, or by Messianic delusions, or by his own deep convictions, the record does not reveal. At all events, soon after the Scopes trial he entered the public controversy with a series of scientific manifestos and theological proclamations assuring the people that he had looked into the matter, and that there was no conflict between *real* science and *real* religion. Beginning with addresses to local church congregations, he quickly broadened his field of publicity to the radio, a national lecture tour, the public prints, and finally books.

What was this *real* religion? There was great curiosity, for millions of sinners had been searching for the true faith for years. Was it the Mohammedan, the Eskimo, or the Chinese? Was it the Christian religion, as understood, taught, and practiced with variations by three fourths of the professing Christians on earth? Oh, no. Dr. Millikan's *real* religion, it appeared, was simply a sort of divine knowledge that one's soul was in tune with the Infinite. That was the *real* religion, and it did not conflict with science. It was beautifully simple. Moreover, Dr. Millikan explained the aims of science and religion. Their aims were identical. That aim was Service. Service, and the subordination of the individual to the good of the whole.

Alas, the good doctor got further and further into the bad lands of theology. The more he said, the more guesses he made; and the more explanations thereof he had to make, until soon he was internationally known as the Great Reconciler. When he got through with science and religion, they were so wrapped up in each other that a Philadelphia lawyer could never untangle them. The closest this great scientist ever came to a definite stand was a full gallop on a supernatural race-track running from Fundamentalism to theism, but his powers of occult observation would have done credit to any crystal-gazer in Los Angeles. In his final philosophical contributions he traveled so far afield into the sweet vistas of unlimited imagination that his original premise, such as it was, was scarcely visible. The whole thing was a conglomeration of metaphysical aphorisms and theological sophistry, suffused in a weird and ghostly atmosphere of obscurantism, with occasional and literal references to Santa Claus.

Dr. Millikan's assurances satisfied many intellectual pussyfooters, but they did not satisfy the forthright and courageous Fundamentalists. After gazing intently at Dr. Millikan's antics for a year, they concluded that the time had come to apply an antidote to all his homeopathic medicine. They resented, as all the faithful of other churches are bound to resent, his talk about the *real* religion. When a Methodist, a Congregationalist, or a Holy Roller, however eminent, starts bragging publicly about his religion as being the *real* religion, he is simply saying that members of other theological sects, Theosophists, Catholics, Hard-shell Baptists, etc., are following an *unreal* religion. Unfortunately, the religion of a Seventh Day Adventist or a Presbyterian is just as *real* to him as Dr. Millikan's religion is to him. So the Fundamentalists resented Dr. Millikan's theological cocksureness. They held most emphatically that there *was* an irreconcilable conflict between religion and science, and, what is more, they immediately demonstrated the fact.

They summoned three pulpit aces to Chicago and then dispatched them to Pasadena, Dr. Millikan's home town. There, in the shadow of Cal.-Tech., playing to standing-room only, the reverend gentlemen made a three-night stand at the Lincoln Avenue Presbyterian Church. The first night Dr. Arthur I. Brown spoke with fire and spirit on " Men, Monkeys, and Missing Links." The second night Dr. Harry Rimmer delivered a scientific masterpiece entitled " Evolution Unmasked." The third night Dr. Gerald B. Winrod went into action. Dr. Winrod is a celebrated emissary of God from the

Kansas prairies, and a leading light of the Bryan Bible League. His subject was "The Mark of the Beast." Hear Dr. Winrod's final shout:

"A hundred thousand members of the Bryan Bible League in California will arouse the Legislature, and a million members in the nation will stir this country and challenge the world. The issue is clear. Shall infidelity in the form of evolution be taught in tax-supported schools? The Bible is barred from the schools of California. We demand that the Bible be taught in the public schools. We demand that evolution shall be barred! Darwinism is an unproven, unscientific, anti-Biblical, and anti-Christian theory, and it must have no place in tax-supported schools. The moral and religious effects of evolution are too disastrous for us to be silent! We must present a united front. We must be organized. With a million members we can say: ' In the name of Almighty God, this modern Baal must go from the schools! ' An aroused populace demands it! Patriotism demands it! The fight is on! "

On election day, which was about three weeks later, the people of southern California went to the polls and voted three to one to put the King James version of the Bible in the public schools of California as a text-book. The bill was defeated, however — by the vote of central and northern California.

In spite of this painful demonstration of fact in his own back-yard, so to speak, Dr. Millikan's intellectual position remains impregnable. He still maintains that there is no conflict between *real* science and *real* religion. And what is his real *science*? I quote from an editorial in the New York *Times* of September 28, 1932, entitled: " Cosmic-Ray Romancing ":

" Your physicist is supposed to be a hard, matter-of-fact measurer who suppresses romantic speculation and talks only of energy, volts, ions and electrons. Confront him with a mystery and he proves to be as human as the rest of us. Consider the cosmic rays. For years Millikan in this country and Kolhoerster, Hess, Regener and others in Europe have been studying them only to their own mystification and ours. . . . And the result? Romance — sheer romance.

" Millikan spins a tale of electrons and protons combining in space, and of resultant cosmic rays that proclaim the continuous upbuilding of the universe, contrary to all the laws of thermodynamics. Jeans holds us spellbound with a poem about stars dying in a fierce radiance and bombarding us with cosmic rays in the process. . . .

" For all the instruments and methods invented to test the cosmic rays, the physicist is still the medicine-man from whom he is descended. . . . That we are actually dealing with something like wish-fulfillments in the cosmic rays is evidenced by the results obtained. Here is Millikan convincing himself that the cosmic rays prove that the universe is self-perpetuating. And Compton, adopting precisely the same methods, reaches the conclusion that the rays are only electrons swerving to the Poles because the earth is a great spinning magnet. What are the cosmic rays? There is no positive answer. We simply try to reconcile what the instruments indicate with our hopes and beliefs and imagine we understand the cosmos."

In using the pronouns " we " and " our " the *Times* is charitable. What it means, obviously, is " they " and " their." The bald truth is that such men are *not even scientists,* in the true sense of that word. They are merely scientific prima donnas. Certainly they are not scientists in the sense that the late Professor A. A. Michelson, whose experiments constitute the spring-board for Dr. Millikan's acrobatics, was a scientist. Professor Michelson was not a medicine-man. One of the few really great men of modern times, the first American winner of a Nobel prize in physics, Millikan's teacher, whose experiments also form the basis of Einstein's theory of relativity, Professor Michelson was a physicist who dealt, oddly enough, only in facts. His successors have added fancy to the business.

At any rate, Dr. Millikan remains to a great many people in southern California — Babbitts and quacks included — the greatest man in the world.

Los Angeles — Today and Tomorrow

*T*wo years ago Will Rogers was asked, among others, to send a message to be read at a Chamber of Commerce banquet in Los Angeles. The banquet was held and the toastmaster read hundreds of messages glorifying the Angel City. Mr. Rogers's solicited telegram, however, was not read. The humorist had wired: " The reason New York is the greatest city in the world is because it never had a Chamber of Commerce."

But Los Angeles, it should be understood, is not a mere city. On the contrary, it is, and has been since 1888, a *commodity;* something to be advertised and sold to the people of the United States like automobiles, cigarettes, and mouth washes. The All-Year Club of Southern California recently announced that in one four-month period it had published " more than 90,-000,000 separate advertisements; 55,000,000 appeared in the newspapers of eighty towns and cities, and 35,-000,000 in national magazines."

Selling Los Angeles is a whole-hearted, hundred-percent civic project, and there is no other enterprise in the world like it. It works twenty-four hours every day in the year, sixty minutes every hour, by every known method of salesmanship, advertising, and publicity. The program of propaganda is tremendous; it is also very expensive, but it brings results, else Los Angeles County officially would not have spent two million dollars, raised by tax assessment, for exploitation purposes every year since 1927. This propaganda goes out to America in a steady flow. For the benefit of the home folks the process is reversed. A six-inch snow-fall in Pittsburgh is a much bigger news story in Los Angeles than a local earthquake.

It is considered very unpatriotic in the City of the Angels for any journalist to spread abroad unpleasant news, such as a hoof-and-mouth disease, a tainted-water scandal, an infantile-paralysis epidemic, a tax trap, or an outbreak of bubonic plague. The idea is to let the tourists find out things for themselves. Any other journalistic view-point is subversive, treasonable, and atheistic. Unfortunately, however, it seems to be impossible to silence the correspondents of depraved Eastern journals.

But if there is no way to gag the spies from St. Paul and Boston, Baltimore and Chicago, there are antidotes, at least, for their malicious venom. After the hoof-and-mouth disease of 1924, when Los Angeles for no sound reason reached the point of hysterics, the *Times* inaugurated a "Friendship Letter Contest." This was a Heaven-sent inspiration, and beautiful in its fulfillment. Every man, woman, and child was asked to write personal letters to persons out of the State, pointing out the glories and the incomparable advantages of living in southern California. The idea caught on like wildfire. Prizes ranging from a thousand dollars down were offered for the best letters. Stenographers, cops, movie stars, city officials, and bootleggers were photographed in the act of writing their "Friendship letters." One banker alone wrote eighty. In what is considered locally a great metropolitan city, boasting a population of more than a million, this infantile movement actually became a civic duty, like voting. The enterprise was a huge success.

It is difficult to imagine the St. Louis *Post-Dispatch*, the Detroit *News*, or, indeed, the Miami *Herald*, asking every man, woman, and child in their respective territories to write personal letters to people residing in other parts of the country in an effort to lure them to St. Louis, Detroit, or Miami! It is even more difficult to imagine the people doing it! The fact that the population of Los Angeles whole-heartedly went in for this project — regarded it, in fact, as a civic duty — shows two things: first, that Los Angeles, a world metropolis of more than a million people, is still in the mental state of "Boost Bellville! — Watch Us Grow! "; and, secondly, that the attitude of the Angelenos towards their city is precisely that of a salesman towards his product, or a football cheering-section towards its team. Here is a spirit of boost which has become a fetish, an obsession, a mania. *Everything* else is secondary to it. A few years ago when the Woman's Christian Temperance Union held its convention in Los Angeles the local members met every incoming delegation at the train, waving flags and oranges, and singing a song to the tune of their famous Prohibition song, which goes:

> Oh, vote for Prohibition
> And you'll outshine the sun —
> And walk the Golden Streets all day!

But the *words* they sang, to the great bewilderment of the visiting White Ribboners, were:

> Oh, southern California
> Is the best place of all —
> The place that Jesus loves the best!

Los Angeles is the biggest " city " in America in area; it has the largest Chamber of Commerce, the biggest woman's club, the largest athletic club, the most sunshine, the greatest this, the loudest that. The boast of the *Times,* indeed, is that it is the biggest newspaper in America; it has more pages and weighs more! The town, moreover, not only has the most of everything desirable; it also has the least of everything undesirable. For example, in a scientific booklet, *The Land of the Beckoning Climate,* by Dr. Ford A. Carpenter, manager of the Department of Meteorology and Aeronautics of the Los Angeles Chamber of Commerce, we learn that " there is less wind in Los Angeles than in any city of its size." The same paper, printed in 1931, pointed out that there was every reason to believe that the weather for the Olympic Games which were to be held in Los Angeles in 1932 would be far superior to the weather for the Olympic Games to be held in Berlin in 1936! There is nothing like getting the jump on these foreigners.

II

Los Angeles is the western capital of the Anti-Saloon League and the Woman's Christian Temperance Union.

On the surface it is the dryest place in America. There is not a respectable saloon in the town. The only places where a person can buy a drink are the Mexican dives and brothels around the City Hall, and a few peep-hole speakeasies, with secret passages. But beneath the surface the town is one of the wettest in the country — a bootleggers' paradise. Apparently, every bell-boy, every taxi-driver, nearly every door-to-door salesman, every tenth motorist, is in the business. They tour the streets in automobiles, making deliveries in brief-cases, suit-cases, sample-cases, and trunks. In Hollywood alone enough liquor is consumed every day to float a battle-ship. In 1925, the last year for which comparative figures are available, 11,290 Angelenos — an average of about thirty-one a day — were arrested for drunkenness. This total did not quite tie the record of Sodom-on-the-Hudson, but for some inexplicable reason it surpassed the record of the sinful and immoral city of San Francisco by three thousand drunks.

In Los Angeles a thing hoped for is a thing to be boasted about to the world as an accomplished fact. For years the city filled the magazines devoted to civic planning, such as the *American City*, with propaganda explaining why Los Angeles was sprawling over a territory of 442 square miles. No mention was made of the real reason — that is, water, the late Mr. Huntington's street-car lines, and the realtors. The propaganda put out was this: " Los Angeles is a planned municipality. It is spreading out to avoid congestion, the curse of the American city." Unfortunately, it has not worked out that way. For it so happens that, no matter how far a city spreads out, the people will congregate in its financial, department-store, and theatrical districts. And it

so happens that all of these in the " planned municipality " are within a radius of eight square blocks. As a
result, the traffic in Los Angeles on Main, Broadway,
Spring, and Hill streets, between Second and Ninth,
is perhaps more congested than that of any other city in
America. All these streets are narrow, the blocks are
short, and all of them have double lines of surface cars,
stopping at every corner. The situation is made worse
by the fact that the traffic lights, set up at every corner,
are not synchronized. Driving in this area during most
of the day is exactly like driving in Pasadena on New
Year's Day. The cars move in low gear a foot at a time;
it requires thirty minutes to go from Second to Ninth
streets. In brief, notwithstanding all the boasting, the
spreading-out plan has been a failure so far as eliminat-
ing congestion is concerned.

III

The chief and great charm of Los Angeles — now,
as yesterday — lies, not in the city, but in the lovely
surrounding country; in the lure of the great out-of-
doors; in the open roads that lead to the mountains and
the sea; in the orange groves, trees, and flowers; in the
mellow sunshine and in the warm, seductive climate.
Unquestionably there is charm in all the bizarre and innumerable novelties, such as lion and ostrich farms and
Egyptian movie cathedrals; in stuccoed wayside lunch-
stands and refreshment parlors built in the shapes of
derby hats and ice-cream freezers; in the spectacle of
fat women rushing to fortune-tellers, and fat men playing golf; in the boundless enthusiasm of the social
climbers and *nouveaux riches*. All of that, together with

AN AIRPLANE VIEW OF THE ANGEL CITY TODAY
IN THE HAZE BEYOND THE MOUNTAINS IS SAN FERNANDO VALLEY

the farmers and the quacks, the tourists and the realtors, the professional patriots and the boosters, the beach resorts and the crazy architecture, make the whole section a sort of outdoor circus.

When you have said that much, however, you have said about everything. When Los Angeles is finally taken up in the hands and squeezed, pressing out of it everything except the substantial fundamentals that go to make up a great metropolis, it is found to be a municipal orange. When the sweet, watery juice is squeezed out, there remains little but a pretty, unnutritious pulp. Daily the Angel City propagandizes itself as "The Athens of the Western World," "The Cultural Center of the West." But it has, in fact, very little to back up its claims except the gushing and gurgling of a multitude of female culture-stalkers, the check-books of retired capitalists, and a publicity bureau.

There are probably more painters in Los Angeles than in any other city in Christendom, but, alas, there is no first-rate artist among all that vast horde of daisy-daubers and dilettante sea-scapers whose easels infest the whole country from Santa Barbara to Laguna. The prize-winning painting in Los Angeles last year was a picture of Angelus Temple, with Aimee Semple McPherson floating in a cloud above it! As soon as the painting was awarded the prize, it was removed from the local Museum of Art as being detrimental to the "dignity" of the city. In a land of gardens Los Angeles is literally a sculptural desert. Musically, it is a place where the president of the University of Southern California bestows the honorary degree of Doctor of Music upon Carrie Jacobs Bond, thus placing the composer of *A Perfect Day* and other musical bon-bons alongside Toscanini. In a city of 1,400,000 population there is not so much as a fifth-rate critic of music, drama, painting, or literature, or one known outside the county. All such work is consigned to safe and hopeless hacks. It is by no mere chance, you may rest assured, that Harold D. Carew, the only competent literary critic in southern California, is with the Pasadena *Star-News*. Los Angeles has no use for critics of anything, except " constructive " critics, which is to say boosters. In the field of beautiful letters Los Angeles is virtually barren. A city one hundred and fifty-two years old, it has no more literary tradition or background or consciousness than Scranton, Pennsylvania. The center of a section as rich in literary materials as any in America, it has produced only one writer of any real dignity or promise, and that one very recently. I refer to Carey McWilliams, whose distinguished biography of Ambrose Bierce came forth somehow out of the welter of lemons, boosters, and Beverly Hills " intellectuals " two years ago.

Here, it seems, we come to one of the *disadvantages* of sunshine, pretty flowers, and orange blossoms. Such an atmosphere may be conducive to boosting and boasting, to daisy-painting and pretty poetry-writing, to playing golf and surf bathing, to long life and a pathological optimism. It is not conducive, it appears from the results, to the creation of worth-while literature. The whole atmosphere of southern California has a great way of reducing the writer of dignity and integrity into a booster, a cheer-leader, and a confector of literary egg-kisses.

IV

At the present moment this great town of Los Angeles — this huge collection of villages — may be appraised without much difficulty. Here is an artificial city which has been pumped up under forced draught, inflated like a balloon, stuffed with rural humanity like a goose with corn. In common with most other American cities Los Angeles has acquired its population largely from the farms and small towns, but there the similarity ceases. Unlike other cities, where this process has been gradual and the subsequent assimilation painless, Los Angeles has lured the yokels so rapidly by the ringing of a bell and the blowing of a horn that the town has never been able to catch up with itself. Endeavoring to eat up this too rapid avalanche of anthropoids, the sunshine metropolis heaves and strains, sweats and becomes pop-eyed, like a young boa constrictor trying to swallow a goat. It has never imparted an urban character to its incoming population for the simple reason that it has never had any urban character to impart. On the other hand, the place has retained the manners, culture, and general outlook of a huge country village. It is highly significant that the people of Los Angeles (population 1,400,000) still speak of going to San Francisco (population 700,000) as " going to the city." In an article on Los Angeles in the September 1931 issue of *World's Work*, Freeman Tilden says: " It is a city hard to lay hold of, and picture; and perhaps the reason is that it is a city not city-minded but rather country-minded." He also compares the Angel City — prematurely, but perhaps with great perception — to Philadelphia.

Superficially and quantitatively Los Angeles *is* a city. It has street-cars, buildings, noise, traffic, theaters, restaurants, department stores, and hotels. Qualitatively, it cannot yet be placed in that category. What makes a city, properly so called, is not buildings, nor the number of people in the buildings, but what goes on inside the heads of the people in the buildings. What makes a place, large or small, actually a village or a city is the presence or lack of a spirit, an atmosphere, of urbanity. " Urbane," says the dictionary, " is opposed to rustic "; and " urbanity " is " the character or quality of being urbane; strictly, the city quality, from the assumption that life in the city results in superior refinement." Thus a community of a thousand urbane people is far more of a city than a community of a hundred thousand rustics. If one were to take a hundred Middle Western towns of ten thousand population each and place them end to end in the prairie, would he have a great metropolis? He would not. He would have a huge country village of a million population, a remarkable sociological phenomenon; and that is precisely what Los Angeles is. It does not have the " city quality." Much has been made over the fact that it has experienced the most amazing growth of any city in America. That, however, is not an asset; it is a liability. The fourteen-year-old boy we read about a few years ago who weighed two hundred and ten pounds and stood six feet three in his socks had experienced the most amazing growth of any person in America, but, alas, he was still in the third grade, and the following year he joined the circus. He was not a Superman, something to brag about; he was merely a freak.

Writing in *Plain Talk* five years ago, I concluded an

article on Los Angeles by saying: " In brief, Los Angeles has now reached the full flower of corn-fed adolescence. What it needs, more than foreign trade or factories, is simply to look in the glass. Some day it will catch up with itself mentally. When that time comes a great, vibrant, world metropolis, worthy of the name, will be emerging as the center of the Pan-Pacific area." I now beg leave to alter that opinion. There is no question in my mind but that the territory known as the " City of Los Angeles " will continue to fill up with people until it has a population of three or four million and perhaps more. But that it will ever be permanently the great vibrant, vital, nerve-center of the Pacific coast I now have grave doubts. The climate is against it. Here is a climate meant for slow-pulsing life; a climate where man, when he gets adjusted to the environment, takes his *siesta* in the middle of the day. Go-getterism in this climate does violence to every law of nature. It is not natural. What keeps Los Angeles " peppy " is the steady influx of people from harsher, more invigorating climates; from the East and from the hardy Middle West. It was a slow town before they came in, and without them it would be as slow and dreamy today as Charleston, South Carolina. The chances are that in a few generations it will settle back to normalcy, and become again in tune with nature, for man has never yet failed to adjust himself to the climate in which he lives.

" More and more," says Mr. Tilden, " as you look at this sprawling giant among cities, you are reminded of Philadelphia. Surely this is the Philadelphia of the Pacific Coast. There are great points of difference, I agree — the face of the landscape particularly. But you have only to travel about the industrial districts, miles upon miles, to see that same peculiarly contented type of workman, the same love of little homes ' across the street from the factory,' the diligence and care for the flowers in the front yard, or the fruit trees and vegetables in the rear, a total lack of the Bohemian spirit, the love of a comfortable, humble existence."

That, as I have said, is not a very good picture of Los Angeles at the present time. But I suspect that it is prophetic. " Los Angeles — the Philadelphia of the West." But let us hope not.

Bibliographical Note

The first five volumes of Hubert Howe Bancroft's *History of California* (numbered XVIII to XXII in his collected *Works*) contain a great deal of documented information about early Los Angeles. Virtually the same facts, considerably abbreviated, appear in Hittell's *History of California*, Vols. I and II. The eight or ten histories devoted entirely to Los Angeles, city and county, naturally treat the subject at greater length. The best of these are James M. Guinn's *History of Los Angeles from Earliest Days to the Close of the Nineteenth Century* (Los Angeles: Chapman Publishing Company; 1901), his *History of Los Angeles*, three volumes (Los Angeles: Historic Record Company; 1915), and *A History of Los Angeles*, by Charles Dwight Willard (Los Angeles: Kingsley-Barnes & Neuner Company; 1901). John Steven McGroarty's better-known *Los Angeles from the Mountains to the Sea*, brought out by the American Historical Society in 1921, in three volumes, presents a colorful and often highly imaginative picture of early Los Angeles and of the development of southern California.

An excellent account of the founding of the San Gabriel Mission (published by the Mission in 1927) is *San Gabriel Mission and the Beginnings of Los Angeles*, by Father Zephryn Engelhardt, historian of the Franciscan order in California. The work is based largely upon Father Francisco Palou's original record, which reposes today in the Cathedral of St. Vibiana at Los Angeles. An interesting monograph on Felipe de Neve, by Orra E. Monnette, was issued by the Los Angeles Public Library in 1930. The early Indians, including the preposterous Yangs, are treated at length, and with careful regard for the scientific facts, in the works of Guinn. Authentic information about the San Gabriel Mission Indians in general is scattered through a series of " Letters " which the squaw-man Hugo Reid contributed to the Los Angeles *Star* between 1852 and 1855. Mr. Reid married the daughter of the chief of the Gabrielino Indians and lived among them for twenty years. A valuable contribution to the literature of early Spanish life in southern California, which also deals briefly with the Yangs, is *Spanish Arcadia*, by Nellie Van de Grift Sanchez (Los Angeles: Powell Publishing Company; 1929). The book is one of a series on " California," edited by John Russell McCarthy.

Colorful and amusing tales of frontier and pioneer life in and around Los Angeles throughout the fifties will be found in *Reminiscences of a Ranger*, by Major Horace Bell. First published in 1881, a new edition of this entertaining book was issued at Santa Barbara by W. Hebberd in 1927. Far more authentic, however, and covering not only the fifties but the whole second half of the nineteenth century, is Harris Newmark's *Sixty Years in Southern California* (Boston: Houghton Mifflin Company; 1930).

In such volumes as *Two Health Seekers in Southern California*, by William A. Edwards and Beatrice Harraden (Philadelphia: J. B. Lippincott Company; 1897), *Through Ramona's Country*, by George Wharton James (Boston: Little, Brown & Company; 1908), and *Adobe Days*, by Sarah Bixby Smith, the reader will encounter much of the color of southern California of the late nineteenth century. A revised edition of Mrs. Smith's work (first published by the Torch Press, Cedar Rapids, Iowa, in 1925) was issued at Los Angeles by J. Zeitlin in 1931. The best book about the Los Angeles of the seventies, oddly enough, is *Los Angeles in South California*, by Louis Salvator, late Archduke of Austria, which was first published in Vienna in 1885. An American edition, translated by Marguerite Eyer Wilbur, was issued by B. McAllister and J. Zeitlin at Los Angeles in 1929.

Other informative books on Los Angeles worth noting are *A History of Los Angeles*, by William A. Spaulding (Los Angeles: J. R. Finnell & Sons Company; 1929), *A History of Los Angeles County*, edited by J. A. Wilson (Oakland: Thompson West; 1880), *Homes in Los Angeles*, by William McPherson (Los Angeles: Mirror Company; 1873), *The Romantic Southland of California*, by Marshall Breeden (Los Angeles: Kenmore Company; 1928), *Greater Los Angeles and Southern California*, by Robert J. Burdette (Chicago: Lewis Publishing Company; 1910), and *The City and County of Los Angeles* and *Los Angeles — Resources, Growth and Prospects,* both by Harry Ellington Brook (Los Angeles: the Chamber of Commerce; 1890 and 1899).

A splendid account of the fight over the location of the Los Angeles harbor is *The Free Harbor Contest,* by Charles Dwight Willard (Los Angeles: Mirror Company; 1900). A brief and judicious review of the Los Angeles and Owens Valley water controversy forms the final chapter of *The Story of Inyo,* by W. A. Chalfant. This important book, dealing with what is topographically, geologically, and in many other ways the strangest area on the face of the earth, was published by the author in 1922 and is now out of print. The Los Angeles County Library has a copy.

The salient facts concerning the Capital-Labor war in Los Angeles during the climacteric two years 1910–12 are set forth in *Dynamite,* by Louis Adamic (New York: Viking Press; 1929). The Capital side of the whole picture was presented in a twenty-nine-page supplement of the Los Angeles *Times,* issued October 1, 1929, under the title, " The Forty Years War." The dynamiting of the *Times* Building is discussed in *The Masked War,* by William J. Burns (New York: George H. Doran Company; 1913), and in *The National Dynamite Plot,* a pamphlet by Ortie McManigal (Los Angeles: L. A. Neale Company; 1913). The second volume of *The Autobiography of Lincoln Steffens* (New York: Harcourt, Brace & Company; 1931) contains Mr. Steffens's personal account of the behind-the-scenes activity at the time of the McNamara trial. Clarence Darrow devotes two chapters to the McNamara case in his *The Story of My Life* (New York: Charles Scribner's Sons; 1932), but what he says, unfortunately, adds nothing to the publicly known facts. What Charles Yale Harrison says about the case in his *Clarence Darrow* (New York: Cape & Smith; 1931) is mainly special pleading for the defense.

For substantial reading on modern Los Angeles the reader will have to go to the national magazines. There he will find a wealth of fugitive material, for the Angel City in the last ten years has furnished the inspiration for more magazine articles than any other city in America. The recent general books on the subject are virtually limited to Mr. Newmark's aforementioned *Sixty Years in Southern California* and a few booster books, written and published locally and put out for home consumption. The best of the latter, and by far, is a 208-page paper-backed book entitled *La Reina*, written by Laurance L. Hill, late publicity manager of the Security-First National Bank of Los Angeles, and published by the bank itself. The book is entertaining and instructive, for its omissions as well as for its inclusions, and is profusely illustrated with photographs, some of them quite rare. The bank has given away three editions, the last of which was issued in 1929.

Mr. Newmark's book deserves special mention. The author, a merchant, resided in Los Angeles from 1853 until his death, in 1916, at the age of eighty-one. He seems to have kept a record of local events during most of those years, and hence his book is a sort of Pepys Diary of Los Angeles. It contains a wealth of authoritative information, most of it to be found nowhere else, about the whole period from 1853 to 1913. The general reader will undoubtedly skip most of this book, for it runs to 744 pages and contains hundreds of names and trivialities of no consequence except to the persons concerned or their descendants. Worse, the present, third, edition has three dull introductions, a preface, a foreword, two appendices, and a confusing index, and altogether is dreadfully edited. Nevertheless, this is a very important and informative book, invaluable to the researcher, and it will remain so, no matter how many books may be written about Los Angeles in the future. The earlier editions were published by the Knickerbocker Press, New York, in 1916 and 1926.

I have no space here for listing or commenting on periodical material, but I make one exception in the case of " Otistown of the Open Shop," by Frederick Palmer (*Hampton's Magazine*, January 1911). It is a competent appraisal of the general Capital-Labor situation in Los Angeles at that time. A chapter on Los Angeles by Florence E. Winslow appears in *Historic Towns of the Western States*, edited by Lyman P. Powell (New York: G. P. Putnam's Sons; 1901), and a humorous critical sketch by Paul Jordan-Smith will be found in *The Taming of the Frontier*, edited by Duncan Aikman (New York: Minton, Balch & Company; 1925). A scientific paper entitled *Southern California Geology and Los Angeles Earthquakes* was issued by the Southern California Academy of Sciences in 1928. There are two or three small books on Hollywood and the movie stars, all of them trash. Valuable source material on Los Angeles will naturally be found in the Los Angeles newspapers and in the *Southern Californian* and *Overland* magazines, complete files of all of which are in the Los Angeles Public Library.

There is a rich store of photographic material on the subject. Most of the photographs used herein are from the superb Historical Collection of the Security-First National Bank of Los Angeles; several were supplied by

the Los Angeles Chamber of Commerce, one by the Pasadena Chamber of Commerce and Civic Association, and four by commercial agencies.

This is by no means a complete bibliography, but it is fairly comprehensive and will suffice here.

BIBLIOGRAPHICAL NOTE

Index

Adamic, Louis, 150–1, 162, 166, 169, 175, 181, 182
Agua Prieta, Mexico, 280, 282, 283, 288
Alabama Hills, 244
Albert, King of Belgium, 218–19
Aldrich, Edward, 299
Alepas, Nicho, 36
Alesandro, Cal., 103
Alexander, Mayor, 160, 161, 169, 173, 176
Alexandria Hotel, 153, 154
Alger, 191
Alhambra, Cal., 294
Allen, Frederick Lewis, 197
All-Year Club, 319
Alosta, Cal., 84
Altadena, Cal., 214
Alta Vista, Cal., 84
Alvitre, Felipe, 48

American Bankers' Association, 160, 172
American Bar Association, 301
American City, 323
American Civil Liberties Union, 217, 305
"American Colony," 67
American Federation of Labor, 143, 145, 147, 162, 168, 169, 172, 174, 188
American Industries, 162
American Legion, 217, 312 –13
American Manufacturers' Association, 145
American Mercury, 150, 217, 229
American-Mexicans, 29
American occupation, 30
"American Plan," 197

Anderson, Paul Y., 131
Andrews, Harry E., 158
Angelus Temple, 273–4, 276, 277, 278, 279, 281–2, 283, 285, 287, 325
Anti-Saloon League, 292, 308, 322
Apia, 190
Appeal to Reason, 162, 165, 170–1, 184
Appleton, D., & Co., 98
Arcadia, Cal., 81, 84
Argonaut, 146
Arlington, Ore., 299
Armory Hall, 50
Armour, Philip D., 88
Arrillaga, 18
Assisi, 5
Atchison, Topeka & Santa Fe Railroad, 71–3, 91–2, 93, 94, 98, 99, 110, 113, 116, 117, 122, 123, 142
Atherton, Gertrude, 9
Atlanta, 95, 98, 170, 172
Atlantic Monthly, 175
Auburndale, Cal., 103
Austin, Mary, 221
Austin, S. W., 227–8, 231–2
Australia, 43, 67
Autobiography (McPherson), 279
Autobiography (Steffens), 180
Azusa, Cal., 83

Babcock, C. H., 308
Baker, Arcadia P., 122

Bakersfield, Cal., 60
Baldwin, Mrs. Anita, 219
Baldwin, "Lucky," 27
Baldwin, Roger, 217
Baldwin, T., 36
Ballona, Cal., 84, 85
Baltimore, 320
Bancroft, Hubert Howe, 13
Bandini, Arcadia, 26
Bar Association, 196
Barrymore, Lionel, 251–2
Barton, Bruce, 291
Barton, Sheriff, 50
Beach, Seneca, 149
Beaumont, Cal., 84
Bella Union Hotel, La, 36, 38
Bell, Horace, 28–9, 38
Berger, Victor, 175
Berkeley, Cal., 176
Berlin, 213, 322
Bernhardt, Sarah, 206, 252
Berry, 124–5
Bethune, Cal., 84
Better America Federation, 197–8, 217, 278
Beverly Hills, 214, 220, 255–6, 326
Bierce, Ambrose, 125, 326
Big Pine, Cal., 243
Bishop, Cal., 224, 241
Bishop, Mme Johnstone, 205
Bishop's pills, 147–8
Bixby family, 66–7
Bixby ranch, 26
Bluefields, W. Va., 216
Body and Soul, 263–5

Bond, Carrie Jacobs, 325–6
Bonita, Cal., 84
Borah, William E., 165
Bordwell, 179, 182, 183
Borica, 18
Boston, 22, 211, 320
Bowles, A. M., 263
Brann, the Iconoclast, 154
Breed, L. N., 121
British Columbia, 74
Broad Acres, Cal., 84
Brockton, Mass., 216
Brook, Harry Ellington, 94–5
Brooklyn, 250
Brougher, James Whitcomb, 308
Brown (Washington correspondent), 125
Brown, Arthur I., 315
Brown, Clara Spalding, 63–4
Brown, Dave, 47–8
Bryan, William Jennings, 304, 305–7, 311–12
Bryan, William Jennings, Jr., 305, 307
Bryan Bible League, 311, 316
Buchanan, W. C., 308
Buenos Aires, 24
Buffalo, N. Y., 98
Buffalo Bill, 191
Buffum's Saloon, 63, 64
Burbank, Cal., 84
Burdette, Robert J., 18, 37
Burns, William J., 160,
163, 164, 166, 169, 171, 172, 173–4, 175, 182
Busch Gardens, 216
Busy Vista, Cal., 84

Cabrillo, 6
Cadman, S. Parkes, 292
Cajon Pass, 72
California: For Health, Pleasure, and Residence, 69
California Building Trades Council, 165
California Fruit Growers' Exchange, 131–2, 133–5
California Institute Associates, 312
California Institute of Technology, 211, 312, 315
California of the South, 98
"California on Wheels," 98–9
California River, 31
California State Church Federation, 308
California Voice, 308
Calle de los Negros, 38, 39, 44, 52, 53
Calle de las Vírgenes, 38, 43
Camille, 206
Camino Real, El, 4
Canada, 70, 297
Canfield, C. A., 129
Cannon, Bishop, 291
Cape Horn, 58, 109
Capistrano, Point, 112
Carew, Harold D., 326

Carpenter, Ford A., 322
Castro, 30
Cata, Leonardo, 20
Catalina Island, 22, 126, 281
Cathedral of St. Vibiana, 8
Central Labor Council, 143–4, 160, 161, 166
Central Pacific Railroad, 58
Century Magazine, 20–2, 70
Chalfant, W. A., 233–4
Chamber of Commerce, 92, 93, 94, 95, 98, 99, 100, 106, 108, 110, 111, 113, 117, 118, 119, 120, 121, 123, 145, 163, 208, 241, 275, 278–9, 313, 319, 322
Chandler, Harry, 140, 156, 158, 162, 180, 185, 188
Chapman, Joe, 24–5, 26, 28
Charleston, S. C., 329
Chase, 8
Chicago, 58, 72, 94, 96, 97, 163, 170, 193, 207, 211, 221, 320
Chicago fire, 51–2, 54
Chinese massacre, 36, 52–4
Church of Our Lady, 18–19, 25, 30, 46, 64
Citizens' Alliance, 143
City limits, 12, 80
Claremont, Cal., 102
Claremont *Courier,* 102
Claremont Hotel, 102–3

Clarke, Harley L., 263, 264
Cleveland, Ohio, 170, 181
Clifford, Pinckey, 47
Cline, Herman, 284
Cody, Lew, 261
Collier's, 175–6
Colorado, 164
Colorado River, 221
Columbia River, 31, 299
Columbus, Ohio, 190
Compton, 317
Connolly, C. P., 175–6
Cooke, Jay, 65
Cooper, Gary, 261
Corona, Cal., 103
Cota, Rafael, 26
Council of Labor, 143
Crabb, Henry, 49
Craighill Board, 117, 118
Crawford, Joan, 261
Crawley, J. M., 120, 121
Crespi, Juan, 5, 6, 7
Criminal Syndicalism Act, 194, 305
Crocker, Charlie, 61, 62, 66
Custer, General, 191
Custer, Mrs., 98

Dana, Richard Henry, 23–4, 107–8
Danube, 26
Darrow, Clarence, 165, 168, 169, 173, 174, 175, 177, 179, 182, 183, 185, 186, 305–6
Davis, Chief of Police, 303

Davis, Arthur P., 228–9
Davis, Cushman K., 111
Davis, Frank H., 122
Davis, LeCompte, 181
Dawes, 110–11
Dayton, Tenn., 304, 313
Deadman's Island, 108, 111
Debs, Eugene, 142, 162, 165, 181, 182, 184
Denver, 143
Des Moines, 132, 136
Detroit, 163, 174
Detroit *News,* 321
Dewey, John, 197
Doheny, E. L., 129, 130–1
Dominquez, Juan José, 19
Douglas, Ariz., 282, 283, 284
Downey, 51
Dume, Point, 112
Duse, 252
Dynamite, 150

Eastlake Park, 75
East Oregonian, 299
East St. Louis, 216
Eaton, Fred, 226–7, 229, 231, 243
Echeandía, 20
Edmonds, W. E., 308
Egypt, 101, 105
Einstein, 318
El Dorado Saloon, 38
England, 3
Enken, Charles, 38

Facts and Figures about Los Angeles City and County, 93–4

Fairbanks, Douglas, 255
Fall, Albert B., 131
Faulkner, Frederick R., 234, 240–1
Federated Bible Classes, 308
Feliz family, 26
Felton, 114, 115
Fermin, Point, 126
Ferndale, Cal., 81
Fisher, Tom, 24, 25–6
Fishlake Creek, 244
Flint, 237
Flintridge, 214
Flores, Juan, 51
Fortune, 263–5
Fort Tejon, 50
Fosdick, Harry Emerson, 292
Foster, Stephen G., 47–8, 49
Fox, William, 263
Fox Film Corporation, 263–5
Francis of Assisi, St., 5
Fredericks, 168, 186
Free Harbor League, 123
Free Harbor Jubilee, 125
Freeman, John R., 240
Friendship Letter Contest, 320–1
Frémont, 28
Fresno, Cal., 60
Frye, 110, 111, 112, 114, 115, 118, 125
Fullerton, Cal., 83

Gabrielinos, 9–11, 14, 27
Gallagher, A. J., 150, 152

Gallows Hill, 48, 50
Gálvez, José de, 3
Garbo, Greta, 261
Gartz, Crane, 217
Gibbon, 117–18
Gladstone, Cal., 84
Gladstone, W. E., 84
Glendale, Cal, 84, 212
Glendora, Cal., 82, 84
Gold Rush, the, 31, 35, 39, 70
Goldwyn, Samuel, 256
Gompers, Samuel, 162, 165–6, 168, 169, 171, 182, 184
Gonzales, Juan, 48, 49
Good Government League, 169
Grand Army Journal, 69, 190
Grant, Ulysses S., 63
Grass Valley, Cal., 218
Grauman, Sid, 258, 259, 260–1
Grauman's Chinese Theatre, 259–60
Grauman's Egyptian Theatre, 258–9
Great Train Robbery, The, 249
Groningen, Johann, 26
Guatemala, 97
Guinn, James M., 13, 36
Gurdane, Tom, 299

Hall of Records, 153
Hamburg, 97
Hamburger's, 146–7, 148, 149

Happy Valley, Cal., 84
Hardy, Carlos S., 285, 290, 301
Harper & Bro., 70
Harper's, 98
Harriman, Job, 161, 166, 169, 170, 176, 177, 178, 181, 182, 183, 184
Harrison, Charles Yale, 175–6, 178, 181, 185–6
Harvey-Elder, Churchill, 156
Haver, Phyllis, 260
Hayes, Cardinal, 291
Hays, Arthur Garfield, 305
Hays, Will, 257
Haywood, "Big Bill," 164–5, 169
Hecht, Ben, 265–6
Helmes, Elmer D., 308
Hess, 317
Hickman, William Edward, 293–303
Hill, Laurance L., 15, 63, 130, 248
History of the Church (McPherson), 278
Hitchcock, 236
Hobby, Gertrude, 132–3
Hollywood, 135, 214, 219, 220, 245, 248–50, 252, 253, 254–66, 278, 304, 323
Hollywood Hotel, 248
Holman, Alfred, 146
Holmes, J. A., 171
Holmes, John Haynes, 291
Holy Rollers, 271, 272
Honolulu, 24

Hood, William, 114, 117
Hoover, Herbert, 290, 313
Hoover Dam, 221
Hopkins, Ernest Jerome, 194–6, 199
Hopkins, Mark, 61
Hot Springs Creek, 244
How We Grow! 95–6
Hudson, G., 271
Huntington, Collis P., 61, 114, 115, 116, 117, 119–20, 122–3, 124, 125, 126, 209
Huntington, Henry E., 126, 312

Independence, Cal., 224, 227, 243
Indianapolis, 92, 163, 170, 175, 185, 188, 211
International Typographical Union, 141, 145
Inyo County, 221, 226, 232, 234, 242
Inyo Mountains, 222
Irvine, Alexander, 176, 181
Italy, 203
Ivanhoe, Cal., 84

Jackson, Helen Hunt, 69, 205
Jeans, 317
Jefferson, Joseph, 252
Joan d'Arc, 278
Johannsen, Anton, 150, 152
Johnson, Hiram, 153
Joliet, Ill., 164

Jonathan Club, 179
Jones, Ap Catesby, 29
Jones, John, 51
Jones, John P., 118–19, 122
Junior Order of American Mechanics, 308

Kansas City, 73, 140, 193, 297
Keeler, Cal., 243
Kennedy, Mrs. Minnie ("Ma"), 270–1, 281, 282, 287
Kern County, 33, 232
Kinney, Abbot, 203–4, 205, 209
Kirby, William, 308
Klondike, 95
Kolhoerster, 317
Krotona Institute of Theosophy, 257

Ladies' Garment Workers Union, 148
Laguna, Cal., 325
Lamar, Cal., 84
Land of Heart's Desire, The, 94
Land of Promise, The, 95
Land of Sunshine, The, 94
Land of the Beckoning Climate, The, 322
Lang, Cal., 62
Latham, 32
La Verne College, 102
Lawrence, David, 187
Laws, Cal., 224, 243
Lelia Byrd, 22

Lenin, 197, 292
Leopold, 300
Lieuallen, Buck, 299
Lincoln Park, 75
Linn, Adam, 36
Lippincott, J. B., 225–6, 227, 228, 231–2
Llewellen Iron Works, 162, 163, 166
Loeb, 300
Loew, 264, 265
Loma Linda Sanitarium, 103
London, 178, 213
Lone Pine, Cal., 224, 243
Long Beach, Cal., 26, 66, 85, 131, 152, 220
Long Valley, 239–40
Lordsburg, Cal., 84, 102
Loreto, Mexico, 3
Los, 42
Los Alamitos rancho, 26
Los Angeles *Citizen,* 146, 161, 167, 217
Los Angeles *Daily News,* 282
Los Angeles *Examiner,* 158, 159, 248
Los Angeles *Express,* 65, 119, 121, 139, 177
Los Angeles Harbor, 107–27
Los Angeles *Herald,* 119, 121, 139, 158, 278
Los Angeles *News,* 58–9, 145–6
Los Angeles *Record,* 288–9
Los Angeles *Star,* 32, 34, 36, 37, 38, 39–40, 41, 42–3, 46, 51–2
Los Angeles *Times,* 69, 80, 86, 93, 95, 119, 121, 125, 139, 140, 141, 142, 143, 144, 145, 146, 147, 148, 152–3, 154, 155, 157–9, 160, 162–3, 164, 167, 168, 169, 170, 171, 174–5, 176–7, 183–5, 186–7, 188, 189, 191, 192–4, 198, 215, 229, 230, 298–9, 301, 320, 322
Los Angeles *Tribune,* 139
Los Cerritos rancho, 26, 66
" Los Diablos," 42, 54
Lovelace, Charles, 156
Lowell, Ohio, 190
Lugo family, 27
Lynching, 35, 36, 40, 50

Main Street, 197
Malibu Beach, 214
Malone, Dudley Field, 305
Manning, Bishop, 292
Manzanar, Cal., 224, 242
Margaret and Mary Home for Orphans, 103
Marietta, Ohio, 190
Markham, Edwin, 11
Mary, Lake, 244
Matthews, W. B., 240
McAdoo, William Gibbs, 256
McCan, David C., 149

McCan Mechanical Works, 149

McCarthy, Patrick H., 143, 150, 152

McCormick, Anne O'Hare, 255, 262

McCoy, Cal., 84

McDermott, Mrs. Clara A., 303

McGroarty, John Steven, 6, 13

McKinley, William, 126, 191

McLeod, 125

McManigal, Ortie, 163, 164, 166, 173

McNamara, J. B., 163, 164, 165, 166–7, 168, 169, 170, 171, 173–4, 175, 176, 177, 178, 179, 180, 181, 182, 183, 184, 185, 186, 187, 188, 217, 305

McNamara, J. J., 163, 164, 165, 166–7, 168, 169, 170, 173–4, 175, 176, 177, 178, 179, 180, 181, 182, 183, 184, 185, 188, 305

McNamara Defense League, 170

McPartland Detective Agency, 164

McPherson, 271

McPherson, Aimee Semple, 207, 270, 271–4, 275–92, 301, 308, 325

McWilliams, Carey, 326

Mears, Joseph L., 205

Mellon, 196

Memphis, Tenn., 148, 170

Merced, Cal., 60, 221

Merchantors' Bureau, 257

Merchants & Manufacturers' Association, 143, 148–9, 152, 163, 193

Methodists, 41, 101, 105, 247, 304

Mexico City, 17, 19, 44

Miami *Herald,* 321

Michelson, A. A., 318

Micheltorena, 29

Miller, Patsy Ruth, 261

Millikan Robert A., 312–18

Mills, Benjamin Fay, 205

Milwaukee, 175

Mina, Cal., 243

Miranda, Antonio, 13

Mission San Diego de Alcalá, 4

Mission San Gabriel Arcángel, 8, 9–11, 12, 13–14, 15, 19, 20, 23, 24, 25, 40, 304

Mississippi Valley, 71, 72, 73, 274

Modesto, Cal., 60

Mojave Desert, 109, 222

Mojave Indians, 223

Mondonville, Cal., 84

Monrovia, Cal., 82, 212

Monterey, Bay of, 3, 4

Monterey, Cal., 14, 24, 29, 31

Monte Vista, Cal., 84

Montgomery Saloon, 38, 50

Mooney, Tom, 150
Morgan, 111
Mound City, Cal., 103
Moyer, 164–5
Mulholland, William, 227, 228, 233, 245
Myer, 265

Nadeau, Cal., 84
Napoleon, 260
National Association of Manufacturers, 161, 162, 171
National Editorial Association, 96–7
National Erectors' Association, 171–2, 173
Neve, Felipe de, 12, 13, 14, 91
Newell, F. H., 228
Newmark, Harris, 34, 50, 51, 52, 87, 98
New Orleans, 70, 172
New York City, 73, 86, 161, 170, 178, 181, 211, 212, 239, 249, 250, 251, 263, 277, 289, 291, 305, 319, 323
New York *Times*, 52–4, 70, 241, 316–17
New York *Times Magazine*, 255, 262
New York *World*, 122
Nicaragua, 109
Nigger Alley, *see* Calle de los Negros
Nietos, Manuel, 19
Nordhoff, Charles, 70, 100

Nordskog, Andrae B., 234–5
Norfolk, Va., 145, 162
Norris, Frank, 60

Oakland, Cal., 124, 283
Ocean Park, Cal., 115, 116, 207, 280
Ocean Spray, Cal., 84
Ochoa, Seferino, 36
Oleander, Cal., 84
Olivewood, Cal., 84
Olympic Games, 322
Omaha, 95, 97, 98
Only Yesterday, 196–7
Ontario, Cal., 84, 132
Orange, Cal., 103
Orange County, 33
Orchard, Harry, 165
Ortega, Guadalupe, 25
Ortega ranch, 24, 25
Osage Indians, 254
Otis, Eliza Wetherby, 190, 191
Otis, Harrison Gray, 69, 71, 86, 92, 140, 141, 142, 143, 144, 146, 148, 152, 153, 154, 158–9, 160, 161, 162, 167–8, 169, 170, 171, 175, 177, 180, 185, 189–92
Otis, Senator Harrison Gray, 190
Our Italy, 98
Our Lawless Police, 194–6
Outlook, 167–8, 313
Owens Lake, 243
Owens River, 222, 224,

226, 229, 230, 231, 232, 233, 237, 239, 241, 243
Owens Valley, 221–4, 225, 226–46

Pacific Palisades, 115
Palace Saloon, 38
Palomares, Cal., 83
Palou, Francisco, 8–9
Panama, 58, 109
Paris, 97, 213
Parker, Marion, 293, 294–7, 300, 302
Parker, Perry M., 293–7, 302
Pasadena, Cal., 27, 82, 92, 146, 160, 211, 212, 213–19, 220, 276, 315, 324
Pasadena *Star-News,* 217–18, 326
Pendleton, Ore., 298, 299
Penn Colony, William, 243
Perfect Day, A, 325
Pettibone, 164–5
Philadelphia, 170, 171, 181, 327, 329, 330
Phillips, Wiley J., 307–8, 310
Pickfair, 255
Pickford, Mary, 255, 286
Pico family, 26
Pico, Pio, 35, 43
Pierce, William, 308
Pilgrim, 23
Pinchot, Gifford, 233, 234, 235–6, 237, 239, 244
Pittsburgh, 181, 320
Piute Indians, 223

Plain Talk, 328–9
Platt, 111
Playa del Rey, Cal., 204, 208
Plaza, the, 12, 14, 15, 25, 30, 35, 37, 38, 39, 46, 47, 63, 64, 75, 77
Plaza de Toros, 44
Point Fermin, 126
Polka Saloon, La, 38
Pomona, Cal., 103
Pomona College, 103
Pomona Valley, 83
Portiuncula River, 5, 12, 15, 86, 128, 224
Portland, Ore., 150, 170, 206, 299
Port Los Angeles, 116
Portolá, Gaspar de, 3, 4–8
Prado, Cal., 103
Prisk, Charles H., 217, 218
Promontory, Utah, 59
Providencia, Battle of, 29
Pryor, Joe, 26

Raker, 240
Ramirez, Cal., 81
Ramona, 69, 205
Rattlesnake Island, 108, 111, 113
Raymond, Cal., 84
Reading, Mass., 26
Redlands, Cal., 103
Redondo, Cal., 113, 116, 117, 118, 119
Redondo Railway Company, 113, 117

Regener, 317
Reid, Hugo, 27
Reinhart, J. W., 123
Reminiscences of a Ranger,
28–9
Reyes, Francisco, 19
Rich, Irene, 261
Rimmer, Harry, 315
Rincon, Cal., 103
Rio, Augustine Del, 36
Rivera, Fernando de, 12,
13
Riverside, Cal., 51
Riverside County, 33
Robinson, James Harvey,
197
Rogers, Will, 241, 319
Rome, 20
Rood, Paul W., 311–12
Roosevelt, Theodore,
167–8, 182, 231, 233,
237
Rosecrans, Cal., 84
Russia, 3, 198
Ryan, Joseph, 284
Ryder, David Warren, 150

Sacramento, Cal., 32, 242,
290
Sacramento *Union,* 234,
240–1
Sacramento Valley, 65
St. George, 190
St. James, Cal., 84
St. Louis, 72, 170, 175, 193
St. Louis *Globe-Democrat,*
123
St. Louis *Post-Dispatch,*
131, 321

St. Paul, 190, 320
Salem, Mass., 26
Salt Lake, 222
Salt Lake City, 57, 148
San Bernardino, 61, 103
San Bernardino County,
33, 80
San Blas, 22
Sanchez, Nellie Van de
Grift, 17
San Diego, Cal., 4, 6, 43,
50, 170, 176, 190
San Dimas, Cal., 84, 103
San Fernando Mountains,
62
San Fernando Valley, 69,
224, 225, 229, 230, 231,
237, 238–9, 245
San Francisco, 31, 32, 36,
37, 42, 43, 49, 54, 57,
58, 59, 62, 65, 66, 74,
89, 98, 102, 105, 109,
113, 116, 124, 143–4,
150, 151, 153, 165, 170,
239, 258, 290, 323, 327
San Francisco *Argonaut,*
146
San Francisco *Bulletin,*
52–4, 148–9
San Francisco *Herald,* 32
San Francisco Typographi-
cal Union, 141
San Francisquito Canyon,
245
San Gabriel, Cal., 40
San Gabriel Canyon, 245
San Gabriel Mission, *see*
Mission San Gabriel
Arcángel

San Gabriel Valley, 69, 82
San Jacinto, Cal., 103
San Joaquin Valley, 59, 60, 61, 65
San Jose, Cal., 11
San Luis Obispo, Cal., 31
San Pasqual rancho, 27
San Pedro, Cal., 6, 22, 23, 26, 30, 49, 57, 58, 61, 65, 66, 76, 92, 107, 109, 110, 111, 113, 114, 115, 116, 117, 118, 119, 120, 121, 122, 123, 124, 125, 126, 127, 210, 215, 221
San Quentin, 152, 177, 183, 185, 194, 301
Santa Ana, Cal., 83
Santa Ana River, 103
Santa Anita rancho, 27
Santa Barbara, Cal., 24, 27, 47, 108, 160, 171, 325
Santa Barbara *Press*, 190
Santa Fe, N. M., 26
Santa Fe Railroad, *see* Atchison, Topeka & Santa Fe Railroad
Santa Monica, Cal., 66, 84–5, 114, 115, 116–17, 118, 119, 120, 121, 122, 124, 125, 126–7, 209, 280
Santell, 264
Santiago Canyon, 50
Sarahsville, Ohio, 190
Saturday Evening Post, 187–8
Saugus, Cal., 245

Savage, George W., 102, 103
Schaeffer, Emma, 281
Schenectady, 175
Scholes, Governor, 36
Schuyler, James D., 240
Schwed, Hermine, 197
Scopes, 304, 305, 313
Scranton, Pa., 216, 326
Script, Rob Wagner's, 255, 256, 260–1
Seal Islands, 190
Seattle, 151, 170, 299
Semple, Robert, 271, 277
Sentous Meat Packing Co., 144
Sepúlveda family, 26
Sepúlveda, José, 43
Serra, Junípero, 3, 4, 8, 247–8
Shaler, Josh, 22
Shame Dance, The, 249
Sheehan, Winfield, 264–5
Sherwin, Louis, 191, 229–30
Shubert, Jacob, 277
Shuler, R. P. ("Bob"), 275, 308
Sierras, the High, 222, 230, 243
Sierra Madres, 7, 68, 82, 222
Signal Hill, 131
Simpson Auditorium, 153
Sinaloa, Mexico, 12, 15
Sinclair, Upton, 194, 217
Sioux City, Io., 103
Sixty Years in Southern California, 34

Sloat, 29
Smith, Al, 289, 290
Sonita, Mexico, 49
Sonora, Mexico, 12, 15, 286
Sonora Town, Cal., 39, 63
Southern California, 95
Southern California Immigration Society, 75
Southern Californian, 36, 49, 102
Southern Pacific Railroad, 58, 59–63, 64, 65, 66, 69, 71–3, 74, 76, 92, 93, 99, 107, 110, 111, 113, 114, 115, 116, 117, 118, 119, 120, 122, 123, 124, 126, 131–2, 133, 171, 284
Southside, Cal., 84
Southwest Museum, 16
Spain, 3
Spaulding, William A., 129
Squaw Lane, 38
Stanford, Leland, 61, 66, 92, 110, 111, 114
Stearns, Abel, 26, 28, 35
Steele, Wilbur Daniel, 249
Steffens, Lincoln, 178–80, 182–3, 185
Sterns, Fred B., 240
Steunenberg, Frank, 165
Stewart, William R., 230
Stockton, 30
Stockton, Cal., 49
Structural Iron Workers, 151, 163
Summers, Mrs. Emma A., 130
Story of Inyo, The, 233–4

Story of My Life, The (Darrow), 174

Taft, William H., 171, 235, 236
Tahoe, Lake, 244
Teapot Dome, 131, 221
Tehachapi Mountains, 61–2
Temple, Jack, 26, 28, 35
Tenth Street Hotel, 90
Terminal Railroad, 113, 117, 121–2
Texas, 104, 206
Tia Juana, Mexico, 3
Tientsin, 190
Tilden, Freeman, 327, 329–30
Time, 140, 189
Times Building, 140, 142, 155–6, 157, 158–9, 160–1, 162, 163, 164, 165, 166, 167, 173, 174, 177, 185, 186, 188
Toledo, Ohio, 178
Tombstone, Ariz., 66
Tomlinson & Co., 59
Topeka, Kan., 247
Toscanini, 326
Tournament of Roses, 211, 217
Travers, C. C., 159
Trowbridge ranch, 242
Tucson, Ariz., 66
Turpie, 111
Tustin, Cal., 83
Tveitmoe, O. A., 150, 152, 165
Twist, W. W., 47

Two Years Before the Mast, 23–4

United States, 29
U. S. Reclamation Service, 225, 226, 227, 228, 231, 232
Upland, Cal., 103

Van Alstine, 125
Vanderbilt, Cornelius, Jr., 257
Venice, Cal., 204–10, 280
Venice, Italy, 203–4, 205, 206
Verdugo, José Maria, 19
Vernon, Cal., 81
Victoria Hall, 273
Vigilantes, the, 35–6, 50
Visalia, Cal., 60
Viscano, 6

Wagner, Rob, 255, 260–1
Walcott, 237
Walleria, Cal., 84
Walsh, Tom, 131
Warner, Charles Dudley, 13, 98
Warner, Jonathan, 26–7
Washington, D. C., 118, 120, 122, 123, 125, 227, 276
Watsonville, Cal., 242
Watterson, Henry, 191
Wellman, 125
Wells, Fargo & Company, 58, 78
West, George W., 217
Wetherby, Eliza, *see* Otis, Eliza Wetherby

White, 124
White Mountains, 222
Whitlock, Brand, 178
Whitney, Mt., 222, 243
Whittier, Cal., 82, 212
Wickersham Commission, 194
Wiggin, Albert H., 263
Wilcox, Daeida Hartell, 247, 248
Wilcox, Horace H., 247, 248
Willard, Charles Dwight, 36, 90, 109, 110
Willebrandt, Mrs. Mabel, 289–90
Wilmington, Cal., 221
Wilson, Ben, 27
Wilson, Mt., 27
Winrod, Gerald B., 315–16
Winslow, Florence E., 14
Wise, Rabbi, 291
Wolfskill, Bill, 27
Woman's Christian Temperance Union, 308, 321–2
Woods, James, 41–2
World's Work, 230, 327
Workman, Bill, 49
Workman, Billy, 75, 76
Workman, Boyle, 285

Yang-na, 6, 12
Yangs, 6, 8, 14, 16–17, 33, 38–9
Yerba Buena, 31 *and see* San Francisco

Yorba, Antonio, 19
Yorba, Ramona, 27
Yosemite National Park, 221, 244
Yuma, Ariz., 42, 49

Zanjas, 40
Zanuk, Daryl, 260
Zeehandelaar, Felix J., 149, 160
Zukor, 265

A Note on the Type in which
this Book is Set

This book was set on the linotype in Janson, a
recutting made direct from the type cast from
matrices (now in possession of the Stempel
foundry, Frankfurt am Main) made by Anton
Janson some time between 1660 and 1687.

Of Janson's origin nothing is known. He may
have been a relative of Justus Janson, a printer of
Danish birth who practised in Leipzig from 1614
to 1635. Some time between 1657 and 1668 Anton
Janson, a punch-cutter and type-founder, bought
from the Leipzig printer Johann Erich Hahn the
type-foundry which had formerly been a part of
the printing house of M. Friedrich Lankisch.
Janson's types were first shown in a specimen
sheet issued at Leipzig about 1675. Janson's successor, and perhaps his son-in-law, Johann Karl
Edling, issued a specimen sheet of Janson types
in 1689. His heirs sold the Janson matrices in
Holland to Wolffgang Dietrich Erhardt,
of Leipzig.

Composed, printed, and bound by The Plimpton
Press, Norwood, Mass. Paper made by
S. D. Warren Co., Boston.